D0551643

TV Commercials

RENEWALS 458-4574

MUHAMMAD LIBRARIES

TV Commercials

How to Make Them or How Big Is the Boat?

Ivan Cury

WITHDRAWN
UTSA Libraries

ELSEVIER

AMSTERDAM • BOSTON • HEIDELBERG • LONDON
NEW YORK • OXFORD • PARIS • SAN DIEGO
SAN FRANCISCO • SINGAPORE • SYDNEY • TOKYO
Focal Press is an imprint of Elsevier

Focal Press is an imprint of Elsevier
30 Corporate Drive, Burlington, MA 01803, USA
Linacre House, Jordan Hill, Oxford, OX2 8DP, UK

Copyright © 2005, Elsevier Inc. All rights reserved.

No part of this publication may be reproduced, stored in a retrieval system, or transmitted in any form or by any means, electronic, mechanical, photocopying, recording, or otherwise, without the prior written permission of the publisher.

Permissions may be sought directly from Elsevier's Science & Technology Rights Department in Oxford, UK: phone: (+44) 1865 843830, fax: (+44) 1865 853333, e-mail: permissions@elsevier.com.uk. You may also complete your request on-line via the Elsevier homepage (http://elsevier.com) by selecting "Customer Support" and then "Obtaining Permissions."

∞ Recognizing the importance of preserving what has been written, Elsevier prints its books on acid-free paper whenever possible.

Library of Congress Cataloging-in-Publication Data
Application submitted.

British Library Cataloging-in-Publication Data
A catalogue record for this book is available from the British Library.

ISBN: 0-240-80592-5

For information on all Focal Press publications
visit our website at www.focalpress.com

05 06 07 08 09 10 9 8 7 6 5 4 3 2 1

Printed in the United States of America

Library
University of Texas
at San Antonio

Dedicated to teachers.

To those who particularly influenced me:
To my father and mother, Joel and Anne, and my sister, Marilyn.
To Mrs. Coveny—3rd grade
Mrs. O'Reilly—5th grade
Mrs. Birnbaum—6th grade
Mrs. Lavy and Mme. Kallir—high school
To Bob Novak, Charlie Irving, and Don Knotts—The B-B riders
To Bill Ball, Alan Fletcher, Charlie Moore, and Edith Skinner—Carnegie-Mellon
Ed Thomen, Ted Kazinoff, and Sam Hirsh—Boston University
To Kit Lucas, Ellis Haizlip, and Lee Polk—WNET-NY
To Jordan Morganstein—Marshall Jordan Associates
To George Zimmer and Richard Goldman—The Men's Wearhouse

To my children; James, Joanna, Peter, and Alex, and to their mothers, Lynda and Barbara.

Contents

Preface

I sang my first commercial for Cream of Wheat on CBS's *Let's Pretend* when I was 11 years old. Later, I sang for Tide. I announced the Oh Henry Candy Bar openings for *Official Detective* and regularly asked, "Where's the LAVA soap?" on *FBI in Peace & War*. I worked on hundreds of commercials. I also played the part of Bobby Benson on *The B-B Riders*, selling kid cowboy merchandise, and appeared as Portia's son on *Portia Faces Life*, which sold such diverse products as Grape Nut Flakes, Maxwell House Coffee, Jell-O desserts, and La France Bleach.

My acting career came to an end when I went to college, but since I was studying theater I felt I was still "in the biz." Upon graduation I worked my way to a position as staff director and then producer/director, first at WNET and then at CBS in New York. Every now and then I got to work as a freelancer, on both programs and commercials. Getting programs to really look right was an enormous struggle. There was never enough time or money. Commercials were different, and I liked doing them.

After a while I got a job writing copy at an advertising agency. I found that most of the time my job was to sell the client's business, which mostly consisted of informing the public about the client's product, and I liked that teaching element. I soon became creative director and then finally a partner in a medium-sized retail advertising agency. I wrote, produced, directed, and consulted for The Men's Wearhouse from 1975 to 2002. Along the way, both for The Men's Wearhouse and others, I shot hundreds of commercials and caused thousands to be made. Making commercials that looked good wasn't always easy, but the cost of airtime was so great that production costs were never as problematic as they had been for programs. The idea was to get the commercial right. Most of the time the struggle wasn't about time or money for production, but about craftsmanship and my own creativity. I also became a professor at UCLA and then at California State University, Los Angeles.

I had a great time writing a book about directing and producing for television, and I thought it would be easy to write a book about making commercials.

Whoops!

When you try to write about commercial production nothing stays in place long enough to be considered "the truth." Things that were true yesterday are no longer true today. Some of the stuff that works on shoots that cost $25,000 will get you fired on shoots that are budgeted at $250,000.

However, there really are enough bottom-line facts to make a book like this valuable. Knowing what's happening at the client's office, at the agency, or at the production company can be a big help in getting the job done well and stress-free . . . or free-er. Often tensions and complications result from a lack of understanding about what that other person is doing. There are far too many times in the production of commercials where one hears some variation of the phrase, "What in the world were they thinking?" I hope this book diminishes the number of times that question gets asked. It is written to serve students of production and business students working in advertising, as well as those actually working on the client, agency, or production side.

Writing this required me to make a number of choices—hopefully good ones. I wanted the book to deal with the actual steps in the process rather than the dynamics of either psychological interrelationships or the design process, except as it affects production. I also chose to let the specific needs of each step in the process be the guide to the discussion of technical subjects. Hardware, for example, is introduced when it is essential to understanding the specific process being described. Context has been the guiding premise in organizing the material. I have added a chapter on crew and some technical matters should the reader wish to use that as a starting point or primer. Chapter 10 may serve in a like manner for miscellaneous forms and information.

Recognizing that no one could possibly know *all* the answers and that my own experience is both helpful and limiting, I thought that I'd be able to get by with some help from my friends. I was surprised, delighted, and sometimes simply lucky at the help I received from the many outstanding clients, agency producers, creative directors, and commercial producers who found time to answer questions, review material, and offer encouragement. Alphabetically they are:

Charlie Allenson—Creative Director/Writer

Jack Brown—Producer/Director—Jack Brown Associates

Barry Berenson—Labor Affairs

James Cury—Writer—TimeoutNY

Peter Cury—Graphic Artist/Designer—*People* Magazine

Drew Daniels—Professor/Inventor/Audio Engineer—Sound Path Labs

C. Texas East—Senior Partner Co-Director, Broadcast Production—Ogilvy & Mather

Alex Gorodetzki—Loyal Kaspar—Director of New Business

Michelle Goetzinger—Producer—B.B.D.O.

John Held—Association of Creative Editors—Administrative Director

Darren Kappelus—Senior Partner, Executive Group Director—Ogilvy & Mather

Blake Jackson—Cinematographer & Professor—California State University, Los Angeles

Jason Jaikara—Sr. Vice President Marketing—Fox Broadcasting Co.

Bryan Johnson—CEO—The Film Syndicate

James Klock—Executive VP—Campbell-Ewald/West

Bob Kurtz—Bob Kurtz & Friends—Animation

Steve McCoy—Association of Creative Editors

Dan McLaughlin—Chair of UCLA Animation Program

Jordan Morganstein—CEO—Marshall Jordan Associates—Advertising

Renee Paley—Association of Commercial Producers

Phoenix Editorial:

John Crossly—Editor

   Lisa Hinman—President, Executive Producer

   Matt Silverman—Director of Effects and Design

   Cathy Stonehill—Technical Manager and Producer

Point 360 Editorial/Duplication:

   Ben Ponzio—Senior VP of Sales

   Shelly Yaseen—Senior VP of Sales

Joe Reich—Manager Casting Administration—Walt Disney Pictures & Television

Julia Rubin—Production Co-ordinator—The Film Syndicate

Debbie Schlesinger—Schlesinger Associates Research

Bruce Silverman—President—Wong Doody Advertising

Art Simon—Producer/Director—Art Simon Productions

Tom Sylvester—Producer/Director—Edendale Films

The Men's Wearhouse

   Richard Goldman—Executive VP

   Jayme Maxwell—VP of Marketing

   Matt Stringer—Broadcast Production Manager

   George Zimmer—CEO, Founder

Joe Tawil—GAM products

Greg Wilson—Creative Director/Director—Red Ball Tiger Films

One can't get a book published without help from an editor who believes in the project and is there to help. For me that person is Elinor Actipis, to whom I am grateful. Thanks too must go to my wife Barbara Harris Cury, who read all the material, made enormously helpful comments, let me make corrections, and then reread the whole thing.

Moral support came from Henry and Diane Feldman, Geoffry and Steffanie Gee, Cynthia Gotlewski, Diane and Peter Gray, Michael Greene and Jan Lustig, Felix Lidell and Paula Woods, Jody Price, Gene Sheiniuk and Eileen Berger Sheiniuk, Barry and Cathy Schifrin, Barbara Spector, and the academic community at California State University, Los Angeles, notably professors Chey Acuna, and Alan Bloom and Dean, Carl Selkin.

I'm sure there are some people who I've left out. I know I'll wonder how I could possible have forgotten the help and advice I've gotten from them. I hope they have a terrific sense of humor and will forgive my lapse.

I found a lot of information on commercial production from books that go back as far as 1956, and many that are "hot off the press." A bibliography appears at the end of the book.

This final note: Although commercial production may be difficult to write about, there have been a lot of pluses, notably the contacts and the research. Besides, one of the terrific things about working on commercials and working with the people who make them is that the landscape does change so rapidly with the newest, latest, and best. Craftsmanship, style, and creative work counts. In fact, even when you work with people who you swear are crazy, you also have to recognize that they either *really do* know what they are talking about, are beautifully connected, or have a very, *very* smooth line. In any case, it's exciting and challenging, and it can pay pretty well.

TV Commercials

1 Introduction

I was a vice president, creative director, and junior partner in a retail advertising company in New York. We were pitching our agency to a leading retailer in the area. We had outlined our media philosophy, shown him our reel, and made some projections about how we believed we could increase their business. It was nearing the end of our interview, and it looked like we had sold the client on our agency and also on using television to advertise its chain of stores. The prospective client turned to me and asked, "So how much will the commercials cost?"

I thought about it for a moment or two. It was the predictable, impossible question that I had come to dread. I knew that this time I was about to answer in a hostile way, but I continued anyway. Instead of answering the question I asked him a question.

"How big is the boat?"

"What boat?" he asked

"Yes," I said, "that's exactly the point. What commercial? Rowboats cost considerably less than battleships, and graphics and an announcer will probably be cheaper than the chorus line from Radio City Music Hall. Before we make any commercials, we'll present you with a few concepts and a general idea about the costs of each of them."

I had made the point. Happily for me, he chuckled, and we created commercials for the client for a number of years. The point of the story is that commercials come in a variety of styles, sizes, and shapes. When one talks about commercial production, it's important to remember that there's no one single model for commercial production. By the same token there is no one single commercial delivery system.

Commercial *production* covers everything from the graphic frames used to identify a participating sponsor on a PBS special to the more traditional 10-, 15-, 30-, and 60-second spots. In fact commercial production also covers half-hour and 1-hour infomercials. The audio/video commercial productions are *delivered* in just three major ways.

1. In movie theaters
2. On television
3. On the Web

Apart from those traditional viewing areas, I've watched commercials while waiting in line at the post office, and I've heard commercials on the radio, in an elevator, and even while on the phone: "Hold on a moment and we'll answer your call as soon as a technician/an operator/a salesperson is available. Meanwhile we're offering a one-time only. . . ."

As a producer and director, I'm most interested in the production of the commercials; however, I know that the work done by the client and the advertising agency has a profound effect on the production. The client and the agency make the decisions about who they believe their audience is, what facet of their product or service is to be sold, and finally, how it is to be sold. If some part of those decisions is wrong, the commercial may not work. The blame is sometimes misplaced. The client blames the agency (poor creative, ineffective media), the agency blames the client (unrealistic mandates, absurd budgets), the production company blames either one or both of the two, citing arguments from both camps. As with any campaign "victory finds a hundred fathers, but defeat is an orphan" (Count Galeazzo Ciano). In most cases the agency writes the script, prepares the boards, chooses the production company, and has the last word on how the commercials get shot. They pay for the work. Sometimes everything clicks; the choices are right, and there is a symbiotic relationship between the client, the agency, and the production company that facilitates really good and effective work. On the other hand, there are times when effective, good work gets done with a great deal of hostility, anger, and pain on the part of everyone involved. Far too often, ego, lack of communication, or lack of understanding gets in the way, and the work suffers.

It seemed to me that if the client, the agency, and the production company knew more about what each area did, what each area felt was needed to create the commercial, it might be more fun to work together, and better work might come out of it. There was a sociology textbook that ended with the obvious statement that the more people know about each other, the better they get along. The same is true for commercial production. No book will be able to help with all the ego problems or bad choices that are possible, but I hope this book helps in making commercials by tracing the steps involved in the total process.

For 25 years I have loved making commercials. That's because of the care expected in making them. Prior to working on commercials, I spent a lot of time as a producer/director in commercial broadcasting, working on daytime dramas, musical variety programs, panel programs, and documentaries, and almost always had to endure battles about spending money to make the production look good. The microphone stands didn't match, we couldn't afford a Chapman crane, there wasn't time to clear all the cables from the floor, no one saw that coffee cup on the band stand, etc. That didn't seem to be as true in commercial production. Although cost was important, the battles about budget were not nearly as severe. In fact, for me, it has been quite the opposite. The creative ideas in commercials are often very good, and very creative . . . often they aren't, but craftsmanship is expected and usually paid for. There's too much money spent on the purchase of air time to run commercials that are anything but "the best" they can be.

In order to see how it all comes together, let's walk through the process and find out what questions need to be asked.

1. The process from the client/agency side
    a. How do clients and agencies get together?
    b. Who generates the theme of what is to be sold . . . and how?
    c. How is it shaped? What is its "tonality"?
    d. How is it shepherded through to completion?
    e. How do those decisions affect the final commercial?
2. The process from the production side
    a. How do production companies and clients get together?
    b. What steps are involved in preproduction?
    c. What steps are involved in production?
    d. What steps are involved in postproduction?
3. Who are the people involved?
    a. The client
    b. The advertising agency
    c. The production company
4. What are the questions that each asks? What are the "given circumstances" that govern the actions that are taken? Who are they? To whom are they selling? Who is the competition?
    a. The client
        Who is our audience?
        What is our message?
        What are we really trying to sell?
        How do we relate to our agency?
    b. The agency
        How do we relate to those in our agency and our creative team?
        How to create that message and give it form?
        How do we choose a production company?
        How do we function between our client and our production company?
        How do we check on what we're doing?
    c. The production company
        How do we get the job?
        What steps do we take in:
            Preproduction
            Production
            Postproduction, including the hardware, the available talent, the money, the sense of style, the audience
            What is the delivery system?
            What is the process: Film or Tape?
5. What are the forms and templates that are set in place to help with the process?

You'll find the process traced throughout the chapters in this book. But first, the history.

There's an old joke that advertising, not prostitution, is the oldest profession. The reason being that if you have something to sell, you have to advertise. Advertising has been around since someone wanted to sell something.

History tells us that advertising started with signs outside business establishments. It's the seventeenth century. Our coach arrives at the Bent Bow Inn or the Sign of the Dove, or for that matter, The Broken Drum (You can't beat it!). We know we're at the local tavern because of the sign. In terms of advertising, there is a significant concept here. When advertising first started, you had to be able to see the sign to get the message. Furthermore, the sign was designed so that you didn't have to be able to read in order to understand where you were. In what was called Yugoslavia through the 1970s and part of the 1980s, a popular tavern was simply known as "?". It was popular with foreigners because they could find it and they didn't need to know Serbo-Croatian. For a very long time, advertising required the consumer to see the ad for it to work.

It's interesting to consider logos in this context. The first major change from "having-to-be-there" was printed ads that could travel to the consumer. This was a new and major concept. The audience didn't have to be on the spot; they could file the information regarding the business and use the information when they needed it. At this stage of the game, it was the printer who was creating the ad. The audience was limited because most people didn't know how to read, but as time went by there were more and more readers, and more and more ads. The ads were glued on walls, handed out in the streets, printed in newspapers, and walked about the village or town by men wearing signboards.

After a while, quite a long while, some bright fellow came up with a brand new idea. If he could get a lot of advertisers together and take out ads on their behalf, the printer/publisher would give him a discounted price on the space for the ads because he would guarantee volume in his space buying. He'd create the ads himself as an inducement to the advertiser. He'd charge the advertiser a percentage of the cost of the ads. The advertisers would be paying for his creative services and for his help with placing the ad. He might even pass on a portion of his savings to sweeten the deal. In any event, he'd make a profit for himself. Everyone would be happy, and he'd have a business. Voila! The advertising agency was born.

At that time the advertising agency offered to create "the ad" and then place it in the best newspapers, with the best position, and at the best cost. Then as now, this was done for a fee that was derived as a percentage of the cost of placing the ad. With enough clients, the advertising agency could buy the space for less money than the client would have had to spend.

At the very least the client got the ads created at no cost. At best the client got effective ads and tremendous savings because of the creative skills and lower price paid for media by the advertising agency. In fact, there are many other costs such as research, billing, and trafficking that the agency provided, which made it sensible for clients to pay for the advertising agency service. This model is now being modified so that the ad creators and the media buyers are often engaged and paid separately.

The client's requirement that the "best" newspaper be used often evolved so that the best newspaper became the "most desired" paper, which was the most "cost-effective" newspaper and not necessarily the most honest or the best journalistic endeavor. Soon agencies were cranking out newspaper ads and flyers, and, of course, billboards of one sort or another for a variety of different papers with different kinds of circulations. In the early part of the twentieth century, newspapers, flyers, and billboards were joined by:

Radio.

As time went on, newspapers, flyers, billboards, and radio, were joined by:

Television. And later:

the Internet.

And in that progression there is a tale of evolution in which the rules and skills that had once worked so well for newspapers somehow didn't work so well and needed change. Radio makes it's own demands on creative talent. It's not enough to simply read a newspaper ad. Radio needs drama, sound effects, and music. So new ways of working and new skills were created and developed. With it there was a passing of power; new talents were needed, and they become more visible and more important to the agency.

Then in 1941, the Bulova watch company placed an ad in a new medium—television. Over the next 10 years, with the growing number of television sets and homes using television, it was the agency that produced most of the major programs, as well as the ads that ran in the programs. But two very significant changes occurred.

At first, the important programs were productions like *The Colgate Comedy Hour*, which featured nothing but advertisements for Colgate products; *The Elgin Hour*, with clocks and watches by Elgin; *The Ford Theatre*, featuring nothing but Ford Motor company products; or *Philco Presents, The U.S. Steel Hour*, or any of a number of similarly named and sponsored programs. Milton Berle became the king of television, and his sponsor, Texaco, was known, as his opening song indicated, from Maine to Mexico. But soon, the first change occurred and ad agencies began to put their clients together so that *noncompeting* clients *within an agency* would share the cost of the production, and the time.

Instead of a production representing one client, the audience was getting productions overseen by the advertising agency and shared by two or more of an agency's clients. *The Jackie Gleason Show* was a good example of this. It was produced by the Kudner Agency and featured ads for a number of the agency's clients, who were identified in the opening and closing "billboards," and by commercials within the program. The station got to place ads from totally different agencies in the lead-in or -out, or sometimes in some of the commercial breaks. Today some syndicated shows still work this way. The major client lost some control of the content of the program, but the cost savings to each client was enormous and the agency did at least as well, and might even find reason to charge one or more clients a premium for placing their ads in a top-rated program. Of course, the stations wouldn't run just *any* program, but the programs that were offered were negotiated and accepted by the stations, usually before much money was spent on the production. *The Hallmark Hall of Fame* productions of today are a good example of this. Hallmark makes the program or hires the production company that makes the program. Hallmark then runs ads for itself within the program, and the station sells time leading into and out of the production. The network is pleased to air the programs since the content is so good. Other such plans abound. For example, some time ago, I directed *Take Five*, which consisted of a series of 5-minute comedy programs created by the J. Walter Thompson Co. Each program consisted of two 2-minute sketches starring the comedy team of Jerry Stiller and Anne Meara. It had a commercial break in the middle. The program was offered free to stations, but the J. Walter Thompson Co. retained the middle commercial slot and ran spots for J. Walter Thompson clients. It was attractive to the stations since the programming was free and offered high-quality entertainment. The local stations sold spots going into and coming out of the program, usually with commercial spots for a local car dealer or food market. Sometimes, however, noncompeting national spots aired at the front or back of the program.

Another big change occurred when advertising agencies gave up creating the programs and instead began to buy existing programming. Agencies simply had their ads inserted into programs offered by the networks. It was certainly cheaper to buy 30 seconds of time from a network or a station in an already existing program than to have to create the entire show. After a while the agency gave up having any voice in creating programming and simply bought time in network or locally produced programming. In the case of sports and special events, the stations still are the leaders in providing programming.

At the beginning of this quiet revolution in the production of programming, it was the stations that were called upon to help create the ads that were interspersed in the programs. For a long time, the stations were the only ones who had the equipment and personnel to make the commercials. While some 35-mm commercials were made for very "high end" clients, the transfer to television was not always satisfactory, and film had to compete with what was then considered the up-to-the-minute feel of live television or, somewhat later, taped productions. Sometimes the commercial was as simple as a dancing cigarette pack, which was a popular 1950s ad campaign for Old Gold cigarettes. Other live spots of that era featured on-camera talent like Betty Furness, who sold the advantages of Westinghouse refrigerators, while the merry men of Texaco sang the praises of that oil company on the most popular television show of the time—*The Milton Berle Show.*

Soon, however, independent production companies found the means to produce first rate commercials and the technology for airing film improved. The stations gave up that part of the business, except for many local spots that still get made at stations across the country.

Some agencies continued to maintain the production capacity to create their own commercials, but that also changed as agencies found it cost-effective to purchase the actual production from outside sources. Currently almost all production services provided to a client come about in one of three ways.

1. Full service agencies. They do it all—create the commercial, produce it, or oversee its production. They then place the media and buy the time or space.

2. Agencies that are specialists. They are involved exclusively with one area—either the creative side or the media side.

3. Clients who manage their total advertising package with in-house specialists.

The Men's Wearhouse, for example, started in 1975 by using a New York advertising agency for its creative work and media placement. In changing to in-house specialists, it first had its creative television work done by a freelance company but maintained the agency for advice, media placement, and buying. Then it dropped the agency and hired its own media placement experts so that the entire operation could be managed through its own advertising department.

The thrust of this book follows the making of the commercial. It deals with television and film. Print, radio, or other media are considered only in relationship to the television campaign. In future-think I suppose that the time will come when television will follow the Internet campaign. Not yet.

The content of this book examines the process involved in making film and television commercials for manufacturers, retailers, and service organizations. Those advertisers work in film, tape, and digital media, in both live and animated forms, with production budgets that range from:

Small: less than $25,000
Midsize: $25,000 to $250,000
Large: $250,000 and up

The scope of "large" was defined by a friend who told about a time when one of his major clients, a soft drink manufacturer, gave his agency the unheard of luxury of an unlimited budget—which, he claims, they exceeded.

Since budget is important, there is this final note about the hierarchy of people in this process. For a while, I worked at FILMEX, a successful commercial production company in New York. They were best known for a Hertz commercial that said "Let Hertz put you in the driver's seat." That line of copy was coupled with a visual in which the "star" of the commercial flew into the seat of a moving convertible. While preparing for one of the commercials, we had a front yard built in our studio. The lawn was created by having truckloads of expensive grass sod brought to the studio and set in place. When the unit manager saw it, he wanted it for his house after the commercials wrapped. Then the studio producer entered the studio, saw it, and suggested it be put aside for him, which meant that the unit manager would not get the sod. That request was followed by the director of photography, the director, and then the advertising agency producer. Each was one step higher than the last, and each would have gotten the sod, until the advertising agency producer, who assigned the job, asked for it. Naturally, he gave out the job, so he was set to get the sod. It was the last day of the shoot, and the client walked on the set. He knew nothing about the requests for the sod, and soon after seeing it wondered, "Could he have it?" Everyone, including the advertising agency producer, was happy to oblige.

The hierarchy is very simple. Whoever is paying runs the show. The client picks the agency, and the agency picks the production company or companies. All of them need to work together to create effective commercials. However, the process starts with the client.

2 Client

It's hardly a surprise that companies as divergent as General Motors, The Men's Wearhouse, and local retailers like Joe's Auto Repair all want to increase sales and achieve higher profits. They want to get a larger percentage of the market, appeal to a larger customer base, and generally achieve greater brand awareness. Quite apart from the budgets, their advertising approaches are very different, as are their needs. Surprisingly, they are also alike in many ways. Those differences and parallels are very significant to clients, to their agencies, and to those who make their commercials.

For the most part, clients with a limited budget tend to come from a local retail or service community, rather than from a national or manufacturing community. A significant number of commercials are regularly made in this price category. One only needs to travel to local markets around the country and watch the news programs to see how good that work can be. (One also gets to see a great deal of second-rate work.) As the price of video equipment continues to go down and the quality of the equipment goes up, there are apt to be more clients using television to advertise. Furthermore, theater, film, television, and media studies programs in colleges and universities are becoming more popular. With that growth, we can expect to see a growing number of college-trained producers hoping to break into the field and creating a strong, if eclectic, talent pool that enters at the lower end of the spectrum.

No matter what the budget is, the client will have to follow these same steps in order to create a "charge" for the agency. The charge seeks to state, succinctly, the goals of the client for the agency.

1. *Define needs. Define the audience. Be specific.* Is this a special sale commercial? Is it a grand opening commercial? Is this commercial seeking a wider audience, introducing a new product, benefits, etc? Who is the audience? Men? Women? Men and women? Is there an age factor? Teenagers aren't apt to buy Geritol, and senior citizens aren't apt to want the latest in skateboards.

2. *Be realistic. Be specific.* What kind of response is reasonable to expect from a television commercial? From the campaign? Can results be measured? How? Will measuring be costly? When does one start measuring? When does one stop measuring? When is the whole process necessary?

3. *Cost.* Questions of cost need to be addressed. Consider if the portion of the budget that can be committed to advertising on television will be sufficient to fulfill those expectations. The president of an agency I worked for once pitched and got the go-ahead to create a spot that would cost the equivalent of $30,000, only to discover that the client could only spend $70,000 on time. We suggested a strong print campaign instead since we felt that the time that could be bought for $70,000 wouldn't be sufficient to make a difference, but a different kind of campaign and awareness might be achieved with a $100,000 print budget. So the important questions are: What's an appropriate percentage of sales to allocate to the advertising budget? What's the best media plan for the budget? What's the best media mix? Should there be a campaign with print and radio too, or just print and television?

Defining needs, being realistic, and creating a charge are often easier said than done. There's no absolute answer to any of the relevant questions, but they do have to be addressed. For our purpose, which is to consider the making of the commercial, we can dispense with some of the headier questions and instead consider what goes into the making of a low budget commercial.

What should the commercial say? Sometimes the answer is obvious. A new store is opening, so it's a "Grand Opening" spot, or a new service has been added, which will take the name of whatever the service is. In retail advertising the promotion-minded retailer has an excuse for a sale every month.

January—The New Year/After Christmas Sale
February—President's Day Sale
March—St. Patrick's Day and Spring Sale
April—Easter Sale
May—Mother's Day
June—Father's Day
July—July 4th
August—Summer Savings Sale & Back-to-School
September—Labor Day
October—Columbus Day
November—Thanksgiving
December—Christmas Holiday

One of my favorite print ads is one that I first saw in *Ogilvy On Advertising* (Vintage Press 1985). It's an ad for McGraw-Hill business journals. It was intended to spur corporate advertisers to consider advertising in business journals, particularly McGraw-Hill Publications. It's a picture of an older man sitting in a chair. The copy says:

I don't know who you are.

I don't know your company.

I don't know your company's product.

I don't know what your company stands for.

I don't know your company's customers.

I don't know your company's record.

I don't know your company's reputation.

Now—what was it you wanted to sell me?

The same is true for low budget commercials. The client must realize that an advertised product has a greater chance of being bought or used than one that is unadvertised. The short saying that covers this is: "It pays to advertise."

Commercials don't have to be about any particular holiday or sale. They can simply exist to encourage the viewer to think about the client at the right time. Need new shoes? Think Al's Shoe Emporium. Buying a new car? Think Joe's Car Lot. Save at 4A Rug Cleaning. Save on garage doors, opticians, etc.

How to Proceed

Once the needs and audience are defined, the budget is in place, and the topic for the commercial has been chosen, there is a question about special circumstances. Is there some special way that this commercial ought to be presented? Will there be a narrator who is familiar to the audience through radio? Will the owner or CEO appear? Is there a logo or some device such as a puppet or animal associated with the company that ought to be included in the spot? Will type running across the screen be adequate?

Inevitably, questions outside of the creative thrust demand an answer. How long does it take to make a commercial? How much will this specific commercial cost? Another important area to consider is the client's time. How much is needed? How much can be devoted to advertising needs?

When should the client be "hands-on" and when should he be "hands-off"? The answer, of course, depends on the client and the commercial. Some productions take longer than others, some cost more than others. An estimate of time and cost is usually included as part of the presentation. Prior to agreeing to the production, the client and the producer ought to agree on all the terms. Then a contract should be drawn up. It can't spell out everything, but it often helps to define what's expected, what's to be delivered, what are the due dates, what are the terms of the payments, how much is to be paid, and at what times in the time line.

At the lowest end of the scale, many transactions are handled with a simple hand shake. A contract that is too long may scare away a first time commercial client. Often a simple contract is all that is possible. At the higher end of the scale, the simple contract shown in

Figure 2.1 is replaced with very specific contracts that spell out the terms in much greater detail. However, most contracts usually spell out:

Who are the involved parties
What's to be done
Who owns the finished material
The payment, and schedule for payment
Allowances for exceptions
Warrants and indemnifications

A basic contract is designed to state, very simply, what will be provided, at what time, and at what cost. In some ways it's intended to impress the client with the realities of creating a commercial and position the work as a business transaction. It's also simple enough to not scare off the client.

This contract defines the method of payment as well. A typical arrangement splits the payments into three periods. One-third of the cost is payable prior to shooting. At the very least this gives the producer an immediate cash flow to begin making purchases on behalf of the client. These are purchases of film or video tape stock, rental of equipment, and hiring the required crew. One-third might be due at the end of the shooting. This will assure the producer payment for the bulk of the cost of editing, even if that cost is simply their time. Lastly, one-third might be due when the spots are delivered, which covers the producer's profit and contingency. Alternately, some producers want to have 50% upon signing of the contract and the remainder upon completion.

One of the things the client might want to consider including in the contract is the right to retain all the original footage as well as production notes for future commercial production.

Choices

There are times, particularly at the lower end of the production scale, when a producer simply offers a particular commercial to a client. The client either does *that* commercial or finds someone else with whom to work. Most of the time there is a meeting between the client and the commercial creator in which the client explains what is needed and expected. Essentially the client is saying: "I charge you with the task of creating a commercial that will accomplish. . . ." After that is spelled out, the creator can go to work and come back with some ideas for commercials.

A moment here to enter this note: Prior to creating that charge, it is well to realize that two of the most common mistakes are:

1. *Superlatives:* They should be avoided. They're usually not true, and they're almost always boring. They're a challenge to which the consumer adds . . . "Yeah, yeah, says you."

ART SIMON PRODUCTIONS
436 S. CENTRAL AVE., GLENDALE, CA 91204
TEL. (818) 486-8888 - FAX. (818) 500-7682

VIDEO PRODUCTION CONTRACT

Client's Name:_____

Proposal Objectives
      This proposal is intended to frame the working responsibilities of **Art Simon Productions** in the development of a video program and provide a payment structure so that work on the project can be scheduled. This proposal represents an approximate working budget based on Art Simon Production's total involvement in creation and production. This includes program design, script development, visualization, video production, computer graphics, animation, professional voice narration, music selection, directing, and editing.

Production
      The primary goal of this project is to produce a

_____

_____

Program Concept & Included Services:
_____

_____

Cost Estimate
      1. Preproduction _____

      2. Production _____

      3. Postproduction _____

Approximate Total Project Cost _____

Payment Schedule:

      ---------- of total estimated budget due at project start
      ---------- of total due at script approval
      ---------- of total due at production
      ---------- of total due at delivery of finished program

Art Simon Productions will provide a final, edited, BetaCam SP Master Tape.

The above terms are agreed to and acknowledged

by _____ date _____.

Art Simon Productions by _____ date _____

Figure 2.1   A typical video contract.

2. *Stuffing:* Trying to put too much into the commercial. Because of the great cost of making the commercial and airing the commercial, the client wants to get full value for the money. Nevertheless a spot cannot say everything. It's better to choose one point and make it well. Unfortunately, if the creator/production company is to get the job and the charge is to "say everything," they may acquiesce and then create what's demanded. The client then gets fulfilling commercials that are too stuffed, too busy, and not very effective.

> We can all do "awful." Unfortunately, we do, because we get a paycheck. And after they don't buy (our version of) "great," you say, okay, we gave it our best shot and now we can do "awful" and we'll get our money and go home.
>
> Greg Wilson, Creative Director—Director/Producer—RedBall Tiger

I once did the following experiment. I was directing a commercial shoot and was standing with the client and the president of the advertising agency as we waited for the lighting crew to finish the setup. We were talking about the length of commercials, and I proposed that I'd start a stopwatch behind my back. I would press the lap button when I thought 30 seconds had passed. They too should call out when they thought 30 seconds had passed, and I'd set the lap button for them.

The results were that the client thought 30 seconds had passed after only 15 seconds. So far as he was concerned, the 30 seconds he was paying for flashed by in double time.

I called 30 seconds exactly right, which I suspect is what would be the case with most producers, directors, and editors who are used to dealing with just the space allowed for a 30-second commercial.

The president of the agency thought 30 seconds had passed after a minute had gone by. Invariably, he'd try to pack a minute's worth of material into a 30-second spot.

Once basic decisions are made about what needs to be said in the commercial, the creative process begins. Some ideas for commercials are created and then presented. Choosing the spot or series of spots to be made can be very difficult. This is particularly true if the creators are doing a good job. Usually the creative team or person presents two or three ideas. The hope is that there will be one standout idea that captures the client's imagination and is a clear choice to be given the go-ahead. Hopefully, all of the ideas are good and finding a criterion to choose one over the other is very difficult. Where money is no object, product testing and focus groups can be used. More often than not with low budget productions, the CEO, or the CEO and friends, or trusted employees make the decision. Sometimes an opinion is sought from any or all of those people. In retail advertising any customers who happen to be around when the creative pitch is being made may also have a voice in making the decision.

Finally, however, one commercial, or series of commercials, is chosen. They may still need refining, but the concept is in place and a basic commercial has been chosen. The spots can be worked on until they're ready to go into production. At this stage of preproduction, whatever the budget, the client ought to become involved with the particulars of the commercial. Again, there are questions that need to answered before the commercial or commercials go to the production stage:

1. How have the requested changes from the original presentation been accomplished?
   The client needs to agree to the changes and sign off on them.

2. Who is the talent? Will there be auditions? When and where?
   The client needs to approve the talent. In the least expensive production, the talent may simply be Uncle Henry and his family. Given a more substantial budget, auditions may be called for and the client may want to go to the auditions. They may also be content to view a video tape of a few select choices presented by the production company after the initial audition process is completed. The client may also simply leave the decision in the hands of the producer. Casting is finalized when the talent is hired.

3. Is there music? What is it? When will it be decided?
   The client may want to have approval of the music, or at least be given a choice.

4. Is there an announcer? Who? When will the announce-track be made?
   The client may want to approve the announcer. Are there audition reels available? The client might want to come to the recording session. When and where is it? Perhaps the client or the producer will serve as talent.

5. When will the audio be mixed? The mix is the process of incorporating the announcer, music, and live elements into one track.
   The client may want to attend the mix or simply have approval of the final mix but needs to be aware that redoing anything adds to the total cost. The cost of the sweetening session, in which the mixed elements are fine-tuned, and for that matter the cost of making changes in any of the elements of the commercial can be, but is not always, significant. The differences will depend on the nature of the work. Is it simple or complex? What kind of hardware is involved; what kind of time is involved? It will also depend on the city in which the work is being done. Is it a highly competitive city like Los Angeles, or not-so-competitive like Butte, Montana?

6. What is the schedule for the shoot and where will it be shot?
   Can the client be there? If not, who will go in his or her place with the authority to make on-the-spot decisions if and when they are needed?

7. What props, scenic elements, or help will the client need to provide? For example, there may be a special prop or visual that resides with the client. The client can supply cars, vans, merchandise, letters of introduction, etc.

    a.   What's needed?

    b.   When must it be delivered and returned?

    c.   Who actually does the delivery and return?

8.   Postproduction. When and where will it be edited?

    The client needs to know about those steps prior to actually editing, which includes:

    a.   The viewing and listing of "footage" in which all the material that was shot is viewed and logged so that it can be found and used when needed.

    b.   The steps to the rough cut in which a preliminary version or "rough draft" of the spots are produced. The rough cut usually has all the scenes but may be missing elements such as music, titles, and sometimes specific shots.

    c.   The steps involved in the final cut.

Producing the Spot

Ideally, everything is arranged before the shooting begins, but that's not always the case. Let us say, rather, that once all the critical issues are in place, the actual shooting can begin. During this stage of the commercial, it's often wise for the client to be on hand. This ensures that someone is always available to make spontaneous decisions about sudden opportunities or surprises that inevitably arise and are a part of all shoots. For example, additional shots of merchandise can be taken for use in subsequent spots. It may be wise to shoot unplanned for, but useful, exterior shots of the storefront, waiting rooms, etc. This footage may then be used for cutaways, in which the editor cuts away from a master shot to show closeups or material that is simply relevant to the master video or audio. (For example, the store owner is saying: "Come on down to our store and we'll show you terrific bargains." The cutaway might then cut away from the picture of him and show the storefront.) Additionally, such footage may be available for future commercials. An actor may propose a line or a bit of business that isn't part of what was planned, and it may be prudent, if expensive, to shoot the additional material. There may be additional costs involved in seizing the opportunity or in solving a problem that arises unexpectedly. Production problems can usually be fixed in one of two ways. The expensive way is almost always the better of the two choices. The "less expensive" choice usually comes with the understanding that it may not "quite" fit the bill, it has "some" drawbacks, and isn't guaranteed . . . etc." The client or the client's representative needs to be on hand to authorize such expenditures and to understand how the costs came about.

    Knowing that there will be issues that come up during the production, it's best to work out a chain of command. Stopping the flow of a production to ask questions can be very costly and can contribute to a less cohesive effort on the part of the director, crew, and talent. Not getting the answers may be just as costly. It's smart to have a plan about who handles what responsibilities and how to handle issues that may come up during the shoot. Often there is a producer/production manager or an assistant available, even on inexpensive shoots, and they may be able to explain what's happening, answer questions, or at least recognize when the flow must be stopped. The danger here is that it puts whoever takes on that job in a delicate position with regard to both the client and the director. The bottom line is that sound judgment and a sense of perspective are valuable. These characteristics are not necessarily guaranteed to anyone, client or "artist/director." Sometimes "muddling through" is the best one can do.

Immediately after the shoot, as things are being wrapped up, or when viewing dailies, it's wise to make note of events and "takes" or scenes that will be relevant to the edit. Those written notes taken while events are fresh in the mind are often a great help the next day, or more to the point, weeks later when the exact order of things and the "whys" and "wherefores" become fuzzy.

"That's a wrap!" signals the end of the production stage and marks the beginning of the postproduction stage. The editing of the spot begins. The process is covered later in the chapter on editing. However, briefly stated, all of the editing will consist of just two major elements.

1. *The shot:* Everything that happens in any single shot or take.
2. *Montage:* The method of getting from shot to shot:
    a. A cut, e.g., we start on a wide shot then cut to a close-up.
    b. A dissolve, e.g., it's a dream sequence, the camera moves into the heroine's eyes and the picture dissolves to a little girl who we assume is her many years ago. Dissolves usually signal a change in place or time that is related to the scene we are watching.
    c. A wipe, e.g., think about old time movies in which we saw both sides of a phone conversation. The reporter on the left side of the screen, and the editor taking notes on the fast breaking story on the right.

The client may attend the edit sessions; indeed some clients insist on being involved in all the steps, but usually the advertising agency, the production company, or the editing company (or some mix of those three) handle all the details. After the rough cut is viewed, notes regarding changes are made, and the spot or spots are then conformed to whatever decisions were made. The editing process is covered in Chapter 6, Postproduction: Editing, and Chapter 7, Post-Plus—Audio/Graphics/Animation.

Once the commercial is complete, a master copy is made in whatever form is deemed best for duplication. Dubs are made, or copies are transmitted, usually by satellite feed, to stations.

Low Budget: Up to $25,000

In the less than $25,000 level of the production scale, the relationship of the production company to the advertiser is apt to be remarkably distanced, summed up by the phrase:

"Leave everything to me!" Often the client is a family-owned and family-operated business. While the business may use the services of a small advertising agency for print work, that agency is not apt to promote the use of television commercials, nor for that matter is the agency likely to be appropriate for creating and running a television campaign should the client wish to do so. Instead, clients with limited budgets find that many stations want to sell time directly. The station will either create the commercial, help arrange for a production company to work with the client, or simply reedit a spot that was produced for the client at some other time.

A production company that works with agencies that have low-budget clients often finds itself involved in the creative process to a much larger extent than is possible with more expensive commercial production. It should be noted that there are major clients with very large budgets who also work directly with their production company.

Let's start by imagining that we are a low-budget commercial client. Perhaps we're a doctor or have a law practice. We might own a restaurant or a hardware store, or a few restaurants or hardware stores. We don't know about the creative end of advertising. We are not very knowledgeable about "media." We know the difference between print, radio, and television commercials, but we don't know the pros and cons of using one rather than the other. If we decide we want to be on television, we don't know about the difference between film and tape. We don't know about market share, or reach, or Homes Using Television (HUT) levels, or any of the other phrases and concepts that are second nature to a knowledgeable advertiser. We know, or feel, we *ought* to advertise, and we've been sold on television. Perhaps we've been offered what we believe to be an outstanding buy on a local cable station, or VHF or UHF station. Now we need a commercial. What do we do? How do we go about getting a commercial? How do we know whom to ask? And with so much money involved, and it's always a lot of money, even if it is a good buy, isn't a second opinion warranted? What's the right thing to do? Television advertising beckons. How do we proceed? How do we find someone to make the commercial?

If the client doesn't have access to an agency that can help with the question, perhaps a small television station or cable station will be able to assist. Locate one that carries ads that are similar in scale to the one envisioned. Even without inquiring, the client may find that a recommendation regarding commercial production will come from a station trying to sell time or a friend who has used television in the past. Perhaps the producer will be a relative or friend. In any event, the procedures in preproduction, production, and postproduction are the same for all levels of production. The differences are in the size and scope. At the lower levels, one usually encounters less research and creative efforts, smaller crews, and a more limited production set-up. To the client, however, all the steps noted earlier in this chapter are relevant no matter what budget is involved. The requirements of working with the production company and the agency, if there is one, will demand an investment not only of time and money, but also of interest in the process. As a cautionary note, over-demanding and intrusive requests in the name of "interest" can become very costly and detrimental to the commercial.

At the lowest budget level, the client is usually well advised to interview one or two producers. Choose one that can work within the budget, and with whom there is a sense of compatibility. Once the job has been awarded, the client is usually best served by accepting the production company's guidance.

Midbudget: $25,000 to $250,000

At the next level of commercial production are clients who spend $25,000 to $250,000 for commercial production. This category is, to say the least, arbitrary. There is no specific cutoff that positively identifies the exact penny at which a commercial goes from being considered low priced to medium priced. Then too, even within this category there's a huge difference between a client who spends $25,000 on the making of a commercial and one who is prepared to spend $250,000. Nevertheless, it's useful to construct this midcategory. Both the client and agency who work in this realm are apt to be different than those working at either the lower or upper end of the production scale. However, the procedures for clients on both ends of this "middle" group are similar, as it is not for low and high end work.

First of all, clients who spend $25,000 and more on commercial production usually have a budget for the placement of the spots that is far greater than the cost of creating the spots. With large sums set aside for placement, clients tend to be aggressive in seeking a more organized, if more costly, approach to their television commercial needs, knowing all the while that there's no guarantee regarding any television commercial.

Most clients in this midlevel category work with advertising agencies, and in that they are similar to the very largest companies. What separates them from the Fortune 500 corporations is the amount of purchasing power they have and the structure they have in place to work with the agency to create and test commercials and then to run them.

The midsized advertiser seeks out an agency in many ways. Sometimes an agency affiliation stems from prior work together, from seeing a good campaign, or from recommendations. Frequently, a client shops among a few agencies to find a match for the product or services. The client's search for an agency starts with the belief that it pays to advertise and with the realization that there are sufficient funds or potential funds to make working with an agency a mutually beneficial endeavor. A call to the sales office of any commercial station in the region will probably yield a list of agencies that handle similar clients or that could handle the caller's request. A look at the American Association of Advertising Agencies web site yields a list of advertising agencies, their clients, and samples of their work. Local or regional advertising councils would offer the same information. Usually, by the time the client is ready to look for an agency, a list of possible agencies is on hand, or easy to find. In fact, the client will probably be besieged with agencies soliciting the account. How to choose the best one, or "what's the best match between client and agency," is the real question.

Let's start by saying there is no correct way to find an agency, nor is there a correct way to make commercials, but there are some parameters to consider. In whatever way the agency has come to be interviewed, the client wants to know as much as possible about the agency before signing a contract. Finding out about the agency starts with asking for a meeting where the agency makes a presentation about who they are and their philosophies. The client may choose a few agencies to make presentations. The client wants to know:

1. What does the agency do? Are they a full service agency? A media placement firm, solely interested in the placement and buying of space and time? Or are they a "creative" agency who suggests others for media placement?

2. How do they work with the client? Create campaigns? Do they test the results of their advertising? How many people are assigned to the account, and who are they?

3. Who are the agency's clients? With what other products or services do they work?

4. What is their philosophy for creating commercials? Is the approach hard sell or soft sell? Is there a way to define their approach to the creative side of the process? What is their philosophy regarding the media side of commercial presentation? Will there be a mix of media? What kind? Do they do testing? What kind?

5. How is the agency structured? Is it a subgroup to a larger agency? What are the advantages and disadvantages of that? Does that help or hurt?

6. Would they be willing to compete for the account?

7. Can other clients be contacted? Essentially, are references available?

On the other hand, the agency wants to know about the client.

1. What is the product or service?

2. How much business does the company do in a year? What are the gross sales? What percentage is allocated for advertising? They need to know what kind of budget would be in operation or how the overall projections might be aligned. Is there sufficient volume or product to consider television advertising? Should some other media mix be considered? If so, what kind of mix?

3. Who is the audience the client already has? What audience does the client want?

4. How does the client manage its brand? Is the client trying to increase the volume of their sales, the dollar amount of individual sales, or a percentage of sales? Is the potential client trying to build new markets or increase its share of the market? Who is the competition? Is the client trying to wrest sales from the competition, or are they adding to the audience they already have?

5. What time line is in place for the creation of a campaign according to the client? Is it flexible? Is it reasonable?

It may be that one agency is chosen to pursue the account. However, it is more likely that a number of agencies will be asked to pitch the account. The client wants to know what the agency envisions for them. In order for the agency to proceed, they'll have to learn more about the client. That can take a week, 2 weeks, or a month for that matter. The expectation is that the agency will come back to the client with a proposal for managing the account. To be able to make such a presentation, the agency will have to study the client's business. The questions they'll need to ask are outlined in Chapter 3, Agency. The immediate question has to do with the client's advertising director and the assistance he or she can provide in helping the agency learn about the company and its needs.

The agency gets its direction for the handling of the account as it begins to work with the client. Ideally, there is one voice who speaks for the company—the vice president, director, or manager of advertising, or of marketing. As the client and the agency work together, elements of the interpersonal or interdepartmental workings of the two companies become apparent. Management issues may come into play that have nothing to do with the creation of commercials, but which will affect the working relationship and the commercial. It may be that the vice president of advertising and the CEO really have different opinions of what is needed. How that is resolved is very significant, but in some ways it is almost irrelevant because ultimately if the agency is going to pursue the account, they will all have to find common ground. The agency will have to find a direction for the commercial and design a proposal for the client. The proposal will include creative efforts such as storyboards for commercials, print layouts, billboard as well as radio copy, and even flyers . . . the spectrum of media placement. If the agency is a full-service agency, one that both creates and places commercials, a proposed media budget will be suggested as part of the plan. Essentially, the agency is saying if you choose us to handle your account, here's how we'll proceed and why:

1. *Research:* Here's what we've learned (or think) about your company. This is our slant on you.
2. *Creative:* These are the ideas we'd promote and why we think they're good ideas that will support the company's goals.
3. *Media:* Here is the way we'd promote those ideas.
4. *Criteria:* These are the criteria we'll bring to measure results.
5. *Management:* These are the personnel from our organization who will work with your organization.
6. *Legal/accounting:* In case it hasn't been discussed, and even if it has, it's sensible to reiterate: These are the terms of our service and its cost.

Most often at this time, one agency emerges as the one that is most compatible with the client, terms are negotiated, and signed contracts result.

At this point there usually is a time line in place. For example, the client wants the commercials to be on the air within a month. The basic ideas have been chosen but may need to be changed or there may be two or even three ideas competing. How does the client choose between the commercials and their variations? At the lowest budget level, the producer offers a limited choice of possible commercials. The decision is almost always made by the owner of the business. As the price of making the commercials and putting them on the air goes up, the steps involved in making a decision may not be so simple. Some clients simply buy into whatever the CEO says. Others may turn to the advertising director or a committee of top executives. Many advertising agencies and their clients believe in testing. Chapter 8, Research, discusses the procedure for testing commercials. For our purposes we will assume that the CEO, the advertising director, and whatever executive, spouse, or relative with a valued opinion agree to a set of commercials. Invariably there will be some alterations or changes that need to be made.

The agency goes to work to make the changes and then presents them for approval. As the commercials go through the various stages of production, the client needs to be available to answer critical questions as they arise. The client also has to take an active role in guiding the agency in the process, alerting them to particular nuances that might not be apparent. For instance, as a neophyte writer for a retail advertising agency, I was surprised to discover that our retail clients hated the word "cheap." This was true even if the price at which they were offering merchandise *was* cheap. The retailer's point was that the consumer might interpret the word "cheap" to mean that the goods were of a cheap quality. Instead we could proclaim that it was "inexpensive," that these were: "discount prices," "great savings," "tremendous value," etc. No matter how specialized the area of work for a particular agency, the client will probably still need to guide the agency in some aspects of its business, or the particular way in which *they* do business.

The initial stage of preproduction is completed when the story boards have been finalized. The client agrees that "*this*" is what will be shot. Of course, changes will occur, but once the final go-ahead has been given, the production begins. Costs for any changes will have to be negotiated. The commercials will probably be shot on film using a single camera. Since the early 2000s, tape or digital media have played a more prominent part when commercials are shot and edited. Digital or film, the commercials would still most likely be shot with one camera and edited later—film style, unless it's an infomercial. The production arm of the agency will begin to solicit bids from various production companies. This process is covered in Chapter 3, Agency.

For the client it is a time when numerous decisions demand immediate attention. As was the case with the very least expensive commercials, the client may want to see the reel of whoever is going to be shooting the commercials. They may want to get involved in the casting choices. They will need to know what product or service they will be required to provide for the shoot. Everyone will want to know how long it will take to shoot the spots and when they need to be ready for air. Now that there *is* a commercial, or series of commercials in place, the client will certainly want to know what the cost will be. The agency should guide the client through the process.

The cost will be based on a number of considerations, including the number of spots to be made, their length, perhaps lead time, and the following:

1. *The Cast:* Will celebrities or personalities be involved? If so, do they need special and costly handling, such as a limousine, personal assistants, personal makeup, hair stylists, etc.? Who pays for this? How many people are in the spot? Is the commercial to be shot under the jurisdiction of the Screen Actor's Guild (SAG—Film) or of the American Federation of Television and Radio Artists (AFTRA—Tape/Live)?

2. *The Crew:* How many crew members are required, and how long will they be needed? Who is available? You may not need a gardener for a men's clothing commercial, but you probably will need extra costume hands. The "A" costume team may cost $500 a day, the "B" team costs $250, and you can get a production assistant (PA) for $75 to $100 a day. Who has been selected?

3. *Time:* How much preproduction time is needed? Locations need to be scouted, arrangements made, props acquired or rented. How many preproduction days will be needed, and how many people at what price will be required during this stage of the process? How many production days? Is the production house bidding for postproduction as well? If so, how many postproduction days? What's included in the postproduction bid? Digital graphics? Film-to-tape transfer? Audio sweetening? And so on.

4. *Operational expenses:* What are the costs for rights and clearances, rentals, insurance, benefits, office space, and similar issues? This should all be covered.

5. *Specialized gear:* How much and what kinds are needed?

Shooting Begins

Whether the project is a single-camera, multiple-camera, or a full-blown all-stops-out, price-is-not-an-object agency shoot, or even a student production, shooting begins only when:

1. The facility or location is ready. The set is in place, the location has been prepared, and permits are in place.
2. All personnel—client, agency, cast, crew, security, and so on—have their calls and have been confirmed.
3. All rentals are set, including cameras, mikes, lights, props, vehicles, locations, costumes, gaffer supplies, special effects items, intercoms, and portable toilets.
4. All legal work is done.

Permits and insurance are in place. Contracts are signed and in place. Union clearances have been completed and the rights have been secured for all music, lyrics, poetry, photographs, stock footage, logos, etc.

Production

Finally everything is in place, and the first shoot day begins. The client is there to help make on-the-spot decisions. As is the case in all levels of production, the client is tempted to voice approval or disapproval or to offer advice to the director as the shoot progresses. However, as is the case in all levels of production, there ought to be only one voice that speaks to the director. That voice should be the agency producer. Too many voices and too many opinions, questions, or suggestions can grind a shoot down to a snail's pace. It can kill creative impulses before they begin.

The actual shoot day, with crew in place and costly rental equipment at the ready in an expensive studio, is a time when things can become very tense and when tact and a sense of proportion are very necessary. It can also be a time when very nice things happen. Whatever the case, the client's best course of action is to work through the chain of command on the set. On the set the director is in charge. The agency bestows that "power" on the director. It's true that that's done on behalf of the client. However, practically speaking, it's the advertising agency, not the client, that is paying for the shoot. And it is the agency that should be the voice that speaks for the client at the shoot. The director will almost always direct his or her questions to the agency producer.

As is the case in all levels of production, at the end of the shoot if it's a tape shoot, or after the screening of dailies if it's shot on film, there is a meeting with the agency producer and creative director, the client, and sometimes the director/producer about the shoot. Opinions are voiced, and notes taken while the events are fresh in the mind. These notes are useful at the edit and later, as material is reused, or to answer legal questions that can arise at a much later date.

Postproduction

The procedure for all commercial production is similar. The production company transfers the material to a tape format or to a hard drive, and perhaps makes a VHS copy for viewing and logging. Sometimes the client wants to be a part of that process, but usually the production company or postproduction company handles the transfer and the logging of material. The advertising agency or the editorial house creates an edit decision list (EDL) and work can then begin on the construction of the commercial. Most often the client *is* involved in the editing process. At the midlevel of production, the production company and specifically the director is involved in the editing decisions. It should be noted that as the cost of production goes up, each segment of the total production begins to be handled by specialists. At the higher end of the production scale the director is often left out of the editing process. Instead, an editing facility is used, and the agency team, creative director, and producer edit the spots with the edit facilities editor, and sometimes the client. It should be stated, however, that there are many directors working on major commercials who insist on editing their own work. In fact, the question of director's cut is one that has been of major significance to the Director's Guild of America and is a significant part of most contract negotiations.

On a personal note, I have had some of my commercial work watered down and blandly presented by unimaginative, though competent, editors. I have also been saved by, and learned a great deal from, extraordinarily talented and experienced editors.

It may be that the boards and shooting are straightforward and the spots are completed within a simple editing session, but that is unusual. Most often what emerges is a "rough cut," which is destined to be refined even further. Additional work is needed in some area that the editing program can't handle or in some area that exceeds the expertise of those actually doing the edit. Such areas might be color correction or audio mixing. In such cases the material is sent to a specialty house. There the editor, the agency producer, and perhaps the client and the producer/director work on refining the specific area. A new corrected tape is made, now color corrected or audio enhanced, and that track is digitally reintroduced to the commercial.

The next thing that usually happens is that copies of the commercial are sent to executives to solicit comments. Sometimes these screenings reveal missing information, sometimes mistakes, and it is best to catch this early. I once directed a set of commercials that required a lower-third super (white type appearing at the bottom of the screen) that indicated that supplies were limited. The client's advertising agency hadn't been made aware of the situation, and the disclaimer, explaining that supplies were limited, was inadvertently omitted. Needless to say, we reedited the spots and added the disclaimer.

In another case, everyone, including the director, the producer, the production assistant, the art director, the editor, and even the president of the agency all signed off on a commercial that had a super that erroneously substituted the word "Atlantic" for the word "Atlanta." It was the CEO of the company that caught that mistake, inquiring at the time if the commercial was some kind of a joke. It was pulled from the dubbing facility minutes before an enormous run was started.

Once the commercial is complete, a master copy is made. Then, in whatever form is deemed best for airing, dubs are made or copies are transmitted to stations.

High Budget: Over $250,000

Clients who wield large budgets when they make commercials are as diverse as any other group. There are usually organizations that have been making commercials for years, like Ford and IBM. There are also those who are new at it but have grown from small budgets to ever larger ones. And there are those, typified by the "dot-coms" of the late 1990s, who suddenly found themselves creating high-budget productions with very little background in the process.

Most of the time, commercials that cost over $250,000 are overseen by clients who know how commercials are made and who have developed some system for defining their needs. They start out by evaluating what they want their commercial to accomplish and what kind of a feeling the commercial should have. They test everything they can along the way. They may ask for line item approval of costs or simply accept a bottom line estimate and invoice. They are usually knowledgeable and prepared to absorb whatever cost is necessary to get the commercial they believe will do the job. They work with advertising agencies that are use to dealing with similar clients. They work with the very best production groups. They are different from each other in their taste and in their philosophic approach, rather than in the actual steps taken during production. Nevertheless, advertisers seem to approach their goals in one of two ways. They say:

1. I don't know what we should be doing. You tell me.
2. Here's what needs to be done. Create a commercial that will satisfy this demand of ours.

Of course different industries have different times of the year when advertising becomes most significant. Sometimes it's seasonal. For car manufacturers, for example, it's the end of the year for current stock, and the introduction of the next year's model. Retailers who sell toys are exceptionally busy commercial producers at Christmas time, as are others whose products might be given as Christmas gifts. By the same token, toy manufacturers need to have completed their toy commercials in the spring if they are to have material to show at the various toy expos. Sometimes the goal of a commercial is to promote a new product. At other times the commercial's function is simply to heighten consumer awareness.

The advertising department of major advertising agencies oversees print, radio, perhaps billboards, in-store promotions, flyers, in-house news, etc. Television commercials are simply one phase of the public face of their client's company. Often there is more than one advertising agency that works with the account. At other times a corporate client's advertising message is brought together under one umbrella. IBM, for example, had a number of different agencies working on various areas from corporate to consumer products. Its overall message had become confusing. It then changed its tactics and brought all its advertising under the one roof of Ogilvy & Mather. For our purposes we'll simply concern ourselves with the television portion of any one major account.

At some time, usually at the end of a fiscal year, management reviews its yearly business plan, as well as more long term plans, for the company. During the review, goals are set. Part of the plan for accomplishing those goals will be a mandate to the advertising department. During the review there may be an examination of the fundamental principles of the company. The prior year is compared to the current year. Management may review its perception of the company with what research suggests the public thinks, and it may wish to change that perception. There are various theories of management and advertising game plans. One of the more popular management theories involves the concept of "brand awareness," which deals with the total image of the company. Brand awareness was made popular in the book *A New Brand World* by Scott Bredlow with Stephen Fenichell. Scott Bredlow is most well known for his work with Nike and Starbucks.

Each company will seek to leave with a focused plan in place. Advertising results are evaluated in terms of volume of business and of contribution to the overall good of the company. Ultimately a plan emerges that will be the impetus for a commercial or commercials throughout the year. In discussing future plans for advertising, they will be considering:

1. What is the volume of business?
2. Do they want to increase it? There may be reasons not to increase the volume of business. A company may not wish to strain a system that is already overworked, or it may wish to control availability of a particular product.
3. Does the company want to increase the amount of money made on each sale?
4. Does the company want to increase the percentage of business in a particular area?
5. Does the company want to increase business by appealing to a wider audience?
6. Does the company want to take business from competition?
7. What are the marketing strategies, and what percentage of marketing funds can be allocated to all their areas of advertising, including television?

The decisions made at this stage of corporate deliberations are then reviewed with the advertising agency, and the agency sets to work to come up with creative campaigns to achieve the desired results. At the agency, the creative department will go to work to create a campaign. The research department will be answering questions to assist the creative process, and, at the same time, the research and strategic planning groups will be developing strategies to implement whatever creative campaign is chosen. The media department will work on developing a media plan.

The chances are that at least two approaches and as many as five will be presented to the client. In order to present ideas for commercials, agencies often prepare animatics of the proposed spots. An animatic is a tape or digital presentation in which the story board is animated and edited into a "commercial." Of course, there's no safe way to guarantee success, and yet a choice must be made, so research may be included on the reaction to the animatics of the proposed campaigns. In some cases, research is carried out only after a campaign is chosen. Chapter 8, Research, explores research and the testing of commercials.

Ultimately a spot or series of spots is chosen. An executive from the client's company, along with a client/producer from the client's company, shepherds the spots through to completion. The executive, usually a brand manager or vice president of advertising, works closely with the advertising agency on creative matters, cost, and media and placement. The executive tracks the relationship of advertising to the well-being of the company. He or she supplies the leadership. The decisions and concerns are based on the company's goals and the total picture. While the executive's style may be "hands on," he or she usually works with someone within the company who has a background in film or television production. This "client/producer" is responsible for the daily necessities of commercial production.

While the vice president of advertising serves the big picture, the client/producer serves as the day-to-day liaison between the agency and the company with regard to commercial production. Some of the client/producer's duties are the same throughout the industry. Others are not.

There is no clear-cut model for the client/producer's role and responsibility. At different organizations producers function in different ways. At The Men's Wearhouse, the producer's job is very diverse. He or she is the brand manager for some of the smaller companies that are part of The Men's Wearhouse Corporation but also acts as a production assistant in some phases of The Men's Wearhouse productions. At other organizations the client/producer's job is very limited and very clearly defined. Titles, however, go just so far. Individual personalities do matter. Steven Spielberg and this author are both directors. Steven Spielberg has more clout.

Fundamentally, the client/producer serves on the creative side. He or she is involved with the making of the commercial. He or she is also involved with media, cost, tracking commercials, and at the very least serves as the first line for information regarding when the spots are apt to get delivered.

Once the spot is chosen, the client/producer is responsible for the detail work involved in getting the spots completed and on the air. The client/producer is usually responsible for:

1. *Checking facts.* This may mean working internally to ensure that the product about to be advertised is at the marketplace by the time the commercial hits the air. It means making sure that the claims for the commercial have been checked and approved by the appropriate sources.

2. *Legal liaison.* The client/producer is responsible for making sure the copy has been cleared by the legal department of the company, and contracts, other than those negotiated by and for the advertising agency, are signed.

3. *Merchandise.* The client/producer is responsible for delivering whatever is necessary for the commercial. This may be goods, displays, company experts, or whatever is needed from the company.

4. *Costs.* The client /producer is responsible for tracking costs.

In a sense the client/producer is a kind of wrangler working for the company, getting whatever is needed. By so doing the client/producer serves the needs of the advertising agency, as well as the production company, while watching out for the company's business. Most of the time, the client/producer is, or gets to be, an expert in production, and since that is the case, his or her opinion is expected and valued.

During the shoot the client/producer troubleshoots for the company and is the first line of defense on the scene regarding production issues. He or she may feel it's necessary to seek higher authority when a problem arises or may be in a position to authorize whatever needs to be done. This person may not have the final word on individual "takes" of the commercial, but his or her opinion is usually solicited.

The client/producer also continues into the postproduction phase of the projects, participating in the editing process by offering opinions and serving as the company record keeper. Along with the agency, he or she assigns code to the spots so that they can be traced through the various systems that handle each spot, e.g., vaults, dubbing facilities, station operation logs, on-air logs. In the past, the Industry Standard Coding Identification (ISCI) code was used. Recently the 30-year-old ISCI system has been upgraded to the Advertising Digital Identification (AD-ID) system.

While the advertising agency performs all of these functions, the client serves as the back up. Serving as the backup and checker of facts is useful in the client/producer's job as the commercial archivist for the company. This function addresses the notion that the current advertising agency may not always have the account and the next agency may need some of the material now being worked on by the current agency.

The client/producer is responsible for maintaining budget invoices. Depending on how the company pays for commercial production, it is the producer who gets the invoices for production, or the bill from the advertising agency, and keeps track of what expenses are to be charged to the production of which spots.

In some companies the client/producer is also responsible for supplying media traffic with the information they need to traffic the commercials. In some organizations, the advertising agency would be responsible for supplying all that information.

3 Agency

The codfish lays ten thousand eggs,
The homely hen lays one.
The codfish never cackles
To tell you what she's done.
And so we scorn the codfish
While the humble hen we prize,
Which only goes to show you
That it pays to advertise.

Anonymous

On the negative side: This quote from an anonymous creative director:

. . . every agency does wonderful work that ends up in the wastebasket, because, one, the account guy doesn't know how to sell it. And the agency doesn't know how to sell it. And the creative guys don't get a chance to go and sell it, or they're not very good at selling . . . And then it gets bastardized and changed and vanilla-ized, and pretty soon . . .

There's no single template that describes the way agencies and production companies work. I directed projects for one client, for example, who started working through a single advertising agency, then they used an in-house advertising agency for creative work and another organization for media placement, and had me direct for them. By 2004 they were using an outside resource for creative work and an internal media acquisition arm. Along the way, they built a store that they expected would do double duty as a retail outlet and a location for making commercials. It has a dark room for the video operator or to change film. It also has audio and video lines running along with traditional power lines. There are special rolling racks for easy placement of product for commercial shoots.

McDonald's creates so many commercials through separate local agencies that it owns a working McDonald's location that is used exclusively by either regional or national advertising agencies for making television commercials. It's booked 365 days a year and has no time to sell hamburgers to anyone.

It's clear why clients are necessary. They have the product or the service. They're the people who pay for the commercials. (Ultimately the public pays for them, but that's an entirely different book.) Why are there agencies? Who needs a middleman? There's a simple answer: In the traditional model of the client-agency relationship, the client knows the client's business and the agency knows the communicating and selling business. The agency also has access to the best rates for the most meaningful media and presumably can identify the most meaningful media. Agencies and their clients agree with that today. The middleman—the agency—is there to create the best message for the best media placement at the best price.

There are, however, a growing number of exceptions in which clients, or boutique agencies, outsource a portion of the work to specialists: research firms, media buying services, creative services, and, of course, commercial production and editing companies, which use both film and tape. The questions, however, remain the same. What's the best message? What's the best media placement? What's the best price for the media? Who can get it? What constitutes "best" is open to interpretation.

Perhaps it is more to the point that the decisions made at the agency level affect what the commercial says, how it gets said, and who gets to produce it. Knowing and understanding the agency, its background, and how it works can be enormously helpful in creating the best possible commercial in a stress-free, enjoyable atmosphere. It also makes sense to emulate the agency's system of work if you, as the producer/director, also have to function as the writer/creator of the commercials. The fundamental approach of the agency has been honed over a long time and is worth knowing. Understanding the agency and how it works helps you to understand why things are happening as they are rather than as they might be.

Since this book is about making commercials, it's important to reiterate the notion that whoever pays the bills is in charge. To the production company, the client is the agency. The agency, not the advertiser, pays the bill. In fact, even the creative area of the agency doesn't really work for "the client." The creative area of the agency works for "the agency." Hopefully, the best interests of the agency's client are also those of the agency, but that is not always the case. Personalities and work ethics do count. A client may be too demanding or disruptive to the entire agency, and that is not in the best interest of the agency. Agencies occasionally do resign accounts.

Someone or some group within an agency may find themselves unable to work with a particular client. At such times the person or group may be reassigned to another client within the agency. As a production company, or as a freelancer working for the agency, the consequences of being unable to work with an agency are far greater. There is no reassignment. If a production company doesn't work well with an agency, they lose the chance to work with *all* the clients at that agency. So it's the agency and not the agency's client that is the most significant voice on the set. In trying to understand how commercials are produced and aired, it may be easiest to assume the classic mold and scrutinize the agency in its traditional role.

Getting Considered

Assume for a while that you are "The Agency." It will help you understand the issues that go into working with a particular production company. Start by pretending that you're trying to get an account. Some of the material in this chapter would be slightly different if the agency already had the account and was creating a new campaign. Pitching for such an account entails much of the same work, but in such cases there's more available research and the personal contacts built up in having worked together create a different kind of balance and urgency.

Agencies get almost all of their accounts from one of four sources.

1. Sometimes the agency is sought out. It's known as being an expert in one area such as retail, automotive, service accounts for stock brokerage houses, or medical services, for example. Or they may be a specialist in media analysis or media acquisition. They may be specialists in broadcast, print, or billboards. An agency may be called upon because they've worked on similar accounts or because they have a popular, fashionable, or "hot" creative presence. In such cases the advertiser comes to the agency and asks them to pitch the account or to accept the account. The agency may not wish to do so for a variety of reasons. It may have conflicting accounts. The advertiser may have a reputation for being slow to pay bills. Such an advertiser leaves the agency cash-strapped and forced to cover expenses incurred on behalf of the tardy client. They may just be difficult to work with and too great a problem for the agency.

    Sometimes, however, chance plays a hand. I was a partner in a firm in New York that was known for its work in television. We had created a number of very successful television campaigns for retail furniture accounts as well as white and brown goods accounts. (White goods are products such as washing machines and refrigerators. Brown goods are television sets, stereos, and stereo components.) Most of our clients came from those areas. We would network with potential clients at trade shows or at regional meetings. As those potential accounts shifted ad agencies, we'd lose one and gain another. In fact, we were often able to maintain what might have been considered competing accounts because there was such a wide difference in the market. For example, we'd have both a low-end and a high-end furniture retailer because neither dealer felt competition from the other. Sometimes location was a determining factor. Retail clients in Connecticut and in Long Island with similar customer bases didn't feel that they were competing for the same customer who lived in New Jersey although they might be represented by a similar media buy.

    As it happened, the most successful campaigns we ran came about not through our expertise in any one area but through "Artie," the younger brother of the company's senior partner. Artie's college roommate, George, had gone into the retail men's clothing business. It was thought that since we worked with retail clients, we might be able to help him. We got the account, which consisted of four retail men's clothing outlet stores in Houston, Texas. At the time we advised our new client not to make his own television commercials because he seemed too young. We also suggested that he consider changing the name of the company since we felt the name The Men's Wearhouse implied a cheap warehouse image. We recommended that they consider a gradual change to: "The Menswear House." They didn't change the name, and it seems they were right about that. I think that, at the time, we were probably right about George making his own commercials. We continued working for the company for more than 25 years. Fortunately, we offered more good advice than bad, and they had the good sense to know which was which. They also had the good sense to make changes when they were appropriate, including, finally, insisting that George really should appear in his own commercials.

2. The second source for an agency to get a new account is when an account is up for review. This can happen because the client is not entirely satisfied with some or all the elements of their advertising and so they want to see "what's out there." On the other hand, some companies regularly review their advertising. Sometimes during a review a few advertising agencies who work on the same, or similar, but not competing, accounts are asked to pitch. Sometimes the agency currently working on the account is able to repitch. The way it works is that a limited number of advertising agencies are invited to learn about the company. After some interviews the field is winnowed down to two or three competing advertising agencies. The advertiser may ask the prospective agencies to prepare some kind of test pitch and may even pay a set amount to each agency to offset its cost. The client does this because they know that the development and production of such a pitch can be very expensive. The speculative work may then range from a simple storyboard presentation to fully produced commercials. The size of the account, the needs of the agency, the current cash flow of the agency, and the history of the companies will play an important role in how they choose to pitch. Most of the time the pitch costs the advertising agency more than the amount that is offered by the prospective client.

3. A new account can also be obtained through an account executive who solicits the account from a cold call, an old friend, or a suggested lead.

4. Finally, consultants may suggest a review, or a particular agency or group of agencies. There are a number of companies that serve as consultants to businesses. These firms are everything from a one-person entrepreneurial operation to established business consulting firms such as Deloitte & Touche or Price Waterhouse.

Once the agency has been approached, however that happens, there will come a time when the agency will have to meet their potential client: the advertiser. If all goes well at that meeting, if everyone gets along and sees potential for working together, the agency is asked to pitch the account. The presentation, or pitch, occurs after the agency has had an opportunity to consider the client's business. At the pitch, the advertising agency will present its suggestions for the client. They will have prepared a proposed media campaign; in fact, they will probably have two or more possible approaches. The proposed campaigns will include speculative creative material, which may include presentations for television, radio, Internet, print, and possibly special events. Proposals for media placement and budgets for the proposed campaign are also presented, along with research designed to back up the proposals. Since we are simply interested in the making of commercials, we can leave the media placement, budget, and research dedicated to those areas to some other book.

Defining the Client's Needs

The agency starts by realizing that there isn't enough information or time in the brief encounters prior to the pitch to come up with a really educated solution. A pitch has to be made, however, so whatever you have is all that there is. Like IQ tests and SATs, which are not always very accurate, that's the way it's done. The strategy that emerges will certainly come from a thoughtful analysis of the client's position. Although there may not be enough information, the chances are that the agencies will know something about the client just from having dealt with the client's product or service. They may be familiar with the client from similar products, retail locations, or services. Or they may have past experience with a competing client. The pitching agency may have the past work of prior agencies as a guide. It will have the input of the client and also may have independent research for study. Most agencies feel that research is enormously important. Most large agencies and many clients have their own research or strategic planning departments. Smaller agencies do their research in whatever way they can. Sometimes an agency's insight into the research redefines the client's needs.

New client or old, there is a time prior to creating commercials when the director of the brand, the client's direct contact with the agency, outlines what the company expects from its advertising. The results are couched in terms of goals, some of which, as we saw in the proceeding chapter, may charge advertising with an increase in the volume of sales. For example, the charge may be to retain the men aged 18 to 49 that the company already has, but appeal to older men, or perhaps both men and women, or open up new territories. The client may even wish to increase profitability by cutting back on advertising costs. Whatever the goal, the research and creative groups at the agency will have to come up with a campaign, or rather a few possible campaigns. Sometimes, despite what the client thinks, the agency may come up with something entirely unusual, "out of the box," and saleable.

Redefining the issue may be the way to change the problem so that it's perceived as a benefit. Some years back, Robert Hall clothiers stressed great savings in their stores based on their low overhead. They made their plain pipe racks and lack of decor into a positive sales benefit. Somehow a message must emerge that places the client's product or service in a desired position. The old adage that covers this is: "If life gives you lemons, make lemonade." If the consumer thinks that they're not getting enough tomato sauce in that little can, explain the wonders of placing eight great tomatoes in one itsy-bitsy can.

An agency was told: "We want people to use our Mexican hot sauce on everything. Put it on eggs, hamburgers . . . everything." The manufacturer thought if people needed to pour the hot sauce on more things, he would expand his business. The agency recognized that those consumers who were of Mexican descent were already using the product in exactly the way the client wanted it to be used. Other populations probably wouldn't. The company needed to increase sales some other way. The agency thought that perhaps they could increase sales by cutting into the competition and making those who already bought hot sauce prefer the client's sauce. Research showed that the major competition was the giant Campbell Soup Company in Camden, New Jersey. The little company the agency represented was located in San Antonio, Texas. The campaign was then built around the notion that people in San Antonio, Texas, knew more about making Mexican hot sauce than people in Camden, New Jersey. They created a commercial that worked very well, and within a few years the company was sold for a great deal of money to Campbell Soup of Camden, New Jersey. The agency must come up with a strategy. Once the strategy is in place, the creative process will flow from it.

Finding a Strategy

The producers of the commercial, the production house, usually have nothing to do with finding a strategy. However, a case might be made for a production company that invents or refines the use of some special hardware or technique. The first users of the Stedicam, for example, inspired the creative departments of many agencies. The early users of such tools as Chroma-key and some editing tools such as kaleidoscope wipes were equally inspired. There may be some creative input as the production gets under way, but for the most part, the production company and the editing company will simply perform the tasks necessary to bring "the boards," which is the copy and artwork presented in panels, usually on a cardboard backing, to fruition (Figure 3.1).

Finding the strategy includes research into who is the audience. Who is the customer? What is the current customer base? Who is the competition? What part of the market will we be going after? What are the legal restrictions? What's been done before, etc.? There are a host of questions that will need to be answered by the agency—often by the creative team working with the data from their research department. Their answers will form the backbone of the commercial and will certainly affect what the commercial looks like.

In its simplest form, the agency knows that ultimately it's going to create a campaign that tries to do one of three things.

Figure 3.1 This is a typical four-panel layout for a storyboard. This photocopied panel was used by the production company. The client retained the original. Storyboards may be anything from stick figures to fully rendered panels and may be simply black and white copies or full-color photo reproductions.

1. *Sell something:*
    a. For the manufacturer that means "buy my product." In order to get you to do that, a manufacturer's commercials tend to promise you a better life. If you use their product, you will feel better, you'll be safer, you'll be a better mom or dad.
    b. For the retailer it means "buy the product at my store."
    c. At one retail agency where I worked, the creative team would get together on pitches and ask: "What are we really trying to sell?" The choice always came down to savings, selection, or service. In fact, we realized that all retail commercials could be reduced to those three points.
        i.   Savings: We sell for less.
        ii. Selection: We may not offer the lowest price, but we have such a large selection that you're sure to get what you want.
        iii. Service: Our prices may be higher than the competition—although that is not always implicit in the "service message"—and we may have a more limited selection than our competition, but we are committed to selling only the best, or the hippest, or the most "kooky," etc., *but* our service is *so* good, you'll agree that spending the extra money is worth it. There's some subtext there as you think about the difference between the service message offered by K-Mart and the quite different service message offered by Nordstrom or Saks Fifth Avenue.
2. *Change someone's opinion:* Vote for Tom, not Dick. Give up Butter, Use Margarine.
3. *Create awareness:* You can buy books online at Amazon.com. You can buy much more than books online at Amazon.com.

If the client has a very limited commercial production budget, the creative team, even if the "creative team" is just you, tends to gravitate toward one of two strategies.

1. A potpourri of shot or fast cuts. It works for food and restaurant accounts or for car parts. In fact you can use fast cuts to indicate a profusion of pots and pans, men's or women's clothing, classes being given, or packages delivered. In the more expensive commercials, the shots are more beautiful than in the cheaper ones. The idea is the same.
2. A stand-up announcement from the president or chief executive officer (CEO) of the company. The look of these spots changes with the stature and message of the president. Look at Crazy Eddie or Crazy Gideon. The name says it all. Then look at the president of the Ford Motor Company addressing the issue of tire recall.

In fact, the potpourri commercial is simply the selection message, and the CEO is usually about saving or service. By now they're overdone. They keep being produced though. We keep seeing examples of the genre, so we can assume that it still works.

There are many ways to go about the actual creation of a campaign. None are guaranteed in any way, and agencies are very protective of their method of work. In some ways this protective stance is peculiar since there are so many copywriters and art directors who move from job to job and who take with them all the "secrets." Some procedures may work better for some people than for others. Different agencies work in different ways.

Chiat-Day constructed the company around the idea of change. There was a desire to eliminate any kind of complacency. The business maintained an office for meetings with clients and for some jobs that positively had to have a home base, but the intention was to create a working environment in which no one had an office. Everyone was issued a laptop computer and worked from wherever they wanted. Chiat-Day provided a number of settings in which people could get together to work, but there were no typical offices for most of the creative staff.

Agency producers, on the other hand, had offices because so much of their work required that they be at the office for so many different reasons. They needed a central location for callbacks, as well as for team screening rooms, client and vendor meetings, deliveries, and many other production prerequisites. Chiat-Day thought that this lack of rigidity would encourage the creative process. As you might expect, it worked wonderfully well for some and not at all for others. Other agencies take a very formal approach to the creative working climate and expect the staff to work in the office.

Research

While Chapter 8, Research, will deal more thoroughly with research, it's important to consider the function of research in the agency's work. Some clients accept the work of research groups and focus groups and some don't. Those that don't, make decisions based on their feelings about proposed campaigns. Those that are interested in research often share past work done by other agencies, including both quantitative and qualitative analysis. Typical of the research considered significant is that of focus groups. Focus groups bring together consumers, and sometimes nonconsumers, who are asked questions relating to the client and the client's needs. The interpretation of those answers may lead to a strategy and a campaign. The data may be risky, however, because of the dynamics involved in the creation of the research. One wants to know what parameters were chosen, who was responsible for the questions, who were the respondents, who conducted the testing, and who tabulated the results.

While I was a staff director at CBS, a focus group was asked questions relevant to a new feminist program that was about to go on the air. The focus group was charged with finding out what concerns were most important to a variety of randomly selected respondents. Amazingly, no one in the group thought sex was an important aspect of their lives.

"Computers are cool for girls too," is a line that changed the nature of computer games for girls and sold millions of dollars' worth of goods. The commercial is now part of the Smithsonian collection. It came out of a focus group done by Mattel, Inc. The analysis of the focus group's responses was done by Tom Sylvester, whose job it was to create a spot for a computer-driven clothes program for a Barbie Doll product.

Sometimes the client has a wrong idea and is insistent about it. Generally speaking, accepting an idea you don't believe in is not a good way to serve a client. In such a case, the agency ought to decline the work. On the other hand, there are number of instances in which an agency accepts a position and then does the best they can with what they believe to be a second-rate idea. In the best-case scenario, the campaign then achieves monumental success. The agency and its personnel are considered geniuses, and the client and the agency become fabulously wealthy and continue to argue over whose idea it really was.

A number of major agencies have created templates to help them generate both the strategy and the concepts for the commercial. This may not work for everyone. Basically the template has a cover page, which first indicates some internal information such as:

1. Who are the team members? What internal team is working on the account?
2. Who's the account supervisor or leader?
3. Who's the creative director?
4. Who's the copy chief?
5. Who's the art director?
6. Who's the agency producer?
7. Who are the specialists in and outside of the agency? Who are the consultants?
8. Who is the traffic coordinator?
9. What medium will be used in the proposed project?
    a. Broadcast: television and/or radio?
    b. Print: magazine, newspaper, outdoor etc.?
10. How frequently will the material be used?
11. What kind of budget might be expected?
12. What are the due dates for delivery of boards, production, air, etc.?

The template may then go on to ask questions that deal with the actual problem of discovering a strategy and/or a campaign idea:

1. What is it that we are selling: the product or service?
2. Who are the consumers? Who are we trying to sell? New customers? New product? New market?
3. Who are the competitors? Who else is trying to do the same thing? How are they working at it?
4. How is our product or service different from theirs?
    a. What is the "unique selling proposition" connected to the client's product or service?

  b. How will it benefit the consumer?

  c. What are the features, processes, technology, etc.?

5. Is there a characteristic that identifies the client's business? Is it elegant? adventurous? labor saving? fun to use? etc.

6. Is there a situation or style that lends itself to promoting the findings?

  a. A humorous situation

  b. A spokesperson

  c. A demonstration

7. Are there legal issues or other considerations that will govern what can be used or said?

8. Is there anything that must be used?

  a. A statement

  b. A character

  c. A point of view, etc.

There are many avenues to creating the strategy. Rosser Reeves of Ted Bates Advertising company is credited with clearly stating the concept that every commercial should provide the consumer with some unique reason for buying the client's product. He called it "the unique selling proposition." Some agencies may change those words. It becomes "Benefits that need to be found," for example. Some agencies or creative teams may feel that the really important quest in finding a strategy lies not so much in the buyer's appreciation of the product's values, but rather in finding an emotional context to what's being sold. To some extent the agency is defined by this aspect of their approach. Of course, the way in which they interpret the results also defines them. Sometimes the answer they get requires that they return to square one and the agency suggests a potpourri of shots showing the client's product or perhaps a statement from the CEO.

Creating the Commercial

Once there's a strategy in place, it's time to create the commercial. A realistic depiction of the working practices of many creative departments can be found in the film *Nothing In Common*, starring Tom Hanks and Jackie Gleason. Tom Hank's creative department is required to come up with a campaign for an airline. There comes a time in this film, and in the lives of many agencies, when all of the creative group working on the account gathers and has a "brainstorming session." This usually starts after everyone has had a chance to absorb material about the client. It's a time when everything is allowed. The doors are closed to everyone but the creative staff, and everyone involved with the creative process shoots out ideas. Nothing is too extreme. Nothing is too lame. Nothing is too gross. Everything goes. It's a time when an attempt is made to think "out of the box," the "box" being acceptance of things as they are. In such sessions an idea may surface quickly, within an hour or two. Sometimes one works for days to come up with the right idea. Often an idea will seem perfect at the moment, only to seem silly a few minutes or hours later. Inevitably good ideas get tossed out with the bad.

Eventually, out of the free flowing exchange of ideas, or the particular phrasing of a strategy, or some element derived from the research, an idea emerges for a campaign or a strategy. From that idea both the script and the look of the commercial develop.

All commercials tend to fall into well-defined types. Many authors have listed the prevalent commercial types. In his book *Ogilvy on Advertising*, David Ogilvy lists some specific categories in which successful television ads tend to fall.

1. *Characters:* Zeke & Eb, two old codgers you'll never forget, along with the product with which they are associated. (This can even be an animal . . . or animated.)
2. *Comedy:* The danger here is that the audience will remember the joke, not the product. On the other hand, the audience may look forward to seeing the joke again as they do with pie in the face. It also builds anticipation for the next joke by the same advertiser.
3. *Demonstrations:* An infomercial is a long demonstration. Commercials for Dentsu Knives and Crazy Glue are shorter ones.
4. *Problem solving:* How do you serve the unexpected guests who arrive 10 minutes after you get home? Easy. Just use the client's product.
5. *Reasons:* Here are three good reasons why you should use [the client's product]. This approach is self-explanatory.
6. *Slice of life:* These may feel trite, but they do work. Often two actors argue over the merits of a product, and finally one is convinced. Sometimes there's simply a question, such as "Oh Madge, how do you get your dishes so clean?" or a statement, such as "Bob, I can't tell you how much trouble I used to have getting a great shine on my car, but that's all changed now." In some ways this may be considered a variation on problem solving.
7. *Talking heads:* A pitchman (someone dressed as a doctor, a mechanic, or a group of women around a table) tells the audience how wonderful the product is.
8. *Testimonials:* Hidden camera technique, as well as stars and personalities. The danger of using stars is that the audience remembers the star but not the product!

There are more, and certainly some that defy such characterization, but these are the most prevalent.

Along the way, issues that seem totally irrelevant may arise and determine whether a commercial concept gets on the air. Here are some examples of strategies and the campaigns surrounding them. The first example is on the air. The second and third examples never got made.

1. *Strategy:* For years, George Zimmer was used as an on-camera salesman for The Men's Wearhouse. His sales pitch revolved around savings. The name itself implies savings. It's The Men's Wearhouse. Warehouses are barn-like places where one expects to find low prices. In order to increase its penetration into its perceived potential share of market, as opposed to the market share it had, The Men's Wearhouse required a new strategy. One of the "givens" was that George would have to be a part of the commercial, however it happened. The new strategy changed the way George behaved—from that of a salesperson selling low price and "guaranteeing it," to a chief executive officer offering an appropriate selection and promising that "You're going to like the way you look! . . . I guarantee it!" The appeal was to a more upscale businessman. The fact that there was a perceived image of low prices probably helped sales to grow given George's new image. Once the idea of featuring George as a CEO was in place, creating the vignettes to help sell that idea became easier. Using George in a voice-over capacity rather than as an ever-present, on-camera personality allowed the commercials to have his presence felt throughout but offered a wider choice of surroundings than his store or office, which had been the locale for most of the early commercials.

   The Ads: When the new campaign started, vignettes were created around businessmen at the office, at social events, at job interviews, etc. It compared and contrasted two types of men. First: "Those who didn't have their act together." That was defined as men wearing jackets that were too big, a guy at a meeting who takes "casual Friday" too seriously and shows up not wearing a shirt, a man in a waiting room whose sloppy socks amuse the receptionist, etc. Second: "Those who did have it together," which were defined as The Men's Wearhouse customers. They were seen in the stores, getting helped, having their jackets tailored, and choosing from a vast array of clothes, and, of course, they liked the way they looked. George guaranteed it. Exactly what he guaranteed was not entirely clear; however, company policy was such that he guaranteed practically everything. Now he just guarantees that "You're going to like the way you look." The company still maintains very customer-oriented policies to back up George's guarantee.

2. *Strategy:* This campaign was created to promote a retailer who was selling brown goods and white goods at significantly lower prices than the competition. His stores looked shabby, though the merchandise wasn't. Also they were inconveniently located. We decided to turn that into a plus by explaining that in an effort to keep costs low, the poor locations and shabby stores were advantageous. With expenses down, the consumer could get the lowest possible prices. Who would locate in such difficult locations and spend so little on ambience in order to get his customers the lowest possible price? "The World's Cheapest Man"—the owner of the chain, and our client . . . we hoped.

   The Ad: The idea was to have some employees and some customers complain about the faults and handle them as if they were in fact part of the cost-saving efficiency. The savings were then passed on to the consumer. Who caused all these trivial problems? The World's Cheapest Man, the boss. One commercial started with an employee saying something like:

"See this short stubby pencil? This is what I've got to use to write up orders. It's because we have to be very careful about our expenses. We want to make sure we can pass our savings on to the customer.

Like this fabulous bargain . . .

(INSERT "SPECIAL 1" OF THE WEEK OR MONTH)

and this one, etc.

(INSERT "SPECIAL 2" OF THE WEEK OR MONTH)

Who keeps our cost down so the customers' savings go up? The World's Cheapest Man. Our boss!"

Cut to Logo with phone numbers.

The client liked the campaign, which included pictures of the pencil to be used in print ads. He liked the other parts of the campaign, which had a customer pointing out that while the parking was easy, the location was not in the heart of downtown. What the client didn't like was that his friends would make fun of him for the campaign. So it was dumped.

3. *Strategy:* We pitched "Nathan's Famous," which sells hot dogs and, at the time, delicatessen. Consumers in the New York area thought that Nathan's was simply a restaurant and hot dog stand in Coney Island in Brooklyn, New York, that sold nothing but hot dogs. We wanted to show selection—that there were many kinds of foods, all delicious, and that they had lots of locations.

The Ad: Our campaign was developed around the idea of "The Nathan's Nibble." We intended to show a series of food shots. The full screen would be filled with first a shot of a sandwich, then a hot dog or hamburger, then another sandwich, etc. Each would have one big bite taken out. It would serve in print, in billboards, and could be used as 10-second TV spots. For television the pictures would be accompanied by a "melody button" in which the words "The Nathan's Nibble" was to be sung by a guy with very low voice and a smart New York accent, predating "The Sopranos" by a few years. (A button is a short musical piece such as "Shave and a haircut, two bits.") For longer radio or television appearances, it could be expanded to explain all the wonderful taste treats that made up the family of Nathan's Famous foods. A competing agency suggested a phrase that indicated that Nathan's was very sincere in the way it cared about food. The phrase they came up with is one that the original owner of Nathan's used to use as a young man when he worked in the kitchen. They got the account. It seemed to be mostly for sentimental reasons. The campaign didn't work, and I haven't seen Nathan's using broadcast in a meaningful way since then.

Sometimes an agency sells the idea for a commercial, then produces the commercial, but the commercial never gets aired. A friend was asked by a leading car manufacturer to produce a commercial that had been pitched months earlier. The problem was that they wanted it to get on air within 5 days. A monumental problem, which was made even worse, because 2 of those 5 days were Saturday and Sunday. The agency did it at great cost, both in dollars and in energy. The client saw the spot, was grateful for the effort, agreed that it did exactly what it promised to do, but then felt they didn't like it. It was shelved.

Also shelved are commercials that were never made for products that never did work exactly as promised. For me that was a motor oil additive. It was supposed to leave a long lasting coat of oil on everything it touched. We were going to get a very expensive car and drain all the engine oil. We were then going to film the car traveling on the highway without any oil for 50 miles. The client never explained why we couldn't make the spot, but they were adamant that it wasn't ready yet and they didn't want us to even think about making the spot.

Once the Account Is "In House"

Finally something works, and a strategy leads to a campaign. Two or three versions are prepared to be presented as part of the campaign, and the agency makes its presentation. It may be a particular ad strategy that gets the account or some other element of the presentation, perhaps the projected time buy.

As in any relationship there may be a kind of chemistry between the client and the agency. Something clicks and the agency gets the account. At that time it may even be discovered that while the client liked the approach to the media, he or she may not wish to pursue this presentation of creative efforts. They may decide to let the agency pitch more creative efforts, or they might wish to seek an outside creative agency. The bottom line is that the agency has the account. Most of the time a new and more informed round of creative sessions follows.

Sometimes successful campaigns come about out of most unusual circumstances, like these two.

"The back-room boys," the nickname for our creative team, had filled a wastebasket with what I, as the creative director, thought was awful work for a sale radio spot. The account executive had to pitch *something* to the client and in a fit of pique strode into our office, reached into the wastebasket, called the client, and read the top spot plucked from the trash. The client then approved the copy as read by the account executive. We made the spot. It was very successful.

One of the writers in that room went on to become the head writer at a large agency in New York. The creative team hadn't come up with anything they thought would really work, and a meeting with the client was imminent. He was asked to stall by creating some "wallpaper." These are ads that have no chance of being made, but which when hung up on the wall (wallpaper) would make it seem as if the agency had been very busy with their creative efforts. Of course, the client loved one of the ads. It was made. It, too, was very successful.

A word here about the executives involved in all this. They don't usually get much praise from the world at large. They may get a raise in pay or a new title, but the contributions of executives are rarely appreciated outside of their companies, certainly outside of their counterparts at other similar organizations. Some of the best campaigns ever mounted were those done in the early 1960s for Volkswagen. One ad showed the client's product with the one word headline: "Lemon." The campaign was very successful, but imagine the internal strife that must have gone on prior to letting that ad run. The advertising agency had to believe in it so much that they would be willing to stand behind the idea. They had to know that it might mean that they would have to forfeit that very large account. The client's ad manager, or vice president of advertising, had to accept an ad that called his product a lemon. He had to hope that the public would read the copy underneath the headline that stipulated a number of reasons why the Volkswagen lemon was such a wise car to own. Later, around the same time, "Think small." was also approved. The highest level of management at Volkswagen, who could not all have had total, immediate faith in the ad, accepted it. They accepted the vice president of advertising's approval. They agreed with the agency, and they ran it. Bill Bernbach, of the very young Doyle, Dane & Bernbach; the copy writer, Rita Selden; and the art director, Helmut Krone, surely deserve credit for the ad, but they had to be very happy that courage paid off and that they had that group of executives working with them.

Once the go-ahead is given, the chances are that a number of spots created along the same central line will be needed. The rationale is that it's wise to have a fallback position should there be some problem with any single spot. It might be an undiscovered legal problem or simply that one spot, which seemed good in script and boards, simply doesn't work well or doesn't work well in a particular area of the country. There are other reasons too. An 800 phone number might be used in large urban markets and a local phone number in a smaller market. Some foods sell well in some markets and not in others. Commercials may be tailored to a particular region's needs. Hot salsa may be a big item in the western regions and mild salsa in the east. Additionally, it's cheaper to make a number of spots at the same time than it is to go through the process of creating a number of individual productions. Whatever the case, there will be many details that must be taken care of.

Let's assume that the client has agreed to the strategy, the campaign, all of the spots, and the media suggestions. What happens then?

First there's a little party.

Then the specifics of the project start being put in place. The agency establishes a time line for the production of the commercials. The media department begins to do specific research, and perhaps secure specific "buys." The art department begins working on whatever it needs to do. That includes accepting and filing material from past agencies, creating or adjusting materials and logos, and generally fulfilling the needs of the new campaign. An agency producer (AP) is assigned to the project and begins working on production of the spots. Throughout the process from preproduction to production and postproduction, the AP serves as the agency's liaison to the client and the production company. If the spots are to be "animated," a separate procedure will be put in place, whenever possible, with specialists in that area.

Scheduling

One of the most significant priorities for the agency producer is staying within the time line. The AP is responsible for making sure that everyone is kept in the loop. The AP will work with the production company, arranging for sign-offs from the agency and the client, and for such mundane matters as deliveries, as needed, in a timely fashion. Of major importance, the AP is responsible for facilitating the legal aspects of the shoot in a timely manner, that is, contracts are signed and in place, and rights, if any are needed, have been secured for music, lyrics, poetry. For the project to be considered ready to shoot, a number of things need to be ready to go, many of which require the assistance of the AP. In Chapter 4, Preproduction, those essential requisites are listed.

Choosing a Production Company

The APs break the boards down in much the same way that the producing companies will. That is to say, each of the panels of the storyboard will be given a number if they don't already have one. Each new location required by the boards will be noted, as will special props or locations. Much of the preliminary work done by the production company will have been anticipated by the AP so that cost can be accurately anticipated. The chapters on producing commercials will cover those breakdowns more thoroughly.

Once the demands of the board are known, the process of selecting production companies to bid on the job begins. The choices are made on the basis of the commercial's requirements; that is, does it require beauty shots, or are there acted vignettes? Will these boards require work with children or with celebrity talent? Those asked to bid on the job will most likely have provided reels that indicate their expertise in working with the kinds of material being shot. At other times an agency and a client will agree to hire a director and his or her production company without any bidding process.

Typically, however, the agency will have a library of reels from directors and production companies, either VHS or DVD. The library will have come to the agency from production company reps, directors, and friends, as well as from direct requests from the AP. The AP will locate some directors' reels that contain work that seems similar to that required by the boards.

Most of the bidding companies will be fairly close in terms of price. Agencies tend to buy into a kind of production look, which usually costs about the same no matter who does the job. It is the same as purchasing a car. Some people travel in Fords and might then be willing to consider Chevrolets or Hondas, and some drive Bentleys or Rolls-Royces, and don't consider Fords, Chevrolets, Hondas, Toyotas, or anything else. When the job is sent out to be bid, the prices of the competing companies fall within the same kinds of parameters, unless the AP is specifically asked to solicit bids from a range of companies whose approach will yield a range of prices.

Imagine that a scene takes place at a little French bistro. Will the crew go to France? Will they hire a full crew in France? Or will they build a set and shoot it in America or Canada? Whatever choice is made will affect the cost of the production. Some directors and production companies might not feel comfortable working with a French crew. Others would. Some directors would insist upon the reality that a real French bistro would bring. Others wouldn't. The kinds of choices the competing companies make will be significant in determining who gets the job.

Once a number of directors, usually two or three, is selected, there is a screening for the account supervisor and the creative team to see if they agree with the selection. Sooner or later a choice is made, and the director or his or her representatives are called and asked to bid on the production. They may simply bid on producing the original footage, or they may be involved with the editing as well. Most of the time, the director on medium- to high-budget projects gets to do no more than a first edit, if that. To a busy director, that may be exactly what he or she wants. An edit-day rate is not apt to be as great as that for a shoot day. Other shoot days take precedence.

The AP has broken down the boards and created a timetable for the project. It's been approved by the creative director and perhaps the account executive and/or the vice president in charge of the particular area. They also agree on getting bids from two or three companies who are asked to examine the boards and bid on the job. At some agencies, all the people who are bidding are brought together at the same time and the job is outlined. Usually, a letter is sent out with the board outlining the specifics of the job, such as the number of spots to be completed, delivery dates, expectations of postproduction involvement, and other relevant matters. The companies are then given a day or two to come up with a bid.

A cautionary word here about the boards and creativity. By the time the commercial goes into production, the client has signed off on the boards. That means the boards were seen in the initial presentation. They were then "tweaked" by the client and the agency. A panel or an idea that didn't quite seem right was changed, and it was then approved by the client's ad manager and the head of the company or division. The legal departments of both the client and the advertising agency approved the words and pictures as presented to them on the boards. *For the most part*, the producer's job, and the production company's job, will be to create commercials that stick very close to the boards. *For the most part*, creativity in the field is limited to those extra shots or bits of business outside of the absolute necessity of the boards that can be done at no extra cost to anyone.

That is *for the most part*. However, there are *some* cases, *sometimes*, where *some* creative input is sought from the producing company. It is, however, rare in the industry. On the other hand, it is less than rare with *some* individual directors who are hired just because they *will* bring a particular kind of expertise or "look" to a commercial. *For the most part, most of the time* everyone sticks to the script . . . or in this case the boards.

As the bidding process continues, there will inevitably be calls with questions about elements of the spot. There may be meetings with the various directors to determine what their approach would be. After a predetermined time, the bids arrive. Along with them will be notes about production elements that each of the bidding companies feels is the way they would handle the challenges offered by the spots.

The agency producer then meets with the creative director, the account supervisor, and perhaps the account manager from the advertiser. They review the bids to select a company to produce the spots. Their discussions will include consideration of the costs indicated in the bids. Cost, however, is not necessarily the most important issue. In the first place, most of the time the bids are similar. But in a larger sense, the cost of the spots is a very small part of the overall cost of the campaign. The purchase of time and space where the ads will be seen will cost a great deal more. Other relevant matters will be considered, including the personnel that will be provided. The preferred company may have a director of photography that is committed to some other job when the shoot is supposed to begin but could be available if the project could be delayed for a short while. Is that possible? Will the agency want to do that? Another company may have taken a unique approach to some part of the production, which changes the total cost or the look of the project. Ultimately, the various bids are considered, and a company is chosen. The chosen company is notified, and upon their acceptance of the job, the other companies are notified that they did not get the job.

At that time, contracts outlining the job are drawn up and signed, and the AP goes to work with the company in the preproduction stage of the shoot. The AP will act as the main conduit and liaison to the production company and the director and will be responsible for arranging the timely delivery of specific personnel and props. Keeping a paper trail of costs, legal matters, and other pertinent information will be another important role. Often there is a call to locate historical elements from past shoots such as old props, notes, or footage. Additionally, the agency will need to assist in locating personnel or current props from the agency or the client's organization. Members of the client's staff may be needed as talent, for research assistance, or for any other matter that facilitates the production.

Casting

The AP is involved in casting decisions and often attends all the sessions. Casting is usually done through a casting consultant who contacts a number of agents to cast the spots. Usually, the actors will be videotaped saying their name and reading the parts for which they are auditioning. Then the agency, the client, and usually the production company will arrange a session to discuss the actors and arrange to have callbacks where a final decision is made. Contracts with the Screen Actors Guild (SAG) and The American Federation of Television and Radio Actors (AFTRA) allow one callback and require that a talent fee be paid should a second callback be required.

Props

The AP is also responsible for getting the client's product to the shoot. Sometimes that's easier said than done. Sometimes special considerations come into play. The classic example of special needs in terms of props is that for years the red, white, and blue of American flags were specially prepared. A dark wine color was used as red and a dark navy or purple appeared as blue, since that was what photographed best. For commercials, specially prepared, color-corrected labels on nonreflective stock are a standard, and there are companies that specialize in the production of specialty products for commercial production.

Underwater products are a good example of those special needs. Products destined to be shot underwater need special care and handling. Colors bleed, glue comes undone, and products float away from their marked and focused position. Without the specially prepared, and inevitably costly "hero product," a production can come to a crashing halt while crew and gear wait around for a solution to be found. It's better to take care of the problem before it begins, even though that can be surprisingly expensive. These substitute products cost as much as they do because they are one of a kind and require unique specialized knowledge and craftsmanship to create. Of course this is one of the reasons for hiring companies that specialize in particular kinds of work. A friend who specialized in underwater production said that he was amused at how surprised most clients were when they discovered how many things simply would not stay down when underwater. No matter if it's the agency or the production company that's responsible for the "hero product," the AP will be vitally concerned in making sure the client's product photographs well.

Audio

One of the key elements that the agency may be called on to deliver in the preproduction stage is the audio track. Sometimes that's done by the production company and is discussed in the chapter on production. However, the AP is very much involved with that phase of the production. There are four audio areas that are of concern:

1.   Voice-over—an announcer or sound bytes
2.   Music—either original music or acquired from a music library
3.   Sound effects—usually from a sound effects library but sometimes created for the spot
4.   Sync-sound—dialogue and/or natural sound

Most of the time the creative director and the client are afforded the opportunity to be involved with all the choices. Most of the time they will want initial approval of the talent hired and then final approval of the completed track or tracks. They usually opt to stay out of the actual recording of most of the audio. If the track is for an animated character, the client and creative team may want to have more of a presence than if the track is simply an announcer saying the client's name or reading an address or a phone number tag. By the same token, if a celebrity voice is to be used, the creative director, account supervisor, and representatives from the client side would be very involved. Sound effect and music tracks, unless of major significance, are usually left to the AP and production company. However, the client and some agency personnel may want to get involved in the final audio mix, where all the sound elements used in the spots are blended together into the final track.

At the Shoot

Once again, as the agency's liaison to the client and production company, the AP is responsible for keeping everyone notified about what is happening and when. APs also attend to many of the details that are a part of any shoot. APs may sometimes step in to perform jobs that should be done by someone else. They may appear as extras, although they may not do so in a production working under the performance jurisdiction of the American Federation of Television and Radio Actors (AFTRA) or Screen Actors Guild (SAG) unless they are members working under contracted conditions. On low-budget productions, APs often act as production assistants as well as talent, cooks, and babysitter, not necessarily in that order. At higher budget shoots, most jobs, including talent, cooks, and babysitter, are covered by specialists, and the production assistant, paid for by the production company, may be sent on errands and perform standby chores to assist in any area where there is no union jurisdiction. Most often APs offer an opinion on material that is shot and serve as the agency's and client's "production eyes" on the set. Ideally, they are the one voice that addresses the production company and director. In fact, it is standard operating procedure that the AP represent the advertising agency on a set. Here's an example. If, while watching a video tap of a shoot, the client wished to make some change, he or she would not go directly to the director. Instead, the client would ask for a small conference with the advertising group or simply pass on the suggestion or request for a change to the AP. The AP would speak to the agency staff, the creative director, and account executive; come to a conclusion; and then represent the client and the agency to the director or production company. When this chain of command is not observed, there is chaos because the director is apt to get notes and information from too many sources and from conflicting sources.

A note here about video taps. Whether the shoot is done in film or tape, the agency and the client want to see not only the live action on the set, but how it looks on camera. The video tap is now the standard tool in the industry to afford that look. Essentially, a video recording is taken from the camera, whether film or tape, and sent to a VHS deck on the set. This allows the takes to be played back, and then decisions can be made based on the tape. In practice the client and agency watch the takes on a monitor and then ask for playbacks. They then indicate when they feel they have material that should be printed or that should be marked as potential "buys."

Along the way the AP is responsible for keeping up with the ever-changing scheduling needs. Often it will be important to bring in the client's representatives, or personnel, or key props at a particular time. Since the reality of shoots often entails unforeseen events, it is the AP's responsibility to inform everyone of changes that have been made. In some ways the agency is less interested in time than the production company. It is the production company that has bid the job and that will be responsible for paying the overtime incurred by a lengthened shoot. If the budget is exceeded, the production company may have to prove that the delays were caused by agency or client requests. The production company publishes its own call sheets affecting crew and gear. Nevertheless, it is the AP who continues to function as a conduit for keeping the client and others at the agency abreast of scheduling matters.

In a typical shoot, the AP arrives early enough to be able to welcome the rest of the people from the agency and from the client side. The AP serves as the point person for the agency and needs to be on location early enough to begin working on any immediate emergency that may have sprung up. It may concern props, casting, costumes, or personnel. The production company goes to the AP with last-minute questions. Can the agency spring for another makeup artist? Is it possible to change the schedule for the color correction because the director would like to be there but has a meeting? Both the agency and the client anticipate that the AP represents their interests on the set. This can sometimes put the AP in a peculiar political position. The nature of the business requires participants who sometimes have strong, and sometimes frail, egos.

Also there are sometimes unspoken agendas. The director of photography (DP) or the director wants to get shots that will look good on their personal reel but are not really necessary for the shoot. The agency may want extra shots that are different from the boards. The director may find himself or herself shooting a number of different versions to accommodate the client and various voices within the agency. Needless to say, these accommodations take time and increase the total cost of the project. There are times when this puts the production company in a peculiar position. Who pays? If the client gets a bill reflecting those overages, how will that affect the working relationship in succeeding productions? Is it better to simply accept the loss or protest? The production company would like the knowledgeable AP to serve as the direct line, a buffer and a voice of reason, between the director/DP and the agency/client. On the other hand, the agency and the client expect the AP to represent them and what they want. Hopefully, everyone is mature and realizes that whatever is being done is being done in good faith for the best possible commercial. It's hoped that everyone's input is being dealt with in a fair and creative way. In fact, it's not that way all of the time. It's terrific when it is.

The AP is also very involved with keeping track of costs. In some contracts the production company's fee is represented by the cost of the production plus a percentage. In other contracts the company agrees to produce the commercials for a set fee, with the understanding that the agency will assume any additional costs. In any case, the AP needs to keep track of expenditures. The production company will be keeping track of the in and out time of the crew, including departments such as makeup, talent, and costumes. They will certainly keep records of the equipment that is rented and monitor the stock that is used—film or tape. While they probably won't keep track of slates as the shoot progresses, they will want to keep track of how time is being used and, perhaps, the shooting ratio. A good AP will try to keep up with the various departments and maintain records of what is being used and when. Being involved in the shoot in such a detailed way also helps with the schedule and any changes that need to be made. It also is useful when questions about billing arise. As might be expected, the greater the initial cost of the commercial, the fewer questions there are about some costs. When there's a $1,000,000 budget in play, a $5000 expense is easier to justify than if the total budget is $25,000.

However, even at some of the largest agencies, producers find that cost consultants have been assigned to various projects, and considerations about cost are very significant.

> Cost cutting is everywhere and production budgets are tighter. Every nickel is carefully watched, and often those nickels are watched by the dreaded cost consultants on the client side. The cost consultants review production budgets and essentially justify their salary by finding little bits of money to pull out of the production estimate in order to "save" the client money.

> Producer 4A Agency

Names and Codes

Along the way the AP will be preparing for the next step in the process, which is the edit. The chances are that the spots already have a name. If not, the AP, in conjunction with the traffic department of the agency, will give each of the spots a name and assign a code. The traffic department is responsible for issuing the actual orders to run the spots and for getting the right spot in the right media (Beta, 1 inch, etc.,) to each station. A short name is better than a long one because it will be filled out on many forms and will have a number of uses. A unique name that implies the content of the spot is also helpful and is important in creating a code name. The actual name and the code name will be used by station schedulers to identify the spots. Working on The Men's Wearhouse commercials taught me the importance of unique names. As might be expected, over the years a number of commercials were made about tuxedos. After a while it became difficult to differentiate between each year's new tuxedo spot. Once you've used "Tux," "New Tux," "TX," "NT," and "TU" you need to find a new code name. We finally used the last digit of the year and the letter "T" to differentiate each set of tuxedo commercials.

The AP or traffic department also assigns a code to the spots. In the 1970s a national kind of code had been developed and achieved popular usage. It was the Industry Standard Coding Identification (ISCI) code (pronounced "is-key"), and it consisted of four letters followed by four numbers. Two or three of the letters, depending on the total annual budget of the advertiser, were used to signify the kind of advertiser, regional or national, and the amount of money they spent on television advertising. The other numbers and letters were codes for the client, the spot name, etc.

The newest form for assigning code is the Advertising Digital Identification system called Ad-ID. In July 2002, O. Burtch Drake, the president of the AAAA, said "Ad-ID will help migrate the current Industry Standard Coding Identification (ISCI) to a digital platform. . . ." Essentially the new system generates unique identifying codes to assist in tracking commercials for scheduling, media placement, billing, and verification purposes. Unlike the ISCI code, it is not limited to eight digits, which were the standard length for computer names in the early days of computers. It can be used across all digital media lines.

However, it's entirely possible to make up your own code and use that. Today most stations are willing to air spots with whatever code you use so long as it's unique to your spots and doesn't interfere with others. Some stations, networks particularly, are very strict about how many letters are used and are adamant about the characteristics of code that is used to identify commercials. The bottom line is that very few stations are willing to refuse the income derived from running spots because of the identifying code, and few advertisers would balk at changing a code in order to get a spot on the air.

Edit Session

This material will be covered more thoroughly in Chapter 6, Postproduction: Editing, and Chapter 7, Post-Plus—Audio/Graphics/Animation, where the emphasis is on the hands-on relationship of the editor to the material to be edited. The role of the client and of the agency is different from that of the production company or the editing company, and although some general knowledge of the editing process is essential to understanding the role of the agency in the postproduction process, the following is aimed at those who represent the agency's point of view.

Either during the taping or soon afterward, the Society of Motion Picture Television Engineers (SMPTE) time code is recorded onto the master as a digital frame of reference, a kind of address that can be located easily by a computer. SMPTE time code breaks time into hours, minutes, seconds, and frames. There are 30 frames per second. Once the time code is embedded on the master tape, special VHS window dub copies are created and sent out for review. These production/editing copies contain the original audio and video as well as a visual readout of the time code, which is usually placed in a window at the bottom of the picture (Figure 3.2). These are sometimes referred to as window dubs.

Prior to editing, the creative director and the AP, perhaps with the client, will look at the takes and make some preliminary decisions about which are the "buys." In some cases a trusted editor has the first go at pulling selected takes and creating an edit decision list (EDL). Sometimes the production company is involved. More often than not on big-budget productions, the production company and its director do not cut the spots. On low- and medium-budget spots, the production company tends to be more involved. They

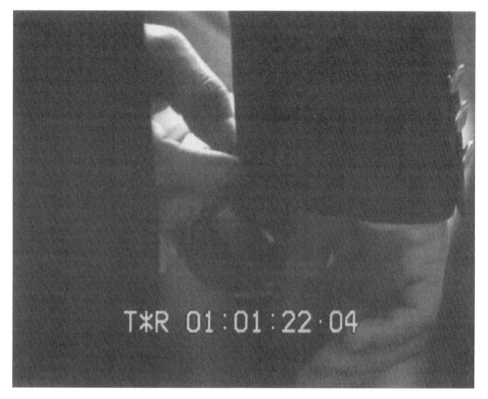

Figure 3.2 A still frame from a window dub. It shows the visible time code. Such a time code would be used to note an in or out point.

have the editing facility and do both the rough cut and final editing for the spot or spots. Sometimes the director is also the editor. The agency producer remains the point person at the edit session unless the creative director is overseeing that part of the project. Whatever the level of production, the steps involved in editing are similar.

1. Shots are logged.
2. An EDL is created.
3. A rough cut is made.
4. Revisions are proposed and discussed, and final decisions are made.
5. The spots are edited to conform to the final decisions.

Up until the beginning of 2000, this would most often be done in an "offline" facility.

Offline/Online

This offline/online mode of operation is now being phased out as cheaper and more effective software comes into play. However, it still persists in many parts of the country. "Online editing" refers to work done in the finishing medium. It means using high-end equipment with all the "bells and whistles" and usually costs about $300 *an hour*, whereas an offline session, with somewhat less than finishing capability, costs $500 to $1000 *a day*.

Here's how the process works. After window dubs are screened and logged, an offline edit session is booked and the spots are edited, discussed, and reedited until they seem right. The notes from that approved or now final cut yield an EDL. The original material is then configured to match the EDL in an expensive online session where special effects and multiple sources, such as graphics and still storage systems, are accessed. New technologies, however, are putting more effect capabilities in the lower end editing programs, and there is little need to go to expensive online sessions for completion.

Once the agency gives their approval of the rough cut, the spot is prepared for air.

1. It may go to specialists in audio for "sweetening" or to a graphics house. At an audio sweetening session, the various audio elements are fine-tuned for air and the AP is usually present. At a graphic session, the AP may also be present, although there is some work that would not need supervision. At any stage along the way, the creative director may want to become involved.

2. It may go directly to an online session in which the EDL, created in the offline session, is simply implemented, and the AP will not be present.

3. It may, instead, go to a film transfer session in which the approved takes are color corrected in a color correction telecine session, which allows for manipulation of the colors. A telecine session refers to a session in which one works with a device designed to transfer projected matter, such as slides or film (cine) to television (tele). While being processed, the signal can be enhanced to correct colors, hues, contrast, luminance, and in some cases framing. A more complete explanation is offered in Chapter 6, Postproduction: Editing. The output of that transfer is then sent to an air master. The air master is dubbed for either network or local station release.

That was then. Now, although the editing hardware and software that are finding favor are still in a state of flux, the primary tool for cutting commercials is still the Avid system. Avid began as a Mac-based system but now runs on PCs as well. It is available in a number of configurations that can be customized for particular projects. There are other similar systems, some of which are exclusively Windows based and some Mac based. Lower cost and less complete programs, such as Final Cut Pro and Adobe Premier, are changing the nature of the hardware/software configurations for commercial and PSA editing. Essentially, they all allow for instantaneous random access of digitally stored information. With these tools, the director/producer or the creative director and client are able to see the commercial (or the program, for that matter) cut in a number of different ways. A scene or shot can be extended, deleted, dissolved, or cut so as to create a number of variations of the same spot. In some configurations, once a version is agreed on, a decision list is generated and used to create the dubbing master at an online session. More and more, however, the material is simply reconstituted in high resolution on the same system that was used for the edit session.

Once the edit session is finished, the now cut commercial goes to the client for approval. If the production was shot in film, the chosen scenes would be color corrected, usually after the final choices have been made in the Avid session. In some cases, all the production footage would be color corrected before the Avid session. This is true if there are only a limited number of takes or choices since color correction is a time-consuming and costly process.

As storage systems become more affordable and accessible, the material is worked on in high definition from the very beginning and is then transferred for dubbing or transmission. Since somewhere early in the 2000s, "Smoke sessions" have cost about $600 an hour. The Smoke system allows many layers to be manipulated in real time at high resolution with the accuracy inherent to digital media. When the master is completed, the project may be dubbed for various markets and shipped to the stations or it may be transmitted to the stations.

Most recently, all material is transferred to a digital format and worked on as digital medium as soon as possible; that is, all film is transferred immediately. Digital formats remain digital, and all material is edited and finished digitally.

Final Details

Agency producers keep track of billable times along the way. They will have arranged for everyone who needs a dub of the spots to get them in a timely manner. They also apprise their internal trafficking department of the master spot names and codes. Finally, they are responsible for maintaining all records related to the production. This includes internal agency records, payment vouchers, and various legal matters, which pertain to the relevant contracts.

4 Preproduction

Regarding television, film production, or for that matter any job working in commercials, the first thing you'll need is a job. "The most important part of being a director is having a job." That's attributed to Eric Von Stroheim, who probably never shot any commercials.

The second thing to know is that while getting the first job is very important, getting the second job from the same client is the moment of truth. It's particularly gratifying if they're nice to work with, need to make a lot of commercials for a long time, pay a lot of money, and you get to be the one who makes them.

There are three phases to film or video commercial production or, for that matter, to production of any kind.

1. *Preproduction:* All the time and work that goes into preparing and submitting the bid, as well as the time and effort spent prior to the actual production. It may also encompass the marketing efforts of the production company.

   Preproduction deals with all the elements involved in bringing the production to fruition: those actions that bring the company to the moment when film or tape actually rolls; locking in a schedule and budget; arranging for crew, hardware, cast, location or studio, props, services, legal matters, and all the other details essential to the actual production.

2. *Production:* The actual shooting of the commercial or commercials.

3. *Postproduction:* The work involved in completing the project.

   For the production company, this means the completion of everything necessary to prepare for the editing of the project. This includes logging the original footage, as well as acquiring any missing elements such as graphics, revised copy and announce track, music cues, etc. Postproduction also includes the various steps involved in the actual final edit. The final edit may include color corrections, addition of graphics and effects, or mixes and can also include the delivery of the final tape or film for air. It may also include delivery of the final project via tape dub, film dupe, or digital transmission. Finally, it includes completion of details such as the reconciliation of the budget and payments, as well as maintaining records of the specifics of the shoot.

This chapter is about the work that goes on prior to production. The preproduction concerns for an agency and production company are very similar. The significant difference is that the production company has to actually go about the business of making the commercial, while the agency has to make sure that the production company is making the commercial to the agency's specifications. It's often the work that's done in the pre-production stage that determines if there is to be a second job from the same client.

Low-Budget Production

Much of the information that is relevant to low-budget commercials is relevant to commercials costing a great deal more. For our purposes I've decided that low budget describes any commercial production that costs up to $25,000. Even commercials that are "free" cost a few hundred dollars for tape or film stock, office expenses, transportation, etc. And while some television stations may include the production of commercials in the cost of the air time, you can be fairly certain that the production cost is then built into the cost of that air time. While it's true that there's a lot of latitude between "free" and $25,000, that's still considered very inexpensive for commercials, particularly since the average network commercial cost over $300,000 in the year 2000.

Who makes these very-low-budget commercials and why? Many very competent local film/tape commercial producers view them as a comfortable, relatively stress-free niche. They may also shoot weddings and other events within a community. Often, however, the producer is a relative, friend, or friend of a friend. It's often those who are young and starting in the business. Typical of this very-low-cost genre are those commercials shot by a director/camera-person who has his or her own camera and can spend an hour or two shooting a local restaurant or retail establishment. They then edit unrelated shots together to offer an inexpensive commercial that helps to establish a general feeling about the wide range of goods or services offered by the client. They will generally use a low-cost music bed from a standard library "buy-out" source, or a computer program like Garage Band, and then edit the resulting cut with Final Cut Pro, which now has its own built-in music composing component, or with Adobe Premiere. These programs are often perfectly adequate to the task. Sometimes these commercials far exceed what is reasonable to expect, but usually it's cookie cutter in looks and style. That's as much a reflection of the client as it is of the creative or production arm. More often low-cost commercials are created for clients who are not very sophisticated in their commercial demands and whose charge is "I want to increase my business. I want to make more money." Making such commercials is a good way for a fledgling director to get a chance to do some work and begin to build a professional reel. It usually also helps the client's business.

Apart from finding such low-budget commercial production companies through friends, stations that sell time may also make recommendations. Here the low commercial production cost is motivated by an available crew and the desire to sell air time. This is particularly true at UHF or cable stations. Since they work with many low-budget or new advertisers, they either have their own staff or need to know producers who can deliver an airworthy product and who are willing to produce low-budget commercials. They try to be helpful to the unsophisticated, agencyless clients that they solicit. It pays then for beginning directors to get to know some of the management teams of cable and UHF stations and to establish a working relationship with them. This is often based on a willingness to shoot commercials at a very low cost. Leaving a sample reel/DVD and some business cards with them is a good idea.

With commercials that cost up to $1000, there is usually a kind of template in place that is similar to commercials that cost much more. The difference is that the spots often suffer from the director's lack of experience and inability to afford the essential but expensive gear needed to make the shoot work as well as they might wish. Instead, the director makes do with jury-rigs, flat lighting, and "almost right." Very-low-budget production excludes expensive lighting setups, art directors, and prop crews to enhance the look of the client's product, and they usually lack the time and skill to get the shot absolutely right. It's not meant to belittle the efforts of many students, neophyte producers, and others who agonize over commercial productions in which they make little or no money. Rather, it is indicative of the limitations with which they live. Often the work is done because the producer knows that he or she needs to get experience and needs to get a good-looking reel. After awhile, they'll take the best shots from a variety of clients and make a demo-reel of that. They know they need to step up the production values so they can charge more, take longer, and afford to do ever better and more expensive work.

Generally speaking, as the price goes up, even within low-budget constraints, the specific concerns are greater. No longer does the script simply call for a "bevy" of unrelated beauty shots of the client's food, dresses, workers, products, etc. Now there are specific shots in mind, and perhaps actors, special gear, and more elaborate lighting is needed. The same concerns prevail as would be in place for a much more costly commercial. The difference will be measured in part by the talent brought along.

Differences are also seen in the gear that a company takes with them. Will the company be shooting in 16 mm or in 35 mm? Thirty five millimeter is more expensive, but will probably look better. Will they be shooting in Hi-Def, DVCAM, digital Betacam, analog Betacam SP, or for that matter, Digital8? Will they have additional "insurance" items: standby gear like extra lighting units, lenses, etc.? Will they bring along additional production help? Those extras are costly but good to have at hand. Waiting for a runner to pick up a suddenly needed item, such as a filter, is more expensive than having that filter available. Conversely, having items "available" can get to be very expensive. It's difficult to determine just how much needs to be spent in order to strike a proper balance.

When shooting for a client with a low budget, the director/camera person, who may very well also serve as the producer/editor, has to work with the client as if they were the agency. The questions that must be asked are similar to the ones that an agency asks as it's preparing to work with a client.

Assume you're that director/producer. You're going to have to ask many of the same questions that would be asked by the research and creative departments of an advertising agency. You need to know:

1. Who, what, and where?
   a. Who is the client?
   b. Who is the audience?
   c. What is the product or service? What are they selling?
   d. What "items" will you have to show in the spot or spots?
   e. What do they want to do?
      i. Do they want to increase business?
      ii. Do they want to appeal to a new segment of the population?
      iii. Do they want to take business from a particular competitor?
   f. What special handling will be required? Legal?
   g. What special gear will you need?
   h. Where are they located?
2. Where will you be shooting?
3. Number of commercials.
   a. How many commercials will you be shooting?
   b. Will the spots be 30 seconds? 60 seconds? 10 seconds? Or will there be a combination? An inexperienced client may not realize that shooting a few spots at the same location at the same time may be more economical than shooting just one. Shooting a few commercials at the same time may not take considerably more time than shooting just one and may offer the client the opportunity to create a few different messages. Of course, doing that helps defray the cost of the shoot. In effect, if one commercial costs $1000, then two might cost $1500. It's a way to justify an increase in the profit on the shoot while giving the client more for his or her money.
4. Airing
   a. Where will the spots run?
   b. What station or stations will run the spots and during what time period? This may affect the creative decisions. If the commercial is running in a "teen" program, a background music track of classical music might be a poor choice. It's also important to know if the stations airing the spots have any special requirements. Networks, for example, sometimes require special coding.
5. Talent
   a. Will on-camera talent be needed?
   b. Who?
   c. Who pays them?
   d. Is voice-over talent required?
   e. Will children be used? If so, the shooting schedule demands special consideration.

    f.   Often the client expects to read his or her own copy. It's best to find out if they can or should do that. Sometimes, unfortunately, they're simply bad. They don't sound appealing. They don't look appealing. They're stiff and awkward. You have to determine what to do if they absolutely insist on appearing themselves. If they do and you feel they shouldn't but still want to do the job, you may want to find a way to minimize or camouflage the damage by cutting their lines or adding music or some other distraction. However, you may be able to turn that liability into an asset. There was a business owner in New York who did his own commercials and was so bad that he began to develop a cult following. He became very successful just *because* he was so bad. Then, too, there are companies like Smucker's jam who used the tag line: "With a name like Smucker's it has to be good!"

6. Location

    a.   Where will the spots be shot? If it's at the client's business, the client needs to know that the elements involved in shooting the commercial will upset the normal flow of things. There has to be very specific communication regarding the demands that will be made. Perhaps a time can be arranged to minimize inconvenience such as a weekend or night shoot.

7. Schedules

    a.   What's the time line for the shoot? Clients often don't know how long things take. It's to everyone's advantage go over the time line with them to avoid, or at least minimize, surprises.

8. Production

    a.   In what medium will you be working?

    b.   Is it film or tape? What kind of tape?

9. Postproduction

    a.   What's the time line for the edit?

10. Medium

    a.   What is the delivery medium?

    b.   Will the stations want Beta copies, or 1 inch, or U-matic for that matter?

11. Costs and legal

    a.   How much money will it take to finish the production?

    b.   How much will the client have to pay? It's best to be firm and candid about this. Arrange to receive at least a third of the money in advance. More if possible. Do *not start* without it. Do *not deliver* the spots without getting paid unless it doesn't matter to you or you know the client very well. Difficult though this may seem, it's really professional to obtain some money before the shoot begins and to be paid in full soon after completion. Get a contract, even a simple one. The act of signing a document lends weight to the transaction. A simple sample contract is included in Chapter 2, Client. It is not offered as a legally binding instrument.

A realistic presentation about all the little things that cost money in a production informs and educates clients who are new to making commercials. They don't think about the van you need to travel to the location, the tape stock and its cost, the office supplies, etc. Sometimes, if you ask about such things, you may find that the client can help with some of those costs or facilities. They have a van you can use. They may be able to offer you the use of their office for making copies, calls, and other things that affect the final cost. All of that increases your profit and may help to reduce the client's out-of-pocket expenses.

Ideally, the client has a good grasp of what is needed and what they can afford. That's not always the case, so it's best to go over things. Traditionally, low-budget commercials run 30 seconds and have three parts.

1. The first 5 seconds say "Attention shoppers!" Even if it's not a retail commercial, there's always something at the beginning of a commercial that's intended to get the viewers' attention and make them want to see the rest of the spot.

2. Then the next 20 seconds say "Here's what's happening!" This is where the pot-pourri of shots happens, where the host walks us through wherever we are, or where we glimpse the many facets of whatever we're supposed to see. This is where the message of the commercial is showcased.

3. Finally the last 5 seconds say "You can get it here" and sometimes "for a limited time only." It may be 3 seconds, but the end of the spot ought to identify the client. Since not everyone pays attention to commercials all the time, mentioning the client's name as well as showing it on screen, a sort of "see and say," helps the viewer to remember the product or service.

In fact, the advice given to teachers and marketing professionals is appropriate for many commercials.

1. Tell what you're going to explain.
2. Explain it.
3. Then review what you've just explained.

As a commercial, that advice for the teacher or marketing professional sounds like:

1. Here's exciting news from the client
   Here's exciting news about the product.
2. Just come to the client's location and get immense savings (which will improve your life).
   Just use the client's product in this way (which will improve your life).
3. You'll find all this at the client's location.
   You'll find terrific results with the client's product.

Usually, if a client is aware of the process, they are more apt to accept lighting setups, walk-throughs, and the other parts of the job that may have seemed like a waste of time. Therefore, it's helpful to assign someone at the shoot to keep the client apprised of what's going on.

The editing process is usually a total mystery to such clients, not to mention a colossal bore. It's best to be specific about what the spot or spots will look like and then show a rough cut that's as complete as you can get it. Do not expect your client to have a sense of the difference between a final cut and a rough cut. What they see is what they will think they're getting. Do not expect them to understand what it will look like when you've added the supers or the music track. Show it to them now with everything in. It doesn't have to be the right font. The music can be copyrighted music that you know you can't and won't use (and you'll have to let them know that), but let them see a "real commercial."

Medium- and High-Budget Commercials

Somewhere about the point when a budget exceeds $25,000 the procedure changes and the productions come about differently. There was a time when the leading production companies were so well known and worked together so well that it almost didn't matter who the director was. The company itself was so good, the crew and gear so up-to-the-minute, that the production company bid as a company. The director was simply another employee, albeit an important one. Commercial production companies like MPO, Filmex, and Centrex in New York were typical of that era. Clients of those companies did have favorite directors and might postpone a shoot in order to be able to work with a director like Howard Zeiff or Marshall Stone, or any number of others, but the company itself was "the star." While that may still be the case in some markets, for the most part that was then. This is now. Now, it's the director that secures the job, and the company serves the director as his or her representative and as the production arm. Some companies represent a number of directors. Much of the time it's the combination of director and director of photography (DP) that defines a production company. Now agencies are introduced and build relationships with production companies and directors through a variety of sources.

Directors come in a variety of styles. Some do their best work with scripts or storyboards that require talent. Some directors work best with food, cars, or retail, or any one of a number of other specialties. Within each category there are subsets. Talent, for example. Some directors work best with children, others with women or nonprofessionals. Some work well with stars or owners-of-the-company. Directors who work well with talent may not work well with animals, or food, or cars, or underwater subjects. It's really no mystery. Woody Allen doesn't shoot Biblical epics, and Steven Spielberg might not fare so well with small-cast neurotic comedies.

So the first thing an agency does, and most jobs at this level come through advertising agencies, is determine what kind of a project is being considered. What kind of product? What kind of script? Who will be asked to bid? A part of that decision will depend on the budget. It's the director's representatives who are most likely to be approached at the upper end of the production scale. At the lower end, it is the director who will have made the pitch for the creative work and perhaps for the handling of the entire account.

One of the nice things about working on productions that come from agencies is that the script will have been written by a group of people who are usually pretty good at writing commercials. Sometimes, of course, the writers need help. Giving that help may require a great deal of tact, and you may be unsuccessful. The agency may feel that its script and boards clearly demonstrate what's required, and that's what they want. The director's job is to bring those boards and that script to life.

It may seem strange, but the more important a director you are, the less likely it will be that you edit the spots. The agency and the client would rather do it without you. Your per day price is too expensive. Besides, you'll have too many other projects to be able to spend time on editing. Usually, the agency is going to start by consulting the director's reels in their library and then contacting the "rep" for that director.

Agents, or representatives (usually referred to as reps), may simply sell a particular production company with just one director. Sometimes a variety of directors are handled by a single representative who may show a reel with the works of many different directors. In the latter case, the rep will try to handle directors who typify a number of different styles of work, a director who works well with children, or food products, or automotive, etc.

In any case, the rep will have friends and contacts at the agencies and/or will make cold calls presenting the works of those they represent. Sometimes an agency, or a client for that matter, may suggest someone because they've worked with that person before. Perhaps they've seen some work they liked and researched who did it. Sometimes recommendations regarding companies are solicited from friends and colleagues at other agencies or facilities. It is an industry that is in constant flux. Clients come and go, and that changes the makeup of agencies. Agency producers often find that they are forced to move from one agency to the next. They take with them a storehouse of information about the work that was done recently, such as who did what job and what were the specific idiosyncrasies, problems, and joys associated with those jobs.

For the production company, the most desirable bidding scenarios are those in which, as a favorite production company, you are simply assigned the job and asked how much a spot or spots would cost. Most often a limited number of companies, perhaps three or four with whom the agency is familiar, will be asked to bid on the cost of producing a specific set of storyboards. They may be asked to price it out, with editing and without editing, or to bid the job on tape as well as on film. The production companies who are asked to bid are usually similar, but sometimes might include a range of options: an established, expensive, experienced, well-known company; a second production company whose work is known and who may be slightly less expensive; and a new company trying to make a name for itself. The least expensive company may not always be awarded the job as is discussed later.

Some production houses, usually very successful ones, have found that since it takes a day or two to make the calls to get an accurate breakdown of production costs, only a broad estimate of cost will be given. If a full breakdown and accurate bid are needed, a small charge is made. That charge is then deducted if the bid is accepted. This is done to prevent what had become the common abuse of using successful production companies to price out jobs for comparison purposes only.

Most of the time, the boards are simply sent to each company to get their bid. Sometimes, however, a formal presentation takes place in which a select group of production companies are brought together to get the details of a proposed job at the same time. The specifics of the spots are outlined and any questions regarding the boards are answered. The companies are then given a set time to work on their bid for the job.

Once the boards are in the production house, they are broken down to determine the cost. Each frame of the board represents at least one shot in the spot, though sometimes a few panels on the board may be used to indicate a number of positions within a single shot. The company needs to know who, what, when, where, and why. Who is involved? What are they doing? When and where, and for how long are they doing it? "Why" is needed to see if there isn't some other better way to do the job. Why are we doing it this way? Could we be more efficient or get better results doing it some other way? The answers determine how much the spots will cost.

> **Typical Horror No. 97**
> One would think that when preparing a bid there is a specific commercial on which to bid. On the lower and middle end of the spectrum, this is not necessarily the case. The president of our agency did so well at one pitch that the client was ready to sign on without even seeing original creative work. Yet again, I was asked how much a series of commercials might cost. We had not even submitted an idea for a commercial. I made a "ballpark" guess. It was based on the general media budget we had pitched, my knowledge of our working habits, and inevitably on twin fears: the client's fear of what things would cost and our fear of what losing the client would cost us. The boards were designed with my "ballpark" budget very much in mind. Creating a commercial with that budget in mind restricted our creative endeavors.

Most of the time, however, there is a commercial or series of commercials in place, and the task is to "cost them out." I include the story where a "bid" is expected for a nonexistent commercial, only to point out how varied the bidding procedures can be.

Bid Template

In the bad old days, bidding a job meant sitting down with pencil and paper and an adding machine. You ran through a series of questions that you hoped were relevant and complete. How much for the director? How much for the crew, the cast, the hardware? Were there unexpected issues that should be addressed? You also asked, "Have I left anything out?" In today's market we usually create a bid using a template that essentially asks questions about the cost factors that need to be added into the budget.

Both above-the-line and below-the-line costs are computed.

1. Above-the-line costs are those costs that stem from the "creative" or managerial part of the production, such as the director, the producer, and the director of photography.
2. Below-the-line costs cover gear, travel if necessary, and all the rest of the people and service organizations who work on the production such as crew, craft services (food), location scouts, fire safety officers, police and crowd control, etc., as well as rentals for the various types of gear and services.

The template considers costs in the preproduction, production, and postproduction stages. The preproduction questions for every single item are:

1. How long will the person, item, or service be used?
2. What is the rate for the person, item, or service?
3. What are the surcharges? Overtime, for example.
4. What is the estimated cost?
5. What is the actual cost?
6. What additional costs should be considered for contingencies and overhead?
7. What is the profit?

The template attempts to create a line item for all the possible people, items, and services required for any production. The Association of Independent Commercial Producers (AICP) has created a Film Production Summary, a template that is specific to commercial production. They also provide valuable guidelines for the various stages of production. They can be found online at www.aicp.com. A sample production bid form is included in Chapter 10, Useful Forms and Reference Material.

Other templates exist for film cost breakdown, such as Movie Magic or DotZero. For postproduction there is a specific template devised and used by members of the Association of Independent Creative Editors (AICE). (They changed their name from the Association of Independent *Commercial* Editors and retained the same initials.) They can be found online at www.aice.org. Both the AICP and AICE programs have itemized line categories that consider most typical costs. They all ripple cost differentials as they are inserted. An example of an AICE template can be found in Chapter 10, Useful Forms and Reference Material.

A template usually offers more categories than one would find in any one shoot. It also leaves out some others, such as underwater photography. Given the standard templates, there is still great leeway in how competing companies bid on a particular job, and various issues make plugging in the numbers very difficult.

Salaries will differ, time estimates will vary, and the commercial's requirements will be addressed in different ways. Does the board require a living room? Will the company go out on location? Which location? How much will it cost? Can a friend or relative's house be used without cost, or is the construction of a living room set necessary? If so, Where? When? What will it cost to build, transport, set up, and tear down? What's the cost for art direction, props, transportation, etc.? Will it require stand-by painters? How many? For how long?

Additional offbeat factors may come to play in bidding out the job. For example, is the production company shooting on a sweep table for a job that is already booked? Can that same table be used the next day for the new job? If the answer is yes, there will be a savings on the total cost of using the table, at least in the cost of hauling the table to and from the production center. In some ways it's hard to complete the work on the template without knowing some of the answers that it is hoped the template will yield once all the work on it is done.

In the early stages of breaking down the boards, a lot things are taken for granted that may be changed as the process evolves. It's one of the reasons the templates are so valuable. It automatically restructures the cost of the commercial as new numbers are inserted. While the running tally may be thought to give one instant access to how costs may be coming along, the fact is that the numbers don't offer many insights until the entire budget is assembled.

When the estimated cost is arrived at, changes can be made on the template, which is essentially based on a spreadsheet program like Excel. It's where the ripple-down capabilities of the program become so valuable. Once a change is made, the program automatically recalculates the project's total projected cost, which allows the user to try a number of different tacks. So if a total budget is $100,000 including a director fee of $10,000, the program will automatically recalculate the total budget to $98,000 when a new director's fee of $8000 is entered.

Let's assume that having created a budget, you now find that the cost is prohibitive. The most likely place to cut costs is to change the location, but doing that will affect the number of days needed to set up, the crew needed, wrap time, etc. Making that one change will require a major review of the budget and cause a ripple effect, which the programmer, not the program, will have to manage.

Along the way, as costs are assessed, questions arise that are difficult to answer. How does one accurately determine the cost of the director if the director is an officer in the firm and is regularly on hand as part of daily business? "Steve, do you think you can shoot the product shot in half a day?" is a typical and legitimate question, and the dialogue is taken for granted. On the other hand, if Steve is a freelance DP and is called to answer a lot of questions throughout the bidding process, he would rightly be expected to receive compensation for his consultation. How does the estimator include the freelance DP's preproduction hours? How many preproduction hours will be needed by the producer and the director? There is no definitive answer, but a number does have to be plugged into the template. Usually, the overall budget of the production, knowledge of the client, key production personnel, and the kind of gear that is apt to be used determines the answer to these questions.

The preliminary bid is put together after all the possible known facts have been verified. It can be extremely costly to make assumptions regarding any matter that could have been checked. Location costs need to be specific, and while it's impossible to lock down crew and talent without a commitment, finding out about availabilities can avert problems later on.

Some of the specific preproduction considerations will play out like this:

1. *The Cast:* Are there stars or celebrities? If so, do they need special and costly handling such as a limousine, personal assistants, personal makeup, hair stylists, and so on? Who pays for this? How many featured players, day players, under-five lines, and extras are in the spot? Are there children or animals in the spot? (If so they will fall under strict guidelines and be available for a limited number of on-camera hours, as well as require additional personnel. The children require a social worker or teacher on set, and the animals may require ASPCA or similar personnel on set.) Is the commercial to be shot nonunion, or under the jurisdiction of the Screen Actor's Guild (SAG—Film) or the American Federation of Television and Radio Artists (AFTRA—Tape/Live)?

2. *The Crew:* How many crew members are required? For how long? Who is available? You may not need a gardener for a men's clothing commercial, but you probably will need extra costume hands. The "A" costume team may cost $500 a day, the "B" team costs $250, and you may get a production assistant (PA) for $75 a day. Who do you select? Your decisions define your company and your style of work.

Note: There is a tradeoff in using inexperienced help. More experienced personnel usually have a sense of studio discipline and knowledge of tools and procedure that is significant to the production. They cost more than inexperienced crew members but can get more done quicker and are not as likely to innocently create problems. For example, a producer friend hired an eager, bright college student to work as a production assistant (PA) on a commercial production. In order to save money for the producer, the PA decided to mark furniture positions on the floor with inexpensive duct tape instead of the more expensive gaffer tape. After the day's shooting, the duct tape needed to be pulled up. It had been a long day and the lights were hot. As the tape was pulled up, the paint on the floor was pulled up along with the tape. This would not have happened with gaffer tape. It cost $3000 to repaint the floor for the next day's shoot. One might wonder why the crew chief didn't protest when the duct tape was being used; however, they may have missed it, and once the first piece of tape went down, the chief may have felt that the damage was done and the rest didn't matter. A $75 PA is more apt to think he would help by using duct tape than a more experienced, and more costly, PA. The person making out the budget will have to assign a monetary value to that experience and hope that when the bid is being considered, the agency or client appreciates the distinction. Recognition of the value of an experienced crew is one of the reasons why the cheapest bid isn't always the one that gets the job.

3. *Time:* How much for preproduction? Locations need to be scouted, travel and personnel arrangements made, production gear and props acquired or rented. How many preproduction days will be needed, and how many people at what price will be required at that stage of the process? For example: Assume there is a scene in a commercial that takes place in a 1950-ish living room set. It needs to be dressed with period props. How many days will it take to make the calls to locate specific pieces? How many days will be needed to see the props? How much time to arrange to have them delivered? To inventory them? To dress them, if that needs to be done? How long are they needed on camera? How much time will be needed to restore them? What personnel will be needed for the restoration? Who returns them? With what vehicles? How much time will it take to handle the invoices for all the props, and who will do it?

Is the production house bidding for postproduction as well? If so, how many postproduction days? What's included in the postproduction? Digital graphics? Film-to-tape transfer? All these questions require answers if there is to be a precise budget.

4. *Operational expenses:* Rights and clearances, rentals, insurance, benefits, office space, and similar issues should be covered. Who's going to be responsible for what? Will the agency be paying for talent directly, or will that go through a paymaster? Will the production company need to pay and keep track of both the session fees and the cycle or residual fees? Commercials run in 13-week cycles. Talent is paid for the recording or filming session and is then paid in advance for a run of 13 weeks. At the end of the 13 weeks, the cycle fee must be paid or the commercial declared finished. Should the commercial then be reused, fees would have to be paid for all the 13-week cycles that had been missed. It's a significant bookkeeping task for commercials shot under AFTRA/SAG agreements.

5. *Specialized gear:* How much, when, and what kind is needed? How does it get to and from wherever it's needed?

Once the preliminary bid is put together with as many items as possible checked out, a production meeting of sorts is called with the principals who will be responsible for living up to the terms of the bid. Usually, this means that the director and producer, and perhaps the director of photography and set designer or location manager, discuss the budget. They may ask for more time or more of one item or the other and will probably indicate where costs might be cut. After the meeting, the changes are inserted into the preliminary budgeting program and the necessary adjustments are calculated. The resulting new information is then ready to be submitted. Perhaps the director will meet with the agency and outline his or her plan for realizing the boards.

The bid will be submitted with a letter indicating some of the assumptions that have been made regarding the production. These would probably be things that had been discussed with the client. "We assume we're not going to shoot this on location in Paris." "We intend to use Actor X as the narrator, or Actor Y if X is unavailable."

Once the Bid Is Accepted

Once the bid is accepted, the preproduction crew goes into action to lock down all the elements that go into the final commercial.

Shooting can only begin when all of the following are in place:

1. The facility or location is ready.
   - Set is in place.
   - Location has been prepared, which means that a contact has been made and that a survey has been completed. If this is the client's office/studio/plant, the advertising agency and client will have to be involved in the arrangements. If not, a contract for use of the location should be signed. In any event the name and phone number for whoever will be on hand and responsible should be made clear.

2. All personnel have their calls and have been confirmed in a timely manner, including:
   - The client and their staff, which means all those participating in the commercial
   - The agency and appropriate representatives
   - Cast
   - Crew
   - Security
   - Location

   The representatives from the client's company should include someone who has the authority and the power to make decisions as needed. It can be very frustrating to wait for a critical response to an unexpected and potentially costly question as the cast and crew wait around while an executive, who isn't present, is located and then asked to make a decision based on details spelled out on a phone call.

3. All rentals are set, including:
   - Cameras
   - Dollies or cranes
   - Mics
   - Lights
   - Gaffer gear
   - Grip gear
   - Props
   - Vehicles

- Locations
- Costumes
- Special effects items
- Intercoms
- Portable toilets

4. All preproduction audio tracks and necessary graphic items are either completed or in an approved state.

5. All legal work is done, including:
   - Permits in place
   - Insurance in place
   - Contracts are signed
   - Union clearances, if needed, have been arranged
   - Rights, if any are needed, have been secured for music, lyrics, poetry, etc.

Some of these permits and contracts may come from the client, such as rights to use materials they own. Some will come from the agency, such as rights to use music, lyrics, and poetry, and perhaps AFTRA or SAG contracts. Some will come from the production company, such as insurance and some union contracts.

Keeping track of those lists is a high priority. Inevitably, the producer/director or production manager spends an enormous amount of time on the phone. Inevitably, he or she leaves messages and has to follow up with additional calls. Calls in response to a message left yesterday are received in the middle of doing something else today and notes are taken on scraps of paper. Those scraps are scattered throughout the master folder for the shoot, or some adjunct folder that was to supposed to remain in the main folder but is now off with an assistant who is trying to track down someone else whose name is on another scrap of paper in the same folder. It's very detail oriented and time-consuming and often very frustrating. It can be somewhat helped by:

1. Putting a date on everything.
2. Creating a folder for each major part of the shoot, such as "People," "Things," and "Services," and keeping notes in that specific folder. I always create a folder called "Mess," which stands for Miscellaneous, but which might as well stand for the mess of unrelated and pertinent information that goes into it. At such times the date on the scraps of paper is a help.

Along the way as people and items are confirmed, the template bid may be addressed to indicate actual costs as opposed to projected costs. As the new numbers are inserted into the form, the totals will change to conform to the new information.

The Go-Ahead

Once the bid is sent out, the agency or client reviews it and makes a decision. While the decision will often be based on price, other considerations are taken into account. For example a low bid from a company that doesn't seem to be as competent in its presentation may be passed over. The desire or ability to work with a particular director of photography may sway a decision. Personal rapport between a production company and a client is often a factor in the decision making process.

Once the production company is chosen, contracts are drawn up and signed. The contract will usually call for delivery of the original material for a spot or for the completion of a spot or spots by a particular day. The contract will try to spell out all the elements contained in the spot. It also spells out the terms of payment, which can be constructed in any of a number of different ways. The AICP offers guidelines regarding the concerns of contracts used for commercial production.

Sometimes production companies are paid on a cost plus basis, in which the agency or client agrees to pay all costs plus a percentage of the total cost of the production. Included in the costs will be the salaries of the principals of the company such as the director, producer, etc. The plus part of the cost will be a percentage of the total cost, which is considered profit for the production company. In such a case, of course, the agency or client shares in the criteria, which were assumed in making up the bid. For example, if a commercial costs $100,000 to make, a 20% cost-plus agreement would mean that the profit would be 20% of the $100,000 or $20,000. The total cost to the advertising agency would be $120,000.

More often, a specific price is named in the bid and agreed to. Usually, when there are changes along the way, the agency and the production company have to find a way to resolve the cost of changes. Most companies protect themselves by factoring in 10% to 15% of the total cost as a contingency fee. For a smoother production, it's wise to have an agreement about additional costs as they occur.

As indicated earlier, most production companies will require a substantial down payment prior to actually going into production. Sometimes one-half is expected before the shoot and the final payment upon conclusion of shooting or completion. Another model is one in which one-third is expected before shooting begins, one-third after shooting is completed, and the final payment is made after completion.

Finally, the production is ready for the shoot. Production begins.

5 Production

As the production level changes, the style of shooting changes. A commercial that's going to be shot in an afternoon for a local restaurant uses a production technique that is vastly different from that used for a major IBM shoot, and that is different from a low-budget regional commercial. Nevertheless, there are some elements that are the same for all three. We'll examine three different kinds of productions and examine their similarities and differences. First, a bit of history that may help explain some general film and video conventions.

Early film cameras and later early television cameras were heavy. Many of today's studio cameras and cameras with long lenses, teleprompters, and assorted other outboard rigs are still very heavy. They need a tripod or other sturdy mount to get a steady shot. Historically, the audience became used to seeing things from a very steady point of view. That concept of shooting is still the way we tend to present material, though it has been changing since the advent of lighter cameras and handheld photography.

In still photography in the early 1930s, Henri Cartier-Bresson popularized the advantages of portable cameras with his brilliant black and white photography. In 1934 a lightweight handheld Bell & Howell Eyemo movie camera was carried on Admiral Richard Byrd's second Antarctic expedition. It was not until 1954, 20 years later, that a handheld video camera could be used at all and another 10 to 15 years before a lightweight portable video camera was available. While it was very expensive, advertisers and television stations were eager to get that "look." With the invention of lightweight portable cameras, cinematographers and, later, videographers could shoot without using a tripod. Photojournalists were among the first to make use of the newest hardware. As they rushed to capture stories, the style of handheld photography began to gain acceptance. Soon, simply by being handheld and shaky, the visual image was infused with a sense of urgency and drama.

Perhaps the most classic example of the excitement and impact of handheld photography was the live footage shot at the assassination of President Kennedy in 1963. The shots taken while a photographer was running to photograph what had happened epitomized the immediacy of the tragedy and the urgency of the coverage. Handheld shots from 9/11 are equally poignant. The look of a handheld camera came to be synonymous with action and excitement. "Shakey-cam," in which the photographer purposely shakes the camera and emphasizes the changing horizon line, became the newest "hip"

style and convention-of-choice for shooting adventure and action pictures and . . .
commercials. It became the visual clue to indicate that "something important" was
happening.

Shakey-cam was a particularly happy convention for producers of low-budget
commercials. It meant that the tripod could be eliminated. That cut out having to carry
the heavy, bulky tripod and reduced the time for setups in which that same heavy tripod
had to be carried from location to location, from shot to shot, and then set in place, leveled,
and so on. Better still, it cut out the cost of a good tripod and head, which amounts to
hundreds, and often thousands, of dollars. Best of all, it excused a host of mistakes, which
could then pass as part of the "look."

More recently, there seems to be a greater need for justification for this kind of technique. Handheld shots are still being used where the story calls for it, but mounted shots
are being used where *they* are appropriate.

Low Budget

Most low-budget shoots have to be done in a short time. They are usually shot on tape
rather than film because tape is cheaper than film. Tape also requires no processing and is
ready to be edited immediately. The low-budget producer is wise to simply shoot enough
footage to get what's needed, but not so much that long hours of logging are needed with
too many choices when creating the edit decision list (EDL). No matter who the client is
or what their product or service is, the amount of lighting used is minimal. Only a few
assistants need to be used. At most, one for audio and one all purpose gaffer/grip/produc-
tion assistant (PA). The chances are that the production will use a schedule that is similar
to the following one.

Travel: 30 minutes

If the location is 5 minutes away, it still takes 30 minutes to load the truck with lights,
camera, and stock, and travel to the location.

Setup (per shot): 10 to 20 minutes

It will take this long unless these are total "grab shots" in which people are eating, or
dancing, or engaged in some activity that won't be lit, and where the camera will be handheld. Even so, it still takes time to get that just-right impromptu scene.

Shoot (per shot) 15 to 20 minutes

Each shot will need to be done a few times. There is usually a moment or two required to
change a light or move its position, and then there are a few takes. Additionally, time is
needed to record a narration track, wild sound, etc.

Wrap: 30 minutes

This includes time to collect all the gear and restore the location to its original condition.

Travel: 30 minutes

Finally, it takes this long to get back to home base, unpack and/or store the gear, and secure the tape.

Transfer to computer and log: 30 minutes to an hour.

Total time: Usually at least half a day.

It's more likely to take a full day to produce the simplest commercial. The producer will have to determine what to charge for out of pocket expenses, his or her time, as well as the time of the assistants and whether to factor in the cost of rental equipment. If editing is a part of the package, that too will have to be considered in determining how much to bill the client.

Here's how the shot is set up:

1. Each shot is set up by arranging the area for the shoot. Desks, chairs, and other objects may have to be moved. Even when nothing in front of the camera is moved, the area behind the camera often needs clearing to make way for lights or for the camera operator/producer who has to move while shooting. People probably won't be placed into the set until the lighting is finished.

2. Three-point lighting is often used. The subject gets
    a. A key light
    b. A fill light on the side
    c. A back light
    Sometimes additional lights are needed to light the walls behind the people. Alternatively, light is simply bounced onto the subject or natural light is allowed to illuminate the subject. Bounce lighting is often thought of as being softer than direct or three-point lighting. Natural lighting has different characteristics depending on the source of the light. Natural lighting may also provide uncomplimentary shadows.

3. Once the subject is lit, you're ready for a few takes. Hopefully no more than 2 or 3 but perhaps as many as 10 takes per setup are shot under normal circumstances. If children or animals are involved, or with particularly difficult subjects, the number of takes can be even greater, which adds to the allotted time. The chances are that the shooting will be handheld. If someone is talking or the shot seems appropriate, a tripod may be used, which will take more time to set up. In any event, no dolly or crane will be used. Once the shot is complete, the next shot is set up and the process is repeated.

At the end of the planned shoot the producer may want to get some "B roll" or "coverage," which is extra shots of merchandise or of people in action. The producer may also want to get room tone for editing purposes. "Room tone" is the sound that is unique to each room or outdoor area when there is "silence." That silence usually includes the hum of computers or air conditioners, the sounds of birds, or maybe the wind through trees. Room tone is all the white noise that is behind all the recorded sound from the commercial. When it is missing from a particular spot in the commercial, usually at an edit point or at a scene that was originally shot without sound, that electronic silence appears. It is very apparent but can be covered with appropriate room tone.

Soon after the shoot, the producer will transfer and log the footage to prepare for the edit session. The sooner that's done, the less likely specifics from the shoot are apt to be forgotten. When the wait is too long, a moment usually occurs when the question is asked: "Why did I shoot this?" or worse yet, "How come I didn't shoot that?"

Medium- and High-Budget Shoots

The process for medium- and high-budget shoots is similar to that of low-budget shoots in that the elements are the same. The production still has to travel to the location, set up, light, and shoot. However, the specifics of each of those is different. For handheld shots, the process is similar no matter how expensive the shoot is. The camera may be different, the lighting is apt to be very different, the operator may be using a gyro mount of some sort, but the process itself is the same. More often, however, when the budget is above $25,000, there are many shots that are set up. Time and care is spent in creating a "beauty shot" that is as close to perfection as the team can achieve.

Once some friends arrived at a studio at 7 in the morning only to find a crew leaving from what had been an all-night shoot. They had been shooting a can of motor oil and had obviously been working for a long time. They were asked how it could be that shooting something as simple as that had taken so long. After all, they all knew how to shoot a can. They agreed that they knew all the regular ways to do that, but since they wanted to do it in a way that had never been done before, it took longer.

Shot Procedure

It doesn't matter if the production is being shot on film, tape, or even on a hard drive. The procedure for a planned moving shot is the same. Once the set is in place and the lights are in their basic positions and are focused and trimmed, the shot procedure begins.

Here's the director's procedure for getting that shot:

1. First set a starting position, a tentative *first mark, and mark it as No. 1.* You can use a piece of gaffer tape and a Pentel for the marks. Set up the camera at that location.

2. Look through the viewfinder and make sure the setting is right. Some things don't photograph well. Others that might seem to have no potential look great. The lens does make a difference. That may be because since the camera only catches two dimensions, height and width; it is the viewer who unconsciously creates the third one, depth. The viewer does that from the symbols that are offered: shadows and foreground, middle ground, and background objects. In doing so, we "see" what isn't there. Our imagination paints in what's implied.

The director is best served by looking at the screen in a painterly fashion. Look at it as if it were an abstract painting. Look at the screen from side to side and top to bottom. Look at the lines created by whatever is being shot. Is it a pleasant composition? Is the light falling well? Where will additional lights go? Are there shadows that are distracting? Is there *anything* that is distracting? If there is, fix it. Fix it immediately. If, for some reason, you can't fix it immediately, take the time to make a note and find someone to fix it. Problems relegated to memory usually fly away as soon as the next disaster presents itself.

It's hard to imagine how the setting will look until it's fully set up, but there's usually a 3-hour savings if you can use your imagination well enough before everything's in place and tweaked.

Nightmare No. 12

One production company kept a list of client nightmares. High on the list was the statement "Well, could you light it first and then let me see it because I can't tell yet." Of course, the client was right, but if the client doesn't like the way it looks after all the work is done, the alternative will probably be to start from the beginning again, which is not only very costly but very disheartening. It's also hard to anticipate such costly requirements when drawing up a budget to present during the bidding process.

Once the opening frame is approved by the agency and client, you have your opening mark. Don't lose it. Mark and thoroughly check all the marks.

1. Mark the floor.
2. Mark the pedestal position.
3. Mark the focus.
4. Mark the pan and tilt positions.
5. Mark the viewfinder.
6. Mark the monitor, if there is one.

Use a grease pencil to outline the key position of elements in the frame. Grease pencil marks on the monitor help the director, the producer, the agency, and client stay aware of

Figure 5.1   This monitor is marked with a grease pencil to indicate the position of a graphic element that will be inserted later.

what would be considered unusual framing if it were not for the addition of graphics that will be inserted in postproduction. Those are the starting marks.

Now move to whatever is the second position of the shot, then the third, marking the pertinent positions along the way. You may want to get approval for each section. If there is a stop along the way, mark and label each section in the same way. If there are more sections to the shot, mark them.

When you move from the first position to the second, you should notice if something in the shot, such as a branch or a prop, has to be moved. That may affect your first position. Go back and make sure that the fix for the second position hasn't hurt the look of the first position. If it has, fix it immediately. Now, continue in this manner until you've come to the final position and marked it. The final mark will be important, even if the in-between marks aren't as critical.

Presumably, the director of photography (DP) or lighting designer has been watching the moves and now needs time to set the lights for the specific marks. When the lighting and set decoration is ready, walk through the shot very slowly. Think: "Slow motion." Use the talent for the first walk-through if possible. If not, use stand-ins. But be careful of working your actors too hard. They may be willing to go on repeating actions for a long time, but inevitably it will take the edge off their performance.

Continue to look at the framing top to bottom and side to side throughout. Check the set props and the lighting and make sure that they work in every marked position and in all the stops along the way. The DP or whoever is in charge of lighting and whoever is in charge of set or art direction should be looking at the shots with you. They'll need to make notes at each point in the shot and make appropriate changes.

It will take time to place all the marks and make all the tweaks that this style of work demands. That time costs money while the crew works on the shot. A different and more critical element is the time the shot itself takes. That is the next thing you'll need to test. Once everything is in place and before the crew works on the fixes, run the shot at "take" speed, making sure it can be done well. If not, additional adjustments will have to be made. Once you're satisfied with the shot at the actual speed needed to make the shot, the crew needs time to make the required fixes. Often the director or producer has to set a time limit on how long the "fixes" can go on. Even though there are some crew members who are never really satisfied with the way a shot looks, almost everyone will accept a reasonable cutoff time. High-budget productions have a greater tolerance for getting everything exactly right than midbudget productions. It's important to realize that even shots that seem simple can take a long time.

Some years ago, Jack Horton, a DP at Filmex in New York, spent hours working on different lighting setups to shoot a pearl dropping down through a bottle of liquid Prell shampoo. The client seemed amazed that it took so long but was even more amazed at the variations that were offered, then shot, and finally discarded. The chosen shot played on screen for less than 5 seconds but became an image that sold the product for a long time.

The attitude toward the time it takes to set up a shot was neatly stated on a stagehand's T-shirt:

It's not the time it takes to take the takes that takes the time.
It's the time it takes to set up the takes that takes the time it takes.

Once the shot is done, many productions will shoot a "protection" shot in case there is something wrong with the master. It's a safe procedure and gives the editor a choice. On the other hand, I have worked with companies who felt it was expensive, time consuming, and tiring.

Most director-producers and most agencies and clients expect to use the playback mode on commercial shoots so that once the shot or take is done, everyone can see it and can be specific about corrections that have to be made. It's interesting to note that in episodic dramas, production companies avoid the playback option, fearing that too many viewers, that is, the producers, key members of the crew, talent, etc., will voice too many opinions, which will prolong the process and add unacceptable cost to the project. Of course the same is true for commercials, but it's better to have everyone approve a shot while every-thing is still set and in place than to have to come back and reshoot.

Multiple-Camera Shoots

There are some events that require multiple-camera shoots; for example, dangerous stunts are usually covered by multiple cameras. They're not the kind of events one wants to repeat. Sometimes funny scenes, a pie in the face, for example, will be covered by multiple cameras. I've shot scenes where a student was learning how the Pac-Man computer game worked. Multiple cameras were used to record the student and the program simultaneously to capture the moment when a kind of light flashed in her eyes as she recognized how individual elements of the program worked.

Most commercials, however, are shot with a single camera and then edited. Most com-mercial productions simply cannot be done in a "one take" multiple-camera format. Some things just don't happen on cue. How, for example, do you get popcorn to pop on cue, or a child to giggle, or a cat to wake up and cross to a bowl? These commercials absolutely demand single camera production. Other considerations such as lighting or number of shots are equally relevant and require a production in tape or film using single camera technique.

Nevertheless, there still are some commercials that *are* shot using multiple cameras. These are usually low-budget, syndicated, or local station productions. Many commercials for kitchen appliances or knives that are destined to be aired on late night television are still shot that way, and of course, there are a large number of infomercials that are shot as if they were half-hour demonstration programs. Shooting with multiple cameras means one has to work around some restrictions. Usually, there can be no light stands on the floor. In a single camera shoot, the order of shooting is established by criteria that are based on a variety of needs: availability of talent or location or client preference, to name a few. In a multiple-camera shoot, every element has to happen on cue in the exact order that it will appear on screen. Multiple-camera shoots do offer some advantages. If the entire 30 seconds of a commercial is shot in a single take, a finished commercial can get on the air quickly, and there have been some local or regional campaigns constructed around this. Cost is often much lower since editing is eliminated. Whatever the number of cameras used, many of the production elements such as budgeting and scheduling will remain the same through all stages of preproduction, production, and sometimes, postproduction.

Keeping a Log

During production, the associate director/stage manager, production assistant, or script supervisor makes careful note of the takes and time codes for each shot. They also make sure that all the material that's supposed to be shot is shot. I once called for a wrap only to be reminded by the script supervisor that I had forgotten an entire sequence. Needless to say I revised the "wrap" decision, endured my crew's derisive remarks about directors who call a "wrap" and then uncall it, and shot the almost forgotten sequence.

If there is no time code, which is rare today, then the slates use consecutive take numbers in which there are no duplicate take numbers. A slate is a device used to identify the filmed or taped material that is to follow. Originally a chalkboard was used to indicate the name of the production, the director, the scene, and take number. Currently, electronic slates and time-code are most often used to track material. Using consecutive slates through-out the shoot is helpful when handwritten slates are used because there can only be one of each take in the entire shoot. Even if you have hundreds of slate numbers, you'll never mistake "Scene Two, Take One" with "Scene One, Take Two."

The production label for the container of the commercial should always show

1. Production name, client, agency, and producer
2. Reel number, particularly if there is more than one reel to the production
3. Date or dates of production
4. Name of the person writing the log
5. The label should indicate whether the tape is:
    a. Original footage
    b. Submaster
    c. Edited master
    d. Dubbing master
    e. Dub
6. A copy of the shooting log should be in the container and show all of the above and add:
    a. The name of the segments or shot numbers, with time code if possible
    b. Notes and comments about each take that were written down as the production was shooting

Additional notes may be added at the end of each production day. These notes will be used in the postproduction process.

Extra Shots and Wrapping Up

During production, certain shots that were not indicated on the storyboards may seem like a good idea. In fact, there are times when whole ideas for commercials come up on the spot, though this is unusual on very-high-budget productions. When these shots or ideas seem appropriate and the agency or client approves, it's sensible to take the time to shoot them. Often something spontaneous works out very well, but some limits need to be imposed. If you have an unlimited budget and unlimited editing time (something I have never experienced), then shoot it all. If there are time and budgetary constraints, you have to consider those constraints as well. There is no rule for how far to stray from the boards. It certainly is done, and some of the best work comes from shots that happened on the spur of the moment.

Whether it's a single- or multiple-camera shoot, it's a good idea to review notes immediately after the shoot has ended, while it's still fresh in everyone's mind. During the wrap, while the bulk of the crew puts away cables, cameras, and lights and wraps various other parts of the gear, the director-producer, the agency, and the client often discuss the selected takes. They may wish to review them with everyone's notes still fresh. The review might also include the associate or assistant director and the production assistant and would surely include a script supervisor if one had been associated with the shoot. There will be time to look at window dubs of the work later, but those first comments are often very telling.

Director's Business

Once the shoot is over, you, as the director, may become involved in the editing session. However, even if you are not participating in the edit, there are still a number of things that should be done. Thank the client and the agency. Follow through on what was done by inquiring about the edit. Maintain contact with the agency. Find out about bidding possibilities on any other shoots that are planned. Arrange to get a copy of the final work. It may be significant enough to add to the demonstration reel.

Take care of the paperwork involved in the shoot. Bill the client. File all the material. Keeping track of notes about who was on the shoot, what was rented, and where it came from can be very helpful in succeeding shoots. Keep track of the various lists that the shoot generates.

You might want to let others who use directors know about your work. Send a release to the local trade papers, but consider the agency and the client. Let them know you're going to do some publicity about the shoot. They may wish to read the copy and may have issues with the publication of your material. By the same token, they may help in letting others know about your good work. Contact other clients for whom you've worked and inform them about this recent job.

This final word. Seem busy, even if you're not as busy as you'd like to be. If you're working all the time, the belief is that you're very valuable. If you're not working, questions arise about your worth. "After all," the thought goes, "if he were really good—really valuable—he'd be working. Maybe he's slipped and I need to call someone who's really busy." You'll also find that, quite often, as your price goes up, your perceived value goes up.

Shoot Basics

While it's possible to define types of commercials—demonstration, testimonial, problem solving, comedy, etc.—commercials are by nature all different, and the production requirements are different for each one. It is, however, possible to examine commercial production by examining a few select commercials and get a sense of how things work.

We can look at three different scenarios for imaginary commercials and see the production procedures that are in place for each shoot.

1. Product shot—made on a low budget
2. CEO stand-up—made on a medium budget
3. Musical—made on a high budget

We'll start by examining a simple product shot. Some of the elements needed here are universal. There are always a director, a director of photography (DP), a camera, and audio of some sort. As each scenario plays out, we can see how various production elements come into play. As the projects become more complex, we'll see what new elements must be added. Start with a simple set of product shots.

There is a wonderful 1954 print ad for Smirnoff's Vodka of a dry martini in a very elegant glass placed in the foreground of a shot that includes the desert and the pyramids behind it. It's a wonderful way to emphasize the "dry" of dry martini. Not all product shots have such elegance. Most of the time, products are shot on no-seam or seamless paper in the very controlled location of a studio. The paper is mounted on a sweep table and then lit in place.

If the spot were being made for the manufacturer, one would expect to see lovely, bubbly clear liquid being poured into glasses filled with lots of ice, and it would probably be shot on 35 mm film. It would have lots of back light against a dark background to emphasize the liquid, or perhaps a light background if the soda were a dark liquid. High-speed photography might also be used to slow down the pouring of the liquid. If a film look was wanted throughout the spots, our taped insert shots could be shot using various filters to create a "film look." The inserts might even be shot on film; however, shooting on film would mean a longer lead time as the film processing would take a day or two. The cost, particularly if it was shot in 16 mm, would probably be the same. In our example we'll assume that we shoot everything on film.

Imagine a storyboard for a grocery chain. It has a high-budget opening and closing shot on 35 mm film. It's designed to feature three regularly changing insert shots about special sale items of the week. These separate product shots will be used as inserts with an announcer voice-over. Essentially, this is a standard "donut" type commercial. A donut commercial is one in which there is a standard opening and closing to the commercial with a "hole" or "donut" into which promotional products are inserted on a regular, or not so regular, basis. Often retailers will get partial repayment for the production and airing of the commercial from manufacturers whose products are featured in the donut. This is called cooperative (co-op) advertising.

The chances are that the liquid will not be moving in this lower budget shot but will instead be a static "beauty shot" of the container of whatever liquid we're selling shown in an appealing arrangement.

Our donut commercials will probably have copy, which reads something like:

"You'll love all the fine products at our store. This week we're featuring
(DONUT STARTS HERE)
Product 1 at price point A.
Product 2 at price point B.
Product 3 at price point C.
(DONUT ENDS HERE)
So come on in now. You'll save as never before."

The requirements for these product shots have to be minimal. A clean, uncluttered look is what we'll be after. Since the shot will be made MOS (Minus Optical Sound or "mit out sound"), an inexpensive, non-soundproof studio would be adequate. Ideally, we would know the running time for each shot, so if possible the announcer's voice track would be recorded prior to the shoot. We'd note the timing needed to announce each product. It might allow for, or even demand, some kind of movement. A typical move would be one that widened out from the product itself, or the label on the product, to a beauty shot that left room in the frame to insert a graphic with our price point.

The agency account executive may arrange for specific products to come from the grocery chain's warehouse or leave it to the production company and their food handler to supply the "hero" products. The agency will be at the shoot almost from the beginning, helping to make decisions about what props might be used in conjunction with each product and how each product should be "dressed." For example, "No, a cup from Tiffany is too up-scale . . . Let's use a small plain white mug, and oh yes, gingham napkins are perfect. . . ." After a few weeks of shooting this kind of insert shot, a "rhythm" for the insert shooting is established, and we may find that the representative from the client doesn't show up at all. The client may simply rely on the agency to make any last minute decisions.

The production company is apt to be represented by:

- A producer
- A director
- A cinematographer
- A production assistant

Figure 5.2 This is a sweep table, made with seamless paper on an ordinary table supplied by the rental facility. The setup is typical for an insert product shot.

Figure 5.3 This is a still of the initial position of the shot. As aired, the shot widened and graphics were inserted.

Depending on the size of the budget, the cinematographer may have:

- A gaffer
- A grip

Additionally, there would probably be a home economist or someone who specializes in food handling, and perhaps a prop person to help with propping and dressing each shot.

A typical schedule might be:

9:00–10:00:	Load in and set up (1 hour to off-load and complete a general set up) Off-load truck or van. Set up; sweep table; rough lights, tripod, and camera.
10:00–10:30:	Set product 1
10:30–11:00:	Shoot product 1
11:00–12:00:	Strike product 1, set product 2
12:00–12:30:	Shoot product 2
12:30–1:30:	Lunch
1:30–2:30:	Strike product 2, set product 3
2:30–3:00:	Shoot product 3
3:00–3:30:	Wrap

If possible it would be wise to shoot an additional product to use the 8 hours of time that would be a minimum call for a full day for the studio and members of the crew.

During the period from 9 AM to 10 AM the crew would be involved in the business of loading in and setting up, getting the day's material in place. The following is what will be needed.

DP

If this is a low-budget production, the DP will be arranging the camera and lighting equipment. On higher budget productions, the DP supervises the setup. In any event the setup consists of the following elements.

Film/Tape

The first decision is whether to use film or tape. Thirty-five millimeter film may be purchased new in 400 (just over 3 minute) or 1000 (just under 9 minute) loads. Tape can be purchased in 10-minute, 30-minute, 60-minute, and in some cases 90- and 120-minute cassettes. The greater film area provided by 35 mm affords a higher quality picture. Alternatively, the use of digital video becomes enticing for cost containment, and it offers a particular kind of look and a currently fashionable style of shooting. (However, digital video does not seem to be used for a majority of high-budget commercials.)

Magazines

The film is loaded into magazines. Prior to shooting, the DP will determine what film stock to use and acquire a sufficient amount for the shoot. A magazine is loaded with a roll of film, perhaps 10 minutes' worth. The load depends on what is being shot and what camera is being used.

- For 16-mm film, the magazines typically hold only 400 feet of film. The film may be purchased new on cores of 400 feet (just over 11 minutes at 24 frames per second [fps]).
- For 35-mm film, magazines come in 500 feet and 1000 feet loads as well as a 2000 foot load for sit-coms and other uses that demand longer takes.
- For tape, the camera is loaded with a tape of sufficient length to shoot the entire day's work. However additional tape stock would be available.

The magazine with the load is then mounted to the camera body, and as the shooting progresses, the magazine will indicate how much film has been shot. Spare loaded magazines are waiting should more than one roll of film be needed.

Body

A camera body capable of shooting 16-mm film is needed. Were this a more costly shoot, the camera body and film stock used would be 35 mm.

Head

The camera with magazine will be mounted to a head that allows the camera to be panned and tilted smoothly. Should this be the kind of commercial where there is a danger that the head might come off, say in a traveling car shot, the camera might be mounted to a rigid support.

One of three types of heads will be used:

1. *A fluid head*, which uses hydraulic fluid and a series of valves and chambers to adjust resistance.
   Or less likely:
2. *A spring tension head*, in which springs of varying tension may be selected to give the proper resistance to dampen movement.
   Or, unlikely for a low-budget commercial of this type:

3. *A geared head,* which requires the operator to turn cranks to make moves. This is the head of choice for 35 mm feature films and high-budget commercials. The operation of such a head requires skills that are specific to that form of camera operation.

Tripod/Dolly/Crane

The camera body is normally first mounted onto the head, which is sitting on a tripod, dolly, or crane. Then the rest of the unit is completed. The magazine is placed on the body, then the film is threaded. Once the camera is ready in all respects, the lens requested by the DP is added.

- *The tripod* is a three legged stand with provisions to raise or lower the entire unit and hold it in place.
- *The dolly* is a four-wheeled, rarely three-wheeled, cart with an arm that can be raised or lowered. The arm is raised or lowered either by a counterweight system or some kind of hydraulic or electronic system. Usually the dolly can also be crabbed, which is to say that it can be moved on its wheels in any direction. Finally, it can be placed on tracks and moved over the tracked terrain. A dolly costs more than a tripod, both as a purchase and as a rental. It might seem wise to use a tripod to shoot product shots, but the ease of positioning a dolly may well make it a better choice. The tripod would be cheaper to rent but would take more time when minor corrections need to be made. The major cost in renting a dolly in some markets is the cost of transporting it to and from the studio. Some studios have their own dollies and simply charge for the rental. Few if any commercials are shot without a dolly or tripod.
- *The crane* is a large dolly. It's often fitted with a kind of jib arm that allows the camera to be swung in a 360 degree arc and travel from inches above the floor to the full height of the crane or jib arm.

Lenses

The DP may mount either a prime lens, which he or she feels will be best for shooting table top photography, or a zoom lens, choosing a setting from the variables that such a lens offers. The most popular lens packages consist of a 10 to 1 zoom (either a 12- to 120-mm or a 25- to 250-mm zoom) and an 18-, 25-, 50-, and 80-mm lens. Various specific commercials might use lenses that are specific to the product. For example, a 300-mm lens might be used to soften the background on a glamour product. One fundamental truth about the choice of lenses is that each choice comes with its own trade-offs. Determining the light source and which lens is best, at what aperture, and at what distance from the subject is exactly the DP's job. If the shoot is done on tape, the camera would probably have a zoom lens.

Figure 5.4 This is the Super Pee-Wee III Plus dolly from Chapman/Leonard and is useful because of its small size. (Photo courtesy of Chapman/Leonard Studio Equipment, Inc.)

Figure 5.5 This is the Hustler IV dolly from Chapman/Leonard that is designed for larger cameras. (Photo courtesy of Chapman/Leonard Studio Equipment, Inc.)

Figure 5.6   This is a Panavision Super Techno 50 (Technocrane). (Photo courtesy of Panavision.)

Instruments

The instruments used to light the production are in the gaffer or chief electrician's area. However, the DP specifies what instruments are to be used and their placement. Generally speaking, instruments are categorized in the following way:

- by their function—key light, back light, etc.
- by the quality of the light—hard edge, soft, etc.
- by the wattage
- by the kelvin characteristics—blueish/daylight, yellowish/studio light, etc.

In ordering instruments for a shoot, great specificity is required as there are many variables relating to each instrument.

Sometimes when a DP and crew have worked together for a long time, the DP simply determines the f stop, contrast ratio, quality of the light: hard, soft, diffused, etc, at which he wishes to shoot, and the gaffer will take it from there, placing the lighting instruments in the right place, with the right wattage and scrims, nets, blacks, etc., to accomplish what the DP required. Most rental facilities come with a variety of instruments, and the company is charged for the usage. At some facilities the company is required to bring in its own equipment. An "electric truck" with instruments, cables, and attendant electric gear is hired, and that equipment is used at a flat rate. The requirements for this table top shoot would

Figure 5.7 This is a TOPBOX, which is a portable collapsible housing for any set of lights. (Photo courtesy of GAMPRODUCTS.)

be relatively small, and the truck rental would be less expensive than that for a musical. At the start of the shoot day, the DP informs the gaffer of the instruments that need to be prepared for the shoot. Since this is a table top shoot, a light box would be needed, and one of the first orders of business would be suspending the light box over the sweep table.

Light Box

A light box is a unit designed to deliver a soft light for table top photography. Imagine a very large open shoe box with a white interior. It's turned upside down and mounted directly over the product. The open face is covered with an opaque fabric, and lights are mounted in the box. Frosted bulbs may also be used to achieve the resulting light, which is soft and uniform and covers the entire product. Light boxes that come in a variety of sizes are exactly like that.

Figure 5.8　The TOPBOX unit includes six PAR lamps within a portable unit. (Photo courtesy of GAMPRODUCTS.)

Grips

Here's what the grips will need.

C-stands

Most studios have a supply of "C-stands" or "Century stands" in a variety of sizes. These are portable three-legged metal stands used as temporary holding devices for various pieces of "grip" gear. The Century Company made the heavy bases used to support standing electric fans. In the early days of film making, the base of one of these stands was pressed into service to support an instrument. The bases soon became very popular, and the phrase "C-stand" became the standard term for any portable grip stand.

Figure 5.9 The MAXLIGHT is equipped with a yoke and can be stand mounted but is used in almost any position including as a top light. (Photo courtesy of GAMPRODUCTS.)

Grip Gear

Some of the gear held in place by the C-stands are:

Barn doors: So called because they look like barn doors. Metal flaps are placed in front of lighting instruments to trim the edges of light coming from the instrument.

Blacks: A device used to hold back light. Blacks are hung like curtains or are stretched on frames. The frames are usually tubular metal in a square or oblong shape and covered with black cloth. Frame sizes begin at 6 × 6 and 8 × 8 feet and go up to 20 × 20 and 20 × 40 feet. They normally require two stands even at the smaller sizes. It's often unsafe to use C-stands with any but the smaller sizes, particularly outdoors, as they act like the sails. (Also see "Flats.")

Cookies: These are metal or wood patterns placed in front of a light source to create patterns such as clouds or leaves. The word comes from a Greek word "cukaloris," which means shadow play. They are sometimes called coo-koos. Sometimes gobos are used in the same way.

Expendables: All shoots require materials that are expendable, such as:

- Gaffer tape—not to be confused with duct tape, though they both may come in gray. Duct tape is not as strong as gaffer tape, leaves a gummy residue, and usually has a reflective surface
- Mylar fishing line
- Colored and frosted gels
- Clothes pins (C-47s)—high on the list of essential grip items are wooden clothes pins used for holding gels in place. They cost little more than a nickel a piece in a hardware store. As theatrical hardware they're called "C-47s" and sell for about three times that price
- Electric tape
- Nails, screws, etc.

Flags: Flags are simply shorter, smaller versions of blacks and are used to trim the edges of beams of light. They come in a variety of sizes such as 4 × 4 feet floppies, 2 × 6 feet cutters, 24 × 36 inch solids, etc.

- Fingers, dots, and postage stamps are smaller blacks. They all come in sets, which include a solid, a silk, a double net, and a half net.
    - Finger sizes vary. The largest is 4 × 12 inches and the smallest is 1 × 12 inches.
    - Dots are circles that come in diameters starting at 4 inches and go up to 10 inches in diameter.
    - Postage stamps are squares of approximately 8 inches to 12 inches.

Flats: Flats are scenic elements. They are frames, often made of wood, usually 8, 10, or 12 feet × 4, 5, or 6 feet, covered with canvas or plywood, and then painted and decorated to resemble some wall element of a set. Blacks may also be stage flats covered with solid black cloth.

Gobos: A scenic element that's used to create the illusion of "looking through" something. Typical gobo elements are cutouts of windows, or keyholes. The gobo, attached to a C-stand or a pair of C-stands, is held in place in front of the camera and the illusion for the viewer is that he or she sees the scene while looking through the gobo window, or through the gobo keyhole.

Nets: A net is a piece of gauzy material or screen, usually black, used to reduce light.

Reflectors: Reflectors are used to reflect light. They can be made of fiberboard, beaverboard, foam core, Styrofoam, or fabric. In fact, a reflector may simply be white oak tag or even a newspaper placed so that light bounces onto the subject. Mirrors are used for hard bounce light. Most often reflectors appear to be boards covered with silvery aluminum foil. Sometimes, a gold or copper foil is used to "warm" the tone of the reflected light.

Scrim: Scrim is a generic term for a loosely woven fabric used in film and television to reduce the amount of light coming from an instrument. The scrim material used in lighting is opaque or white and usually mounted in metal frames. The purpose of scrim is to dim the light without changing the color temperature or quality of the light. Scrim is also used in theatrical productions, usually as a foreground painted drop that becomes translucent when a scene is lit from behind the scrim.

Sweep table: Presumably the studio will have such a table. At the least it would be a long folding table, the kind that's available at most retail office supply outlets. Ideally, we would be shooting in a facility in which there was a permanent studio sweep table specifically constructed for such work. Ideally it would have a top made of white opaque Lucite that sweeps up to form a background for the product. The use of Lucite allows for lighting from beneath the product. Its color would be determined by the gels used to light it. If necessary, any table can be covered with colored seamless paper.

There are over 55,000 sites to be found on the Internet under the general heading of "grip rental equipment." The sites represent grip rental locations around the world. One can also search the Production Equipment Rental Association (PERA) site. This is an organization that represents a variety of suppliers and rental facilities used in television production. They can be found online at www.productionequipment.com.

At the Sweep Table Shoot

Props

Prior to the shoot the prop crew goes over the products that will be used and offers suggestions to enhance the shots. We examined the shooting of clear liquids earlier in this

Figure 5.10   This Lucite sweep table is in its shipping position.

Figure 5.11   Here the table has been raised and is in the position in which it will be used.

Figure 5.12 A product on the sweep table. In production, the table and product would be lit. As this is a Lucite table, the product could be lit from underneath.

chapter, now let's assume our product is orange juice. Fresh oranges and a mug of coffee might be placed near the "sale" juice carton. The prop department would get together with the food handlers, director, and agency producer and go over the chosen products and accessories to match up specific props to the product. In the case of the orange juice, for example, they might bring a dozen or so different mugs and cups from which to choose.

It will probably take the full scheduled hour to offload, store, and then select and begin to set up the first "hero product" and matching props. The prop department will need a storage place for the many accessories it brings as will those working with food. Cartons of orange juice require fewer hero products than actual oranges, but with three or four products to shoot in a day, it's important to have a storage room, out of the light and out of the way but still convenient to the set.

Well before the merchandise is put in place, a decision has been made about the background color of the sweep table. The color is chosen to work well with the products. Are we selling oranges? Chances are the sweep table won't be red. Will we want to shoot other products on the same color background, or will we want to change the background for each product? Our choice will affect the amount of time needed for setup and perhaps for lighting. Once the seamless paper is in place and the camera mounted, a beehive of activity ensues around the sweep table. Various arrangements and configurations of merchandise and props are set in place and alternate arrangements tried until a setting is approved. The food and prop crew step back and lighting begins to work.

Food

Food handlers will have found a kitchen or at least some area where there is clean running water and begin setting up their table filled with the products that will be featured in the commercial. They will have brought sufficient product to offer a choice of so-called hero products. This will allow the client, the agency, and the director a choice of goods to shoot. They will want an early decision on which product is most likely to be used so they can prepare it for its moment on camera. The food handlers with whom I've worked have an amazing ability to make the food product look good. It starts with their personal relationships with produce markets. Those connections are regularly enhanced by the high prices they are willing to pay for the just-right hero merchandise. In all cases, the food must be real and edible, but once the camera is in place, the food handlers use a collection of special devices and tools to enhance the look of the products. This may mean polishing or waxing the product or scoring it with a wood burner if it's supposed to be a grilled steak or chicken. They'll use an atomizer with water or glycerin to give fruit, such as our oranges, a "dewy" look. They'll have sprigs of perfect greens to use as decoration. They'll probably travel with a portable stove or heating element and any number of rarefied kitchen chemicals and tools. Those lush steaming steaks that are featured in various food ads may get that steamy look from acid that is dropped on them just before the camera rolls. At this writing, there is a limit as to the amount of nonedible chemicals allowed to enhance a shot of food products.

In a major production the DP assigns the crew to prepare for the first shot. The first assistant camera would be setting up the camera and the gaffer would be working on the lights. For this low-budget example, the DP might fine tune the camera mount while a rough lighting setup is being set in place according to his or her instructions. This would mean that C-stands were mounted and instruments placed on them, ready to be focused and gelled or scrimed. Special lighting units and grip equipment would be brought to a nearby staging area should they be needed.

In our low-budget production the DP places the lights, perhaps with some help, and refers to a light meter and to the camera's viewfinder along the way. Essentially, there is a half hour scheduled for the rough setup of each shot and an hour's time scheduled for each shot. That isn't a lot of time considering the fact that each product will be a different size and color. Nevertheless, the product should be ready to be shot within the time allotted. Prior to shooting, the director, the agency, and the client look through the viewfinder and approve the shot. Perhaps a few takes are shot to bracket the f stops and afford a choice. If there were a video tap, and it would have to be very low budget indeed to not have one, the director, agency, and client look at the shot and approve the take.

A video tap is video recording taken through the lens of the camera while the film is being shot. The mechanics of doing that revolve around the video camera having access to the viewfinder picture. On a low-budget film commercial, a production company might feel it's wise to avoid offering the video tap as an option. If the product was shot on tape, tape playback would be mandatory.

After the last take of a particular shot is made, the takes and picks are noted on the camera report. The DP examines the gate of the camera to make sure that it's clean. In our more expensive production, the first assistant cameraman would examine the gate. Once an OK is given, the rest of the crew strikes the setup for product 1. After it gets taken down, work would begin on the second shot. Each successive shot follows the same procedure.

Medium Budget: Location Shoot

Storyboard

Office scene: Chief executive officer (CEO) speaks from her desk and walks to a map.

The Champs Elysées in Paris, France, and the dockyards in Brooklyn, New York, are both remote locations. Saks Fifth Avenue and K-Mart are also remote locations. Which is to say all locations are different with different requirements. In fact, the same location is different on different days at different times of the day from sunrise to sunset. So, while it's easy to speak about shooting on location, as is so often the case, the devil is in the details. Which location and what product or service you're shooting on the location determines:

1. Who's needed for the shoot
2. What's needed for the shoot
3. How much the location is going to cost

If the location requires extended travel, the budget would include location fees, permits, car rentals, airfares, hotels, and per diem expenses. The logistics inherent in that kind of production are greater than our needs for this example. We're going to be working on the client's premises. We could be in a store, corporate offices, or company workspace. It doesn't matter. We're going to disrupt business, no matter how innocuous we'd like to be.

Let's assume that we'll be shooting in the CEO's office. She's going to deliver the sales pitch herself, and we'll be cutting away from her during the spots to exciting cover shots of her workers and product in action. For now we're just going to shoot her. There are many commercials that are done like this. Elements of this particular scenario may change, but the fundamentals of the shot are commonplace. We're going to make some convenient suppositions: adequate time and a willing CEO who is able to take the time to get the best possible work. Often there is insufficient time and an executive who is unable or unwilling to cooperate as fully as one would hope.

In this commercial we've added some elements that were present in the sweep table example. The most significant differences are the addition of sync-audio and talent. For the most part the crew and their gear will be similar, but there is more of both.

Schedule

A typical schedule might be very similar to the one used for the sweep table. We'll assume that there is a trucking shot of the CEO as she walks from the front of her desk to a map on the side of a wall. The wall is on the inside of the building facing windows. A second shot will be made in which she walks from the wall back to her original mark. Another assumption is that our CEO can do this well. There are very successful executive officers of companies who can't walk and talk at the same time or who do it so badly that it's best not attempted. Making such executives look good can be a genuine and rewarding challenge. It can also be a nightmare. The creative team may need lots of leeway in creating spots using a CEO who doesn't work well on camera. Conversely, there are many CEOs who are remarkable in their ability to perform for the camera.

9:00–10:30:	Load in and set up
	Off-load the truck or van. Run a rough rehearsal with the talent or with the director so that the crew can proceed with the setup. This will include the setup of tracks, dolly, and camera. The crew needs to gel the windows with Color Temperature Orange (CTO) so that the kelvin temperature of the lights from outside matches the tungsten lights that would be used inside. Kelvin temperature is a measure of the relative color of light. Daylight is blue, approximately 5600 kelvins, while theatrical tungsten light tends to be yellow, approximately 3200 kelvins. As an alternative to that, the DP might use halogen-metal-iodide (HMIs) or a similar type of instrument that gives a light that more nearly matches the blue of daylight and would not require gelling the windows.
	Lastly, if the windows don't appear in the shot, they might be covered with blacks and no daylight would be used. The choice is based on the feel of the boards and the desired look of the spot.
	At an hour and a half, this setup is a half-hour longer than was allowed for the sweep table because this setup is more complex. Even more time isn't allowed as the additional members of the crew can help, so the load-in is apt to go faster. Another assumption is that the amount of time allowed with the CEO of the company would be limited. In fact, a stand-in might be used for the rehearsals to aid in setting up the shots.
10:30–11:00:	Walk through the first shot and make corrections
11:00–12:00:	Shoot the first scene
12:00–1:00:	Lunch
1:00–1:30:	Walk through second scene
1:30–2:30:	Shoot second scene
2:30–3:00:	Wrap

Setting

The setting in this case is the CEO's office. We'll assume that it's a large office. If not, we probably wouldn't shoot in the actual office. Her staff would have been informed of our arrival and their assistance might be sought to help in the creation of whatever look we are after. At the very least they will have to hold the CEO's phone calls. Additionally, if things need to be neat, the staff must be the ones to put everything away instead of our crew, or there's apt to be a mini-disaster when the CEO or her staff tries to locate important papers after we're gone.

Assuming that one wall of the office is a window, we'll put blacks up over the part of the window we don't shoot and use a gel on the part of the window that is in the shot. The office will have a "lived in" look, which means some papers should be left on the desk, but only a few as the office ought to appear to be neat. While one might like the papers to be a light baby blue, or off-white, there's really no way to avoid a lot of stark white on the desk. Nevertheless, that mass of white on the desk may need some toning down because it may be too bright in the picture or may reflect too much light on our seated CEO. Props should be able to help with this, either with a gray spray on disposable documents or some prop color-correct documents. If there is an art director or a dedicated crew person working on set decoration, they might have prepared for the office scene by getting a ream of light gray paper and printing an appropriate amount of irrelevant but impressive-looking prop documents for a busy and color-correct look.

Our CEO moves from her desk to the wall. Therefore, we will be looking at the background all along the way. She stops at a map approved by the DP prior to the shoot. If it had not been seen and approved, we would have acquired a number of maps that could have been checked for camera prior to our arrival on the set. We might hang a few different kinds of maps to see which works best.

Additionally, it would be wise to have a copy of the script on a lens-line prompter for the CEO. Lens-line prompters project the copy on a piece of clear glass in front of the lens. The reader appears to be looking into the lens, but the copy is not seen by the camera.

One of the first things to do, even before the crew begins to set up, is to have the CEO work with the prompter and walk through the shot. If the prompter isn't mounted yet, she can hold a script and walk through the shot. This will help determine timing and affords the director, DP, and audio chief the opportunity to see what problems might arise. For example, rather than sitting at the beginning of the shot, can she lean on the desk and simply walk to the mark, or is there some obstacle in the way? Does the track of the walk have overhead lighting fixtures that will interfere with the boom?

Almost as important as getting the on-camera set ready, is the area off-set. This is where the camera tracks will be laid and where a host of people and their gear will have to stay. The chances are that the body of people and things needed for the shot represents more volume than is usually found in the office. There will be:

1. CEO*
2. Director*

3. Producer, perhaps
4. DP/operator*
5. Camera assistant to pull focus, perhaps
6. Audio*
7. Gaffer
8. Key grip
9. Dolly grip*
10. Makeup*
11. Hair
12. PA/script supervisor, perhaps
13. Prompter operator (with a video tap—may work out of sight of the talent)
14. Video tap operator so that the CEO and the agency can see the takes in playback

This means there is a minimum of 6 crew members (indicated with asterisks) and perhaps as many as 14 people in the office, apart from lighting gear, scripts, lens boxes, extra film magazines, extra tape for audio, etc. While some of the jobs might be doubled up, the room is still very likely to be very simple in front of the camera and very busy behind it.

We also need room to maneuver. Room will be needed to lay tracks. The camera dolly will need to be moved, and the dolly grip needs room to move. The lens needs to be at least 6 feet away from the subject, and probably will need to be farther away. If it isn't, we'd be shooting with a wide angle lens, which is not very flattering.

DP

The DP will have chosen a camera for the shoot. It will probably be a 35-mm camera that runs silently and can handle sync sound. A set of lenses, including a zoom lens, will be part of the complement included in the package.

While the on-camera office is being set up, the unneeded office furniture is removed, including couches, coffee tables, and side chairs. Once the room is clear, the DP and director will go over the move for the shot. The crew then lays track, and the camera assistant mounts the magazine and preps the lens, cleaning the front and rear elements and checking the gate and claw mechanism of the camera. Mounting the lens may be delayed until the camera is mounted on the dolly. When the tracks are in place and secured and when there is room to maneuver, the dolly is mounted on the track, and the head, camera, and lens are mounted on the dolly. Once the camera and lens are mounted, the prompter can be put in place.

Audio

Audio will set up the tape deck and a fish pole boom to hold the microphone. Audio also works with the assistant camera (AC) and/or script supervisor to confirm the relationship between film roll, audio tape, and the time code to be used for the day. During the day's shooting at least 5 seconds will be allowed from the beginning of the tape roll so that the audio deck is up to speed. Both audio and camera will use a time-coded slate to keep track of sound and picture.

A note here on how sync-sound will be maintained throughout the day. Each time a scene is shot, an electronic slate will be placed in front of the lens. It contains a readout of the time code running at that time. The time code may be based on a 24-hour clock or started and stopped with the hour representing new rolls of film. For example, the first roll shot in the day is considered hour 1, the next roll is hour 2 and so on. Later the picture of the time code is matched with the recorded time code on the sound track to achieve sync-sound. In the case of a tape shoot, sync is inherent, but the time code is useful for locating particular takes.

Gaffer/Key Grip

At arrival time the grips and electricians will bring their equipment, probably rental equipment, into place. The cost of all the various pieces of gear needed for production is too expensive to purchase and not use every day. There are also so many items that it is almost impossible for any one production company to have everything that might be used for every shoot. Rentals are a regular part of commercial production. In the top 100 major markets there are usually a few rental facilities with which local crews work. In smaller markets, television stations, and freelancers are usually willing to rent whatever gear they can. After a while crews get to know where to locate specific items. They also get to know how well (or not) the gear is maintained, and the various peculiarities that are pertinent. That's one of the reasons a more expensive rental house may be the first choice.

Set/Props

In our case the set is the office. A prop master or scene or set decorator dresses the set. One of these crew members will provide the dulling spray for papers or color correct documents for the desk. They would also be responsible for having alternate maps for the CEO. Additionally, the prop master would have either seen pictures of the office as it is normally or made an in-person visit to the office to determine what other props might be used to "dress" the set. This might include plants and additional desk sets, picture frames, and books.

While the various departments are setting up, the talent, which in this case is the CEO of the firm, would be having her hair and makeup done. The producer, director, and perhaps PA/script supervisor as well as the agency representative would most likely spend a portion of the time with her to review the script and procedures for the day and to help alleviate any fears about appearing on camera.

Once the set, camera, and sound are ready, a walk-through with talent would be called for. This is the first time the talent might meet the crew so introductions are in order. The director blocks out the movement, and the CEO walks and reads the lines without a script in hand. It might be the first time she used a prompter, and these rehearsals will help to make her comfortable with the way the unit works. It sometimes takes a while for those who haven't used a prompter to realize that the prompter doesn't lock them to a particular speed. Instead the copy will go by at whatever reading speed *they* choose. After the walk-through, the production of the shot proceeds very much as it would as outlined earlier in this chapter.

High Budget: Musical

In 1999 the Association of American Advertising Agencies (AAAA) published figures that stated that "In the 1999 Survey, 1,232 of the 1753 commercials in the database, or 70 percent were 30 seconds in length, at an average cost of $343,000, up 16 percent from $296,000.00 in 1998." Obviously some cost more and some cost less, and the intervening years have only added greater numbers to the total cost. This section describes commercials that are produced in an entirely different way than those in the first two categories. The big difference is the approach to the budget. In a sense, producers of commercials at this level forget about money. Instead, they start by asking: What do I need? What else might I need? What am I omitting that might enhance this production? How can I make this the best possible production? The budget comes after that. The production company is going to be evaluated on their judgment of what is the best and their ability to produce "the best." There are no excuses for anything. Whatever the commercial costs is the cost. The budget includes rentals, services, salaries, and everything else that's needed. On top of whatever number that yields, the work is then marked up to include a profit for the company and contains a contingency fee should something have been left out.

In the old days Busby Berkeley would get an audio recording of the music for a dance number he would be shooting. He rehearsed the chorus, and when the production was ready, he brought his cast and crew together on the set. A wide master shot was made, then insert shots that highlighted segments of the master shot followed. It hasn't changed a lot since then, although the master shot may or not may not make an appearance in the final production. We'll compare the making of the master shot to a musical commercial. This will be a high-budget commercial and requires a larger number of people working on the project, an extended amount of time to do the project, and a wide variety of gear and specialty items to fulfill the job. The size of the cast, of course, affects the total cost, but so too do the salaries of the director, DP, choreographer, performers, and those responsible for the music.

Storyboard

A chorus and two lead singers cross from a "sky" limbo area at the left to a wide "suburban front porch" set on the right. The singers are singing as they walk. The dancers are dancing in front of them and will arrange themselves on the steps of the porch.

Cast

One male singer
One lead male dancer
One lead female dancer
Six female chorus dancers
Six male chorus dancers.

Schedule

This high-budget musical shoot requires either a location or a set. If we used a location, we would have to assume extensive prepping. We very well might need to bring in all the necessary power lines, water, heat, and refrigeration. We'd need to consider the vehicle requirements for a small army of talent and crew. Whatever location we chose would need to be prepared for the onslaught of our production. We'd need to become involved in construction of either a set piece, crew platforms, or access routes. Since the particular nature of problems that are a part of location production are outside the scope of this book and won't add anything to understanding the unique aspects of a high-budget production, we'll assume that the production is housed in a studio.

The studio has to be large enough to house a cast of 2 lead dancers, 12 chorus dancers, and a lead "star" singer. It will need to have space for those who work with the cast such as makeup, hair stylists, and wardrobe, as well as our crew.

It need not be soundproof since the work will be done to a played back track. That may bring down the cost of the studio rental. Studios such as this exist in New York, Los Angeles, Chicago, Miami, Houston, Dallas, Nashville, and many other cities across the United States and Canada. Each stage has its own peculiarities, which can be a challenge or a joy, and the specifics of the boards as well as the demands of time and availability help to determine the choice of studio.

Often a television studio can be rented for a film production. Sometimes working in a television studio brings work to a crashing halt for a short portion of the day when the studio reverts back to being used for local programming. This would probably not be the choice for a high-budget production in which the interruption of a shooting schedule can mean the loss of key talent or crew. For the most part the technology is similar in all the studios in the United States, although many studios are still using older equipment, which may hinder a production. Similar studios and arrangements exist in many countries around the world, although the method of working in many countries is not similar to ours.

A number of years ago I worked in Cairo, Egypt, and found that the studio procedure for trimming lights was that a stage hand simply hammered wooden barn doors onto an overhead walkway that was used to hold the lights. There were no plugs for instruments. Instead, bare wire was plugged into a grid, and one avoided the electric arcing that resulted from such crude connections. Some countries prefer using boxes to raise and lower the camera, rather than work with a moveable tripod or dolly. This, however, will not be our problem in this imaginary production.

A major element in some studios is a cyclorama, or "cyc." A cyc blends the walls and floor, usually in a corner of the studio, into a seamless area. It gives the illusion of infinity. Some cycs are small and some are huge. Sometimes the cyc is painted and must be restored at the end of a shoot. Sometimes it's simply painted with light. Our cast of 12 chorus and 3 principals requires a large cyc.

Today, most musical productions would probably consist of a series of fast shots strung together. In our example we'll want to create a longer shot that offers a few more possibilities for our study. We'll intercut lots of cutaways later. Let's assume that we'll have a fantasy trip in which the cast dances from an area with a cyc, which we'll call shot 1, to a stylized front porch in a suburban community, which we'll call shot 2, although it will be shot in one continuous take. That means that:

- The cyc will have to be prepared—painted and lit for our background.
- The floor on which they walk will need to be prepared.
- A set, consisting of a front yard with grass and picket fence, and a wide front porch and building facade large enough to accommodate our large cast will need to be put in place.

In order to work out the logistics of the schedule, it may be best to start at the end and work forward. We can assume the time required is as follows.

1 day	Tear down the set, restore the floor, and return the props used in the shoot.
3 days	Shoot the commercial. One day will be used for a master shot and two days for inserts.
2 days	Load in the set (1 day), and put it up (1 day). This might be done in 1, but it's safer to allow 2.
1 day	Touch up and light the set.
7 days	Total

A typical schedule might start with construction of the set. Simultaneously other elements of the production, for example, casting, crew decisions, and rentals, are beginning to be put together. Once the plans are approved, and they must be approved by the client, the advertising agency, and the production company, construction can begin. Let's assume that it will take 5 days to build and paint the set.

Given panic situations and high budgets, 24 hour-a-day projects can be mounted. However, one of the hallmarks of high end commercials is that they build in appropriate times, deadlines, and fees. They wish to avoid the higher cost of a 24-hour project, but more important, they wish to avoid the inevitable rushed and often mediocre or unsatisfactory decisions that such haste dictates. In this example the time frames are intended to indicate what would be expected under normal circumstances. In order to get the approval, a designer probably needs time to:

1 day	Look at the boards.
1 or 2 days	Come up with a proposal for the set. This includes not only a sketch, but also a bid, which means that the designer has to create the design and then research the elements.
1 or 2 days (at least)	Get approvals from the agency and client.
2 days	Draw up the plans and then submit the project to a few shops to get bids on the job.
5 or 6 working days	Total time for the designer, prior to having the set in the shop.

The relevant matter here is that it will take a minimum of 1 week to get the plans into the shop, another week to get the set onto the studio floor, and 2 more days before shooting can begin. If everything runs smoothly, and it seldom does, we need a minimum of 12 working days to get the shoot ready. Let us assume an additional 3 days for various changes, and we find that at least 3 weeks are needed for the set before we can begin to shoot. During that time we'll be creating the sound track, casting, getting costumes, and doing many additional tasks. Each of those tasks will require its own position on a flowchart. It will take at least a week to cast the dancers. Before we can cast the dancers, we'll need to hire a choreographer, who can't begin to work until he or she has heard the music. The choreographer can't hear the music until it's recorded, which, of course, means that the music has to be approved by client and agency first. Presumably, in a production of this kind, the track would have been accepted very early on in the process. It may be that someone other than our "star" did the vocal, in which case we would redo the sound track, but the remake would adhere to what the client initially bought. Let's assume the track exists. We find our choreographer, and the casting takes no more than a week to accomplish. There may have to be auditions, but the choreographer probably already knows which dancers are appropriate to appear in the commercial and needs to find only one or two additional dancers. A week before the first rehearsal, the dancers would need to be fitted for costumes.

One day, perhaps even half a day, is all that's necessary for the dancers to learn what they need to know for a simple project like this. A rehearsal hall is required with a tape of the track and playback unit for the rehearsal. Ideally the choreography is being worked on at the same time that the set is being placed into the studio. The closer to the shoot date that the dancers and the lead singer work, the more likely they are to remember what they learned in rehearsals.

Throughout all of the preceding, the director visits the set, even while in construction, to monitor the progress and make sure that there will be no surprises and that the set is as he or she imagined. In fact, the hard reality of the set is often different from the one imagined in plan. There may be changes that need to be made, and it's easier to make them while the set is still in the process of construction. The director will also be working with the costumers and with the casting of the dancers, which will probably require some auditioning. Once in rehearsal, the director will want to see how the actual dance is performed. The client and the agency may also wish to be present at the rehearsal and will arrange a time to arrive with the choreographer and director.

Let us then examine the actual shooting day schedule. I have allocated 3 days for the shoot. No doubt many high-budget companies would require five or more.

9:00–11:00	Set up shot.
	The cast and crew walk through the master shot in rehearsal clothes. Instead of using a simple dolly, the chances are that a Technocrane will be used. The Technocrane allows moves that are impossible with a simple jib arm. The crane's arm telescopes and allows the remote controlled camera to move fluidly and be easily placed wherever the director desires. Even so, spots will be marked on the boom arm and floor for each move along the way. A video tap may be made of the walk-through to check positions and lights. Audio will test for playback.
11:00–12:00	Get cast into costume and makeup.
	Fix lights.
12:00–1:00	Shoot first takes of master shot of dance.
1:00–200	Lunch.
2:00–5:00	Shoot second set of master shots of dance.
	Shoot insert shots with dancers if possible.
5:00–6:00	Wrap: cast leaves.

There would probably be a second and third day of shooting to get insert and product shots. We'd want to shoot our lead singer in a variety of shots . . . close up, waist shot, etc. We'd also want cutaways of dancers' feet and hands, their faces, shot one at a time, and a pan shot as they danced. We might need a fourth and fifth day. Whatever the case, if rentals need to be extended, or if the production went into overtime, charges would be incurred. Tearing down the set, restoring the studio, and cleaning up would be planned for a straight time day. The budget would include at least one postshoot day as a line item. It also includes provision for postproduction administrative work, including time to complete accounting for the project. This includes arranging for payments, billings, and a comparison of actual costs with budgeted costs.

Let's go back to day one and see what all the departments are doing during the shoot.

Setting

While the shop was working on the set, following the blueprints and color scheme of the designer, the director, the choreographer, the production company's producer, and perhaps the costume designer and a producer from the agency would probably visit the shop to see how the work was progressing. The costume designer might bring color swatches of costume material to see how they go with the paint that's to be used. If the dancers step onto the set, the choreographer will want to get a feel for the actual set. Can the dancers jump onto the steps or will they have to walk on the steps? Is there any foreshortening in the set, in which foreground objects are constructed on a larger scale than those in the background? How will that look if the dancers get close to the wall?

The studio was rented on a starting date that offered sufficient time to load-in the set, and a load-in and setup crew needs to be at the studio to receive the set. In some cities, the setup crew picks up the set at the shop and hauls it themselves. In other cities, separate crews are needed. A day would probably be dedicated to construction and touch up after the set was moved from the shop, and another day to hang and prelight the set.

The DP will be busy in the preproduction stage getting the crew and the hardware needed for the shoot. That crew will probably consist of:

Camera operator: Handles the pans and tilts. Frames the shots as indicated by the DP.

First assistant camera: Handles focus and sometimes operates the zoom. The assistant is also responsible for checking the gate on the shutter after each shot. Since the shot is a trucking shot in our example, the first assistant camera person may need to change focus as we truck across the room.

Second assistant camera: Keeps the camera reports and brings and removes magazines. They may also be responsible for tracking the zoom.

Loader: Loads and unloads the magazines and is responsible for slates.

Technocrane operators: Runs the crane and camera on which the camera is mounted. Marks the focus, zoom, boom arm, and the floor. In this case a large crane would be in order and that would require at least a two person crew. One person would drive the crane and handle the remote settings of lens and focus. The other operator would mark and handle the boom arm.

Chief lighting technician (gaffer): Assigns instruments to the switchboard and along with his crew, is responsible for the hanging, focusing, trimming, and dressing of the lighting instruments. Confers with the DP regarding the number of electricians needed to assist with the lighting and which ones are preferred.

Key grip: Confers with the DP regarding the number of grips needed.

Particularly on a union shoot, grips do not perform electrician duties nor do electricians perform grip duties. There are severe penalties for those who do. A nice way to remember who does what is:

Electricians place lights.
Grips place shadows.

Audio

In this production the singer is lip-syncing to a track that would have been made prior to the shoot. Audio would supply playback of the prerecorded material to the floor. The singer sings out loud along with the track, so that his or her lips and breathing match the natural look of someone singing. Live sound recording during the filming would not be a part of this shoot. However, if we assume that there will be some time in which sync sound is a part of the production, then a full audio package would be in order. That might consist of a mic or mics, a recorder, along with all the attendant cables, cable connections, headsets, and related gear.

Set and Props

A prop master and assistant or assistants are responsible for acquiring the props needed for the shoot, and then maintaining and making them available as needed. After the shoot they would require time to return all the props.

Makeup

Five or six makeup artists are needed. There are six female dancers, six male dancers, and a lead singer. It takes more time to make up a woman than a man. If it takes 30 minutes to make up a woman and 15 minutes for a man, then we can assume that five makeup artists (and possibly six) are needed to get the talent out of makeup in one and one half hours. Here's how that breaks down.

Three of the makeup artists make up the female dancers. It will take at least an hour to do six. The fourth makeup person works on the men and might get through with four in an hour. The last hour would be used to make up the remaining men. The fifth makeup artist would work on the two lead dancers and the lead singer. The lead singer may have contracted to have his or her personal makeup artist on them. In this case, there would be six makeup artists. During the filming, the makeup artists will stay near the set and touch up the talent as needed. Dancers will surely need it. At the end of the shoot day, the makeup department will provide oil, cream, or a makeup remover to help remove the makeup.

Costumes

There will be a head of wardrobe and assistants. How many are needed depends on the costumes involved. It's likely that the celebrity lead singer has his or her own wardrobe person. This is either someone who is supplied by the production company or, more likely, someone who is part of the celebrity's staff. The lead dancers might require the same individual attention. The chorus dancers might have two assistants for the women and one for the men.

Prior to the shoot, the cast meets with the head of costumes to be fitted. Even if the costumes were to be bought, there would still be a time set aside to make sure that the costumes fit properly. This might take place at a dance rehearsal studio. If it did, sufficient time would have to be allowed to make any necessary adjustments.

Once the dancers meet at the studio, they are assigned dressing rooms. Costumes are either in the dancer's dressing room or in a costume room. The costume department keeps track of who gets what costume and then makes sure that the costumes look fresh throughout the shoot. They might even elect to have a second set of costumes so that the dancers can change out of anything that began to look too haggard as the day went on. The wardrobe personnel have access to cleaning and pressing tools and are responsible for keeping the costumes looking good throughout the shoot. At the end of the shoot, they return the rental costumes.

The next days are spent shooting insert and product shots, which would probably have been a part of the storyboard. Each day's shoot is arranged to call only those dancers or the singer required for particular shots.

At the end of each day's shoot, footage is sent to a lab for processing. From there it goes to a transfer house where a digital print of the material is made and forwarded to an editing house. Dailies would be viewed each day.

The day after the shoot is finished, the set is hauled to a dump or stored, and the various rental pieces would be returned on a straight-time day.

6 Postproduction: Editing

Editing is the process by which the elements of the commercial are put together to form the completed spot. Shots with and without sound are strung together via cuts or special effects such as dissolves or any one of a number of different wipes. Graphic elements and animation are added as are various sound tracks. Editing puts together all the elements of the commercial, including effects, until the final commercial is completed.

Throughout this chapter "the editor" stands for the actual editor as well as whoever is working with or supervising the editor's work.

In theory, the editor follows the storyboards and puts the shots in consecutive order until the spot or spots are made. It *does* work that way sometimes. Most of the time, however, choices need to be made. When there are a number of "takes" for each shot, there are subtle nuances and sometimes not-so-subtle nuances among the takes. While the shoot was in progress, opportunities presented themselves so that the director shot additional material or slightly different material than was indicated by the boards. At the edit session there are more shots than the board shows. A choice has to be made about what to use and about where a particular edit should happen. The timing—when to make the edit, what kind of edit, and the montage, which scene in what order—affects the total impression.

In practice it works like this. The editor selects the actual shot, and that's as it has to be since the board can't really show action and the shots are seldom exactly as drawn on the boards. The editor determines the timing of the shots, which is sometimes mandated by the audio track. Sometimes the editor sets the way the viewer is taken from shot to shot. Will it be a cut, a dissolve, or a wipe? If it's a dissolve, how long will the dissolve last? Where does it start and end? If it's a wipe, which wipe? Where will it come from? Right to left, or top to bottom, or some other way? How are the colors handled? The editor must make a number of artistic decisions that affect the look and feel of the commercial. That's the real business of the editor.

How are the client, the agency, and the production company involved in the editing process?

The Client: For a low-budget commercial, the editing is probably done by the company hired to produce the project, and the input from the client will be very limited. For expensive commercials the involvement of the client is often direct and on-going.

The Agency: At all levels, the advertising agency strives to bring together a harmonious team to complete the commercial. The agency's involvement includes either finding the edit facility, in those cases where the production company isn't completing the project, or working with and supervising whatever editing or finishing companies are involved. This includes companies that specialize in graphics, animation, and audio.

The Editor: In today's market, editors are unlikely to be proficient in all the available systems but are usually employed at an edit facility or are freelancers who work at any one of a number of similar facilities. They probably work with a favorite system with which they are most familiar. When editors need experts in audio, graphics, and at least some animation, they either outsource the work or have personnel and facilities on-premises.

At the lower end of the production and postproduction scale, the editor or the producer/director/editor probably knows one or two editing programs and is most comfortable with one. They also need to know one or two graphic programs, a music program, and an audio mixing program.

Some freelance editors know a variety of editing systems and are able to work on whatever system is available. The work module that is becoming ever more popular is one in which freelance editors are hired to work on a project, either using an editing system on the agency's premises or at a rental suite. Usually the work is done on an Avid system, but there are other systems, both high and low end, that the freelancer must be able to use.

Timeline

An understanding of how editing evolved may help in understanding today's postproduction methods. Let's start with television before there was video postproduction. Of course, even then there really was video editing. As the program aired, the director faded up camera number 1. That was a dissolve. Sooner or later the director then said: "Take 2." That "take" in television parlance is "edit to" or "cut to" in film. Ultimately, some of today's choices are based on decisions and customs that may have made sense at one time and now are simply accepted. A dissolve, for example, can mean "meanwhile," or "at the same time." A fade to black means "it's over." Why not a fade to blue?

When television began to be used as a medium to deliver commercial messages, the production techniques were exactly the same as they were for the programs. In fact the director of the program simply ended on one of the cameras and moved the other camera to the "commercial area" for the commercial break. The director "took" that camera, "cued" the talent appearing in the commercial to begin, and then shot the commercial. The set for the commercial would probably have been a commercial display of the sponsor's product. The talent stood behind a table with a large art-card, or next to a refrigerator, or a giant jar, or can of Reddi-whip, Fox's U-Bet syrup, Texaco oil, etc. At the end of the commercial, the director faded to black, came up on the other camera in the studio, and cued the talent at that end of the studio to begin.

After a while, clients and advertising agencies wanted more control over the look of the commercial and so hired special commercial directors. This director would work with the agency and rehearse the talent at a rehearsal studio prior to shooting the commercial. Costumes, special props, and music cues were often part of the commercial. When the program was on the air, the director of the program slid out of the chair and the commercial director slid in. The commercial director directed the commercial—live, then faded to black. The commercial director then slid back out of the chair as the program's director slid in to continue the program.

Television commercial production continued to be a "live" event for many years. In order to get a program seen from coast to coast, kinescope films were made. Kinescope films, usually referred to simply as "kinescopes," were single system films shot directly from a monitor while a program aired. They were then "bicycled" around the country. They made very little difference to commercial production because most, if not all, commercials were still shot live as part of the program.

In 1957 video tape became a reality, and videotape editing grew out of the tradition that most International Brotherhood of Electrical Workers (IBEW) engineers then knew: audio and audio editing. Video tape was physically cut, spliced, and handled in much the same way as audio tape. There were, however, significant differences between video and audio tape. Most audio tape was, and remains, $\frac{1}{4}$ inch wide. (Although for a while, prior to the advent of computer manipulated audio, 2-inch multiple-track audio decks were very much in use.) In the late 50s, through all of the 60s, and part of the 70s, video tape was 2 inches wide. It needed to be that wide because it had to carry more information than simple two track audio tape. Then, as now, video tape made use of multiple tracks on the same piece of stock with information stacked at the same location on the stock. At that time, any one frame of the 2-inch stock had video, audio, control, and cue tracks lined up vertically to the tape. This was 2-inch quad recording. It was called that because the record heads were configured as the four points of a cross that was spinning as the 2-inch-wide tape was pulled across the tape heads. The concept of vertical alignment mirrors the alignment used with audio tape.

Synchronizing audio and video was difficult. It was engineered so that the audio was off set. It was synchronized to the video 7.5 inches, or a half-second away from the video tracks. That's because, as is the case in film projection, the head that read video and the head that read audio couldn't be at the same physical location on the tape deck. It made editing difficult: you had to find an edit spot with a half second of silence or nonsync sound.

By the early 1960s, a number of systems were developed that took advantage of video's control and cue tracks. The control track is a constant pulse that marks each complete television frame and is recorded onto a separate portion of the video tape. Its function is to keep the tape playing at a constant speed. In order to make a physical cut, which was the first kind of television editing, it was essential to cut between control track beats. The beats, or pulses, could be seen with a microscope if flux had been put on the tape. Flux is a liquid that when applied to the tape allowed the editor to see the pulses.

Here's the way editing worked in that very primitive time of actually physically editing video tape. The program was played and the editor stood by the stop button. When the desired spot was located, the director or producer would yell out: "Edit!" The editor pressed the stop button and then marked the spot with a Pentel or Magic Marker placing the number 1 at the tape's tension bar. Then the editor took the tape back at least 8 seconds, started it, let it get up to speed, and 8 seconds later, as the mark went by the tension bar, the editor would clap. If the clap was too early (or too late) a new mark would be made at the tension bar and labeled number 2. Again the tape was played. Again there would be a clap, and adjustments would continue until the director/producer felt that the right edit spot had been found.

Once the edit spot was located, the editor turned the tape emulsion side up and put some flux on the marked spot. Looking through a microscope, they could see the control track pulses that the flux revealed. They found the pulse closest to the marked spot and made sure that they were not cutting on a pulse, which would disturb sync. They then sliced the tape on a massive edit block which could hold the 2-inch-wide tape. Finally, they connected that outpoint to the inpoint of some other piece of tape that had been handled in the same way.

To find particular scenes, the tape counter was zeroed at the beginning of the tape, at the start of bars and tone. The editor's very inaccurate notes made from the very inaccurate tape counter were used to approximate the location of the next scene. Actually, this is still a good way to work on analog machines if there is no time code. Obviously, it's still inaccurate, but now as then, it's better than nothing.

The first electronic tape editor allowed edits to be performed without physically cutting the tape. Essentially, a new tape was made with just the selected takes from the master reel recorded in exactly the order it was to be aired. The new tape on which material was to be recorded had to be prepared by having a sync signal, usually black video, recorded first. It permitted the editor to "insert" material on the tape without disturbing the control track. The editor recorded material in the insert mode from a playback deck up to and a few seconds beyond the point to be edited. Once the edit point had been located, the editor inserted a pulse or tone onto the cue track. That triggered the record deck to start recording in the insert mode. Then the editor located the inpoint on the playback deck. Both the record deck and the playback deck were then backed up 10 seconds, started simultaneously, and 10 seconds later, when the record machine "heard" the tone, it started recording again. Thus the first edit of the program was made. The rest of the edits were made in the same way.

As time went by a few inventions helped these first electronic tape editors. The first really important development was Editec, a device that allowed the tape to be advanced or retarded from the tone by up to 15 frames, which meant a half second in either direction. This made syncing up the record and playback decks easier.

Another major development was the development of helically scanned tape. In this format, the heads contact the moving tape on an angle rather than vertically. This allows the same amount of information to be stored on narrower tape. In fact, rather than using

2-inch tape, 1-inch tape could be used. One-inch tape was easier and cheaper to manufacture. It was less subject to tape shredding and drop-outs and required smaller, lighter recording and playback machines. Those machines were cheaper to manufacture. One-inch tape soon became the industry standard.

By 1972, the Society of Motion Picture and Television Engineers (SMPTE) adopted a system incorporating earlier editing systems, notably the Electronic Engineering Company of California (EECO) system, which itself had been adapted from a military application. SMPTE time code became the standard of the industry and was an enormously important advance in editing. The code, a series of pulses, was placed onto the cue track area. It broke time up into 24 hours, 60 minutes per hour, 60 seconds per minute, and 30 frames per second. It meant that each 30th of a second on a video tape had a unique address, which coincided with the "holes" (or pulses) in the control track. Furthermore, a way was devised to make the code available as a readout.

At that point, the exact place at which you wished to make an edit could be found and indicated with the time code number. The editing device read the spot on the encoded SMPTE track represented by that number and made the edit at the correct spot, and it was able to do this over and over again. That made it possible to lay down video, then go back to the same place and lay down audio. You could make what was then called an "L" cut and delay the video or the audio. SMPTE gave editors more control over what could be done.

However, scenes had to be edited together in a linear fashion: first scene one, followed by scene two, followed by scenes three and four. If you wanted to remove scene two, it was necessary to redo everything that came after it. That was a major effort as you got deeper into an edit session. You didn't want to change edit number 6 if there were 112 edits that would need to be redone.

In those days the editing process started by viewing and logging all the shots/takes, and that practice continues today. With the advent of the $\frac{3}{4}$-inch U-Matic system, offline editing became a reality. Now, after logging the takes and having a sense of how the commercial was to go together, an offline editing session would be arranged. In an offline editing session, the selected takes are strung together, still in a linear fashion, on VHS or $\frac{3}{4}$-inch tape, which was cheaper to use than the standard 2-inch, and later 1-inch, tape. Unlike film, you couldn't take scenes out from the middle and then replace them. You couldn't add scenes anywhere but at the end of the last edit. Later digital video changed that.

The offline session might not allow all the effects of the commercial to be seen, but one could get a good idea of what was to happen. Once that rough cut was approved, an edit decision list (EDL) was printed so that the original material could be taken to an online session where the spot was conformed to the EDL. At the conformation session, all the effects that were to be part of the commercial were added. This included dissolves, wipes, type, etc. It also included zooms, realigns, and a host of possible audio sweetens.

The advent of digital video, which became the standard in the late 1990s, changed the way editors worked. With digital video, the signal originates in a digital format or is changed from an analog format to a digital one. Essentially, digital video handles the television signal somewhat like the digital audio of popular musical CDs. It's like the change from $\frac{1}{4}$ inch tape or cassette to a CD. The ramifications are profound. Using digital video means that almost instantaneous random access to material is possible. Simply input the right SMPTE code numbers into the computer, and start and end sessions by the numbers. Best of all, the edit process no longer needs to be strictly linear. Digital technology affords editors and director-producers the opportunity to manipulate the material. The picture can be resized, recolored, repositioned, or replaced, to name but a few of the video options. Audio can be removed, sweetened, and then be replaced with frame accuracy.

Digital technology dramatically shortened the time and reduced the hardware needed for achieving many of the video effects created through the special effects generator. It allows sound to be manipulated in much the same manner. The lower cost of digital cameras and digital editing equipment has made access to the technology more widespread and encouraged experimentation, which is leading to new ways of working with the medium.

These advances have made the job of editing easier. However, now, as then, the director-producer has to know exactly where to begin the first scene—both audio and video—and where to end it. He or she must be able to locate both the video and audio "ins" and "outs" for the next scene or edit until the production is completed.

Current Practices

The process of editing remains the same no matter what budget is in operation. Some productions go to an online session immediately. Commercial tagging sessions in which commercials are prepared for regional markets are typical of this kind of production. Tags and slates, too, can be downloaded from any one of a number of graphic programs or database programs and dragged and dropped onto a commercial base for use in multiple markets.

The Avid system, and there are many variations, currently offers the most popular programs. The Avid family includes systems dedicated to working with specific kinds of media. The Avid Media Composer, for example, is designed as the standard in digital nonlinear editing systems. The Avid Film Composer is used for film-based projects. Other specialty programs are designed for news operations as well as media management and archiving.

Adobe Premiere, which works on both a PC and a Mac platform, and Final Cut Pro, which only works on a Mac platform, are popular at the lower end of the editing scale. These two low-cost, easy-to-use editing systems have opened the door to students, directors, and producers who, in growing numbers, are editing their own projects.

Somewhere out there in the land of commercial-making, there is sure to be someone who is still using a movieola to cut spots. Somewhere they are editing shoots that were produced on a sound stage with three video cameras. For the most part, however, that isn't the way it's done. For the most part, the commercials at the lower end of the scale are shot using digital video and are then digitally edited. They are then transferred to digital tape and sent to stations for airing. At the upper ends of the postproduction scale, most mate-rial is transferred from film rather than from a video or digital original. The film is then transferred to a digital media, digitally edited, and released using the same procedure as commercials produced at the lower end of the scale.

Until now we have been looking at projects from the point of view of the client, the agency, and the producer. We've chosen a low-, medium-, and high-cost production as the criteria for separation. A more realistic approach for editing would be to examine the process based on the material to be edited. No matter the level of production, the com-mercial was shot on either film or tape. The tape might have been shot in an analog video format, but was more likely in a digital format. Shooting directly to a hard or floppy drive is still unusual but may well be the wave of the future.

If the commercial is edited by the producing company, the commercial was probably produced on a low budget and shot on tape, probably digitally. Higher budget productions are usually shot on film and edited by a specialty editing company rather than the pro-ducing company.

Editing Work Styles

It's probably obvious, but important to state, that editors work in different ways, even when they work with the same program. That's because editors bring to their work the same kind of personalization that one brings to setting up one's own word processing program. Per-sonally, I like dates that remain the same once I've entered them. Some people like the new date to override an original date. I like to use keystrokes. Some people like to use the mouse. Most editing programs offer editors a number of different ways to accomplish tasks. The choices they make are personal, based on their work styles and idiosyncrasies. Even when I know that I have a better way of accomplishing a task, I have found that it's best to let the editor complete tasks in whatever way is most comfortable to him or her. Changing the work habits of the editor usually doesn't work very well and can be very frustrating to everyone involved.

Low-Budget Commercials

For the low-budget commercial, it is likely that the producer-director will also be the editor. The timeline for completing the editing stage of the commercial begins as the editor loads the production material onto the hard drive. No matter what medium was used, from film to analog tape, the material is digitized and then edited digitally. It's also likely that the commercial was shot in a digital format, which would afford a simple FireWire transfer. The editor probably logged the material as it was being transferred. Since the material was shot to a specific script and storyboard, perhaps a storyboard that existed simply in the mind of the producer/director/editor, choosing the select takes is a fairly straightforward task. The question the editor is answering even as they are logging the material is: "Which shot that I shot is best to fit this sequence that I wrote?" Once the choices are made, the EDL is compiled, and the editor goes to work putting the project together. If it's typical of the kind of projects that fall into this category, the commercial has:

1. A 5-second opening that could be categorized as: "Attention Shoppers"
2. 20 seconds of pitch that defines whatever is being sold
3. A 5-second tag to tell the viewers where they can buy the product or service and explains that it's best to "act now!"

The editor will do his or her best to complete the commercial so that it's as close as possible to the final "air" version. This is because most of the clients at this end of the production scale are not knowledgeable about the steps necessary to complete a commercial. Given too many options, they begin to "direct," and the edit session can become an interminable, and unpaid for, nightmare. As the cost of commercial production goes up, clients often become increasingly more knowledgeable and more involved with the decision making process. At the most expensive levels, approvals are needed at all of the "key steps" along the way. Key steps change with the type of commercial so different types of commercials—animation, live action, live action/children, fashion, food, etc.—will have different key steps. Then too, as the cost of the commercial goes up, the cost basis goes up. The editing bid is based on a different criterion than it is for a client using television for the first time.

To edit the commercials at the lower end of the production scale, the editor is most likely to use either Final Cut Pro, Adobe Premiere, or a low-end Avid system. Adobe Photoshop might be used to include and manipulate still images, and Illustrator or Quark Express would be used to compose them. Should there be a need for simple animation, Adobe's AfterEffects, Apple's Shake, or a similar program might be used. Finally, a music bed could be developed using Adobe's Audition, or the Macs sound programs, Soundtrack (Final Cut Pro, version 4) or Garage Band, or on a PC platform with Sony's Acid (released through Sonic Foundries). All of the sound might be mixed, if it were simple, within the editing program. Otherwise, Cool Edit by Adobe or Pro Tools by Avid might be used to make a mix that could then be imported into the editing program and commercial. All of these editing tools are readily available. New programs are introduced almost daily and many are, relatively speaking, inexpensive.

Once the commercial is edited together, the client is called in to approve the spots and indicate whatever changes they believe are necessary. The changes are made, and the spots are then duplicated and shipped to either stations or a dubbing house for multiple copies.

Middle and High End Commercials

By the time a client reaches a level of spending in which commercials cost $25,000, they tend to become very involved with the postproduction process. The involvement may start with the choice of postproduction companies that are to be used, but that choice is more likely to be made by an advertising agency. At this level of production and postproduction, there is usually someone from the client side who understands the total production process and wishes to be involved in the key decisions about the commercials. Some commercials go directly from production to a finishing suite where the commercial is readied to be dubbed or aired. This is true in cases where great haste is warranted or there is a standard commercial that is simply being edited with new tags, changed dates, revised logo, or some other similar small change.

Most of the time, however, the first step is to create a rough cut of the commercial. The rough cut contains all the elements of the commercial, but many of the "finishes" such as type or music are absent or merely indicated. It should also be noted that at many larger agencies the client doesn't enter the postproduction process until the rough cut has been assembled.

In fact, there really is no one standard procedure for the editing process. Each commercial, each client, and each advertising agency sets its own priorities and timeline. Different agencies, clients, and postproduction facilities advocate procedures that may be similar but not identical. For example, at some high end commercial production facilities, negative film is cut, retransferred, and then color corrected. Other high end editing companies simply transfer original footage to a high-definition medium and never again work on the project in a film format.

The procedure and process used at high end editorial companies represents exceptional attention to detail and provides archival results. To the client and to the agency, much of the technical aspects of the editing process take place in the background. They are apt to work on the creation of the rough cut and on the audio and graphic steps along the way to completion but do not get very involved in the various transfer processes. Production companies, on the other hand, may become very involved with all the steps in the process.

For the editorial company it begins with a bid for the job. The company will use an editorial estimate that has been customized to meet the needs of their specific services and equipment. The chances are that it was derived from a form that closely follows the one from the Association of Independent Creative Editors (AICE). A copy of the AICE form is included in Chapter 10, Useful Forms and Reference Material.

Once the client agrees to completing a commercial or series of commercials, contracts are signed and delivered. Essentially, the process is much the same as the contracts between clients and agencies, and agencies and production companies.

Actually there are two contracts.

1. The contract is the estimate, now signed by agency/client and returned to the postproduction house.
2. The purchase order generated by the agency/client signed by the postproduction house and returned to the agency/client.

Typical concerns addressed by the estimate are:

1. Identifiers: the parties involved in the contract
2. The specifications: names of the spots—code numbers; number of spots to be created (two 60 seconds and two 30 seconds); format 35 mm, etc.; format of delivered product
3. To be offlined (rough cut) *from* when *to* when with *final approval* expected when?
4. To be onlined (finishing) *from* when *to* when with *final edited master* expected when?
5. Elements to be furnished by agency/client
6. Terms of payment
7. Delivery to whom and how

Apart from these concerns, there are a number of other legal matters that would probably be defined in the contract concerning changes and variations, ownership, insurance, and a variety of other issues that are boiler plate and derived through legal counsel. Often the process begins before the contracts are signed, particularly where a long-standing relationship has been established.

A typical editing job starts when the production "takes," usually shot on film, are transferred to a video format, usually either $\frac{3}{4}$ inch or BetaSP (also known as video dailies), and then loaded onto an Avid hard drive for editing. Sometimes VHS or other dubs of the material with time code are made available for viewing so that a select list can be formulated without being at the loading session. A select list is a decision list with all the takes that should be considered. Sometimes a select reel is made.

At some editing facilities, usually at the upper end of the postproduction scale, the editor is left alone to make choices, comes up with the select list, and may even create an initial rough cut prior to the first meeting with the agency or agency and client. There are some situations in which the client may wish to be involved in the choices made for the select list. However, viewing all the takes and logging them can be a very tedious process. Most of the time the client is pleased to view the dubs of the original material to get a general idea of how things look but is willing to let the creative director of the agency and/or the director of the production or the editor bring together the material that will be used in the commercial, based, of course, on the boards.

There may very well come to be three versions of the boards: the agency's, the client's, and the director's, and possibly a few alternates of any of them. Those versions come from different, yet relevant, concerns; for example, the client may think that the commercial ought to be a little more serious in nature, while the agency is convinced that it should be funnier. The director, on the other hand, may be after something entirely different, which is perceived as being irrelevant by both the client and the agency.

Then, too, the nature of the commercial may mitigate against any preconceived idea of how to precede. A commercial in which there are children ad-libbing, for instance, might see the client involved in choosing what child is best suited for the spots. For the most part, it is either the editor and/or the agency's creative director who creates the select list.

At some postproduction houses, choosing the selects is part of expected editorial service. In fact, the company's reputation may be founded, at least in part, on it's ability to do that well.

Once the selects are chosen, the editing begins.

Editing Process

1. The original 35-mm material is processed, and a "one-light" video daily is made. A one-light print daily is a transfer in which the negative simply passes by a single light source of one predetermined intensity, yielding a transfer that is not corrected for bracketing or any peculiarities of exposure. Later a color corrected transfer will be struck in which the best possible exposure is made for each frame of the commercial. This too may be manipulated both as film and in a digitized format, but more of that later.

2. The one-light print is transferred to BetaSP, which is a component high-quality analog video tape format. Component video are used rather than composite video since the color and luminosity information is separate, providing more bandwidth for both, which results in better picture quality. When that one-light BetaSP print is made, various "windows" are added to assist in the editing process. The first window is the time code of the video itself. Additionally, the film edge number or key code is added in the next window. If there is sync-sound, a third window is added. It contains the time code from the production audio, which is usually a DAT recording. When the DAT audio is synced to the one-light Beta print, the audio is denigrated to an analog signal and is married to the one-light print and is thus considered a scratch track. The BetaSP to be used in the edit now contains high-quality video and audio. It also has everything in the right place including the scratch audio track and the time codes, which make the print not airworthy.

    Phoenix Editorial in San Francisco, and perhaps other organizations as well, requests that a duplicate of the DAT audio be made. This is to provide a protection copy for the client. This duplicate DAT, however, is created matching the time code from the video, as opposed to the original DAT time code. This specially time-coded DAT will be used for efficiency's sake at the end of the editorial process. Its numbers now match the video code, although the original code is still visible in the BetaSP windows in case there's a problem with the audio. Now, when batch digitizing only the final selected audio at the end of the editorial process, a separate EDL list for the audio selects isn't needed since the audio time code matches the video selects.

3. Only the BetaSP is digitized with scratch track audio for editing. The dupe DAT is loaded to prepare for the mix after the edit is complete. A pristine digital copy of the audio can then be laid off to the final cut.

A BetaSP version of all the footage and the DAT are then digitized and imported into an Avid system, and the rough edit is done.

Usually a set of commercials will be done at the same time. Four to five is the average number, but there are times when as many as 18 or 20 may be produced. The rough cut editing process for a typical set of four or five commercials may take 7 to 10 days.

Prior to beginning the rough cut and sometimes continuing through the process, graphic and animated elements of the commercial need to be completed if they do not already exist in final form.

4. Once the rough cut is accepted, a negative cut list of the takes that are to appear in the commercial is compiled. This is sent to a negative cutter who creates a "flash to flash" negative. "Flash to flash" refers to the entire "take" including the slate of any scene that is used in the commercial. The outtakes are spliced and retained. The select takes are then sent to a film transfer company where they are critically color corrected and transferred to a digital betacam tape, which is the usual broadcast standard. This film transfer process is sometimes called a data transfer because essentially the film is scanned and can be retained in a variety of digital formats, including video or data tape, and loaded onto a hard drive.

Grass Valley's Datacine "Spirit" is a high end telecine transfer unit. The Rank "Ursa" is another film transfer unit, which is still in use in many parts of the country. The Rank Cinetel was the standard for color correction, but the General Micro System (GMS) DaVinci currently seems to be the most widely used high end color correction unit. These telecine components are capable of creating digital files that allow an extraordinary amount of control in rendering color, hue, contrast, and luminance.

To understand the telecine process, look at simple black and white photography. Black and white photography consists of black, lots of different shades of black, and white, lots of different shades of white, as well as an infinite number of shades of gray. The telecine artist looks at a black and white film frame and commands the telecine to assign total black to anything on the "black" side of the scale and white to anything on the "white" side of the scale. Once the separation is made, and it's an instantaneous process, the telecine artist has the ability to change the amount of black or white in any given area of the screen to yield the amount of gray required.

Essentially, the color process is identical except that all color is broken down to the primary colors of red, blue, and green. Those colors are separated, divided in the same way that the black and white elements were divided, and they can then be manipulated to change the values of the color, hue, contrast, and luminance of any shade of red, blue, or green in the same way as the black and white image was changed. The colorist is vectoring in on a specific wavelength of color and is thereby able to manipulate that one shade's value without affecting the rest of the picture.

5. Some high end editorial companies choose to transfer the output of the enhanced select negatives to a digital betacam format and then load that into a Discreet Logics' Smoke editing system. Smoke is advertised as being "a random access, uncompressed, broadcast quality, nonlinear editing system." The material can be transferred to any format, such as digital betacam, or BetaSP, and then loaded/digitized into the Smoke editing system. The EDL from the approved offline session is also loaded. When a company uses Smoke, it serves as the finishing suite. The Smoke conforms the digital betacam transfer automatically based on the EDL. The audio, however, is still the scratch track from the rough cut, so the digital audio is sent to an audio finishing suite, and once it's mixed and sweetened, it's laid back to the final picture.

It is then sent to a duplicating house or transmitting facility to get the final project to the stations.

7 Post-Plus—Audio/ Graphics/Animation

Almost every commercial made requires special postproduction work in the area of audio, graphics, and animation.

Audio: Working with narration, sync-sound, and/or adding music and perhaps sound effects.

Graphics: Adding titles, the client's name, phone numbers, legal notices, disclaimers, lower-third supers, etc.

Animation: Animated graphics or type, or a totally animated spot.

This chapter is intended as an introduction to these three enormously important areas, in which attention to detail is paramount. It outlines what the client, agency, or production company producer needs to bring to the audio suite or to the graphics or animation company.

Audio

It doesn't matter how much the production costs, audio elements remain the same. How the sound gets produced, inserted, and then integrated into the commercial often helps define the commercial.

Audio in commercials consists of just four elements:

1. Voice-over—an announcer or sound bytes
2. Music—either original music or that acquired from a music library
3. Sound effects—usually from a sound effects library but sometimes created for the spot
4. Sync-sound—dialogue and/or natural sound

Preproduction

Production necessities dictate the order in which the audio track is produced. Most of the time the commercial's bed is either the voice-over announcer or dialogue, but that's not always the case. There is, for example, a history of commercials using well-known popular tunes to make a point. In the 1970s Carly Simon's version of *Anticipation* was used to help sell the slow pouring of ketchup. In the 1990s Nick Drake's music was used in a Volkswagen commercial. Bing Crosby, or a great sound-alike, could be heard singing in 2004 to help boost car sales. Other artists have lent their music to the commercial cause, usually for a great deal of money. In such cases the music bed preexists and is the driving force of the commercial. Whatever the case, the audio starts with the script.

To see how audio is used in commercials, let's assume we have a commercial that uses all four elements: voice-over or narration, music, sound effects, and sync-sound. In our imaginary script we'll assume:

1. An announcer introduces a problem as a voice-over. That's the narration.
   A cat brushes against an open bottle of liquid soap.
2. A sound effect (falling bottle) ends the introduction.
   The soap bottle falls.
3. A couple solves the spilled liquid problem in a dramatized, humorous little sketch.
   A couple decides to use the client's very absorbent and all new towel to clean the mess.
4. A custom-made music bed runs throughout the commercial and finishes with the company's signature sign-off.
5. The commercial ends with a voice-over announce track naming the product and the slogan that goes with it.
   "Our Product: Building on the dreams of tomorrow!"

Voice-over

In our example, the announce track is made first. It might be possible to create the dramatic elements first and then work on the announce track, but I think it's safest to work the other way around. Once the timing is available for the narration track, the producer will know how long the dramatization can last. A number of readings may be required from the announcer, with different timings to allow the dramatization to expand or contract in length. Preparation for this narration recording demands that the copy be set and approved prior to recording the announcer's material. The agency will probably have an announcer in mind for the commercial and will have decided if the voice-over is to be male or female.

Should there be the desire to engage an announcer that is not familiar, announcer tapes that are maintained by the agency are auditioned. Additionally, the announce track producer could listen to tracks over the Internet by logging onto any one of a number of announcer/voice-over agent's sites, where tracks are available. The agency may then decide to conduct live auditions to find the voice-over spokesperson. Once a choice is made, and it may be made with input from the client, the agency, as well as the production company, a recording session is set up. Ordinarily the creative director of the agency or the director of the production runs the recording session.

At the lowest end of the production scale, the announcer may be a friend of the producer, or the producer or client, and the session is run by the producer.

Ideally, the voice-over (VO) session is done in a soundproof environment. That means that it will have a somewhat different voice characteristic than the dialogue, which will be recorded on a live set. The reason for recording the announcer's voice-over track in a soundproof environment is to create a sound track without extraneous sounds. Zero tone is recorded at the start of the recording session so that it can be matched during playback. An audio oscillator built into the audio board emits a tone, the volume for which is set at zero on the volume unit (VU) meter. This is called "zero tone." The recording is then made at that level. Each take is assigned its own take number, with pickups being slated just as clearly. While a soundproof booth is the most appropriate setting for announcer recordings, one often has to make do. There have been times when I have had to record a VO track while standing on the floor of a client's business or office.

Different mics have different recording characteristics, and that affects the quality of the recording. When working in Europe, I found that audio engineers tended to use microphones that emphasized bass response. That's what they liked, so I accepted it. The same recording quality might not be acceptable in America. The end result must ensure that the VO recording and the dialogue recording are compatible; that is, they can be used in the same commercial without calling attention to differences in sound quality.

Once the spot or spots are completed, the material is duped for safekeeping. To be safe, one copy remains with the recording studio. Another copy or series of copies are made and used by the editing facility, who may later send the material to a mixing suite for a final mix prior to the completion of the spot. More about the mixing suite later.

Music

In this imaginary commercial we're constructing, we completed the announce track first. However, there are some commercials in which the first thing to be prepared is the music bed. That's particularly true if the commercial is based on a song. If the commercial has a music track that's supposed to run throughout, the producers will usually wait for a timing of the elements of the spot so that the music can be prepared with consideration of that timing. They may compose the music with natural rises not only in volume but in phrasing and intensity as well. For example, imagine the range of musical dynamics to a commercial in which a dramatic dialogue intro ends, having a low-volume music bed under the dialogue. The dialogue is followed by a small music sting and announce copy with product shots. That is followed by the announcer's tag, which has a signature music phrase that plays the commercial out. The "play out" phrase might be something like the original "shave and a haircut . . . two bits." The 1970s gave us "Plop-plop Fizz-fizz," and more recently we've had Chevrolet's "Like a Rock."

The process for creating music for a commercial would be the same at the lowest end of the production scale as it is at the highest. At the low end it's the producer or friends who might write material for the spot and then record it. Final Cut Pro version 4 has a built-in program for creating music beds. Other programs such as Apple's Garage Band are also available. Essentially these are short loops of various instruments that can be strung together to make a track with accents.

On the upper end of commercial production, specialists in writing music, often famous artists from the pop, jazz, or classical music world, create the music beds for commercials and then arrange to record the material. These sessions are produced in the same studios using the same musicians one would hire to record popular or much of the classical repertoire. Multiple tracks are used to create these tracks, and a working premix may be arranged to get a feel for the final product.

Since the creation of a music track is so specialized, the client usually remains out of the process, while the agency producer and creative director take an active role. Once the recording session is finished, copies are retained to be used in the final mix. Work copies are also struck for the client and for the production company so that there is a general idea of the mood and timing of the music bed.

As an alternative to the process of creating an original music bed, stock libraries may be used. There are some that are available at little or no cost, and many can be found on the Internet. Most of the time the material is not *really* free. It's listed as "Royalty-Free Music," which means you can use the music after having paid a fee. The fee payer then has permission to use the track for an unlimited royalty-free time. These are similar to music libraries, which may or may not offer music royalty-free.

Music Stock Libraries

Music stock libraries, often referred to as production music libraries, license material for use in various media. Once a fee is paid, the music is cleared, and it can be used for air or for other agreed-upon release. Without a license a copyright infringement suit is entirely possible. Judgments in the area of $10,000 and up are usual in major markets.

Music libraries, and for that matter stock footage companies, charge by the amount of material used and the breadth of the expected distribution. For example, background music for a 30-second commercial running in a small local market for a 13-week run will cost less than the same music for a full network 30-second commercial with no time limit.

Music libraries often, although not always, charge a modest "listening fee." The listening fee pays for some of the library's overhead and buys the time of a librarian who knows the music cues and can help find a piece quickly. Music libraries also charge a "licensing fee," which allows the music to be used under carefully stipulated terms. The licensing fee pays the owner of the material for its usage. This licensing fee may also include compensation for the licensing agent as well as composers' fees, artists' fees, arrangements, property searches, etc. It releases the material to the buyer under the stipulated terms, or licensing agreement—13 weeks in a local market, for example. It usually also pays for delivery of the material in a manner suitable for the production, either on 1/4-inch audio tape, tails out, or a DAT cartridge.

Music library cues may be cheaper than original music, but library cues are often familiar to the audience. The chosen library music can easily be the very cue that was recently heard behind some other spot, perhaps a competitor's spot. The use of an inexpensive music library may then detract from the message. It's also very difficult to find a stock music cue that's "just right." After a while, something that's adequate or just acceptable begins to look ever better, and a "just okay" music bed becomes the cue that's used.

Sound Effects

Ideally, anything but the dialogue will be added in postproduction, but in working with a dialogue track, there is a great deal more sound than the dialogue. First there is the "room tone" itself. Each room has it's own sound, it's own tone. Shut your eyes and listen to whatever room you're in for 30 seconds, and you'll hear that tone. Sometimes the room tone is carried over and mixed into the sound of the narrator so that the switch in ambience from the acted dialogue recorded in a room with it's own sound characteristics to narration performed in a soundproofed booth is minimized.

Other sounds from the production may also need to be considered. Was the talent in the kitchen moving pots from place to place? We may then expect to hear the sounds of those pots moving. Are they working at a computer? We may or may not want to hear the clicking sounds made by fingers working on the keyboard. Often, we do want to work with those ambient sounds. They may or may not occur naturally. Most of the time it's better to add them in postproduction. That way the levels can be manipulated to enhance rather than distract from the message. I have directed a number of productions in which couples are dancing in the background, while the dialogue takes place in a foreground shot. It is always strange to walk on stage and see the couples dancing to whatever beat is supposed to be in the music when there is no music playing. Later, "in post," we add the music to which the dancers are dancing, but at a level that allows us to give prominence to the scripted dialogue.

Obviously other sounds are strictly postproduced. The kids hit a baseball through a window, and we see the look of terror on their faces. The breaking of the window is a sound effect. There's a pesky mosquito trailing our heroine. That buzz is a sound effect, as is the sound of the dripping faucet, thunder in the background, and the cell phone ringing on cue. They're all sound effects. Sometimes they're made on the spot by the recording studio, but most often they're bought from a company that specializes in the production of sound effects.

At the lower end of the production scale, stock sound effects from a sound effects library can be used. The cost for the sound effect depends on the effect itself, but there are many that are free. In my experience sound effects always seem easy to find until one actually has to locate the particular sound effect. There are so many ways any given effect can be executed. Frequently, the choices are entirely different from what had originally been discussed. Finding exactly the right effect can be very difficult, particularly if you are on a tight budget. Once the production scale is elevated and more precise effects are needed, specialty houses are contacted to find just-the-right thunder clap, bell ring, or crowd background. In any event, a fee of $85 an hour for a professional search and $50 per sound effect is close to standard in Los Angeles and New York.

In our case we need the sound of a bottle filled with liquid dropping from a counter. We can do that on the set and listen to it, and if we like it, use it. However, it will probably not actually sound like what it is. The studio floor will have the wrong texture and the sound will be muffled, or the bottle won't sound like a bottle, or perhaps it's supposed to break. We might use a special "break away" bottle for the video portion of the shot, but our real bottle won't break the right way and give us the sound we need. To get the exact sound we want, we'll use a "Foley stage," which is a sound stage used to create sound effects. It's named after Jack Foley, who was the head of a group at Universal Pictures; he used a special stage to add sound and sound effects to pictures in the early days of Hollywood. The stage on which he worked was called the Foley stage, and the concept remains with his name on it.

Dialogue

Dialogue is often just as prominent as the other elements of the commercial. Here too, a zero tone is used to set level. The idea is to record just the dialogue. During the production, the audio team strives to get the microphone placed as close to ideal as possible, as close to the actors as the camera will allow. Unless the script calls for the dialogue to be read into an on-camera microphone, some concessions have to be made because the speaker's mouth cannot be in the exact right place for the microphone. However, there is almost always some way to get the sound, even if it has to be added in postproduction. It's important to make certain that recordings made at different times and places can eventually be mixed into a compatible sound bed.

Horror Story 374
I directed a series of commercials over a number of days. It was a location shoot, and I had never worked with the local crew. I didn't pay sufficient attention to the sound quality or the mics that were being used at the various locations. When we came to piece the shots together, there was an enormous difference in the sound quality from scene to scene. It never really sounded right despite a very long mix session.

Post Sound

Sometimes a narration track is added after the commercial is done. The legal department may discover that more disclosure or a new tag of a different length is demanded. A shorter or, for that matter, longer tag may be needed. If that's the case, it's handled in the same way that it would be handled were it to have been recorded prior to production. Knowing exactly how long the narration can be is a luxury (and sometimes a terror) that postproduction narration affords.

There are overdub studios that specialize in recording dialogue that has to be added or changed after the actual production has concluded. Foreign films that are dubbed into English are the principal users of such studios. However, the same techniques and technology are often used to alter audio under any of a number of scenarios. For example, there may have been a problem in the recording that was inadvertently missed at the time of recording, a change in copy may be needed, or perhaps the voice quality of one of the performers needs to be changed. In such a case a scene can be played on a work print loop or video loop without any sound. The audio talent watches the lips of the talent appearing in the loop and then reads and records the copy while trying to match what they are seeing.

The Mix

We know that the audio portion of a commercial is apt to contain these four elements:

1. A voice-over or narration track
   It may be just the client's name at the end of the commercial.
2. A music track
3. A sound effects track
4. A dialogue track

The four tracks are blended together at a "mix" session.

At the lower end of the production scale, the parts are simply added to the audio portion of the commercial using a program such as Final Cut Pro. In this case, the editor places the various parts onto a time line on the audio track, or tracks. For example: "The commercial starts with dialogue. There's a window crash here. Music starts here and immediately is taken down until it crescendos at the end. The narrator track with the store name and hours goes here at the end."

As the production cost goes up, a mix session is usually carried out at a sound mixing facility. Here each element of the mix is tweaked. Was there a little hum during a portion of the dialogue? Perhaps that hum can be removed by taking out a small portion of the high end of the audio spectrum. Perhaps Dad's voice can be made a bit more ominous by adding a little reverb. At this kind of mix, each element is worked on individually and then blended until a final mix of all the elements is agreed upon. Throughout all of this the material has been handled with care and diligence. The best speakers and headphones have been used to hear every nuance that was recorded. Now, at the end of the session it's likely that the material will be listened to one last time through the kind of speaker that an average listener has in his or her home television set. Some additional work may be required to offset the poor quality of sound that is likely to be a part of the home listening experience. Finally, the completed track is sent back to the editing house with time code in place to match the visual portions of the commercial.

Graphics

A graphic artist handles a wide variety of projects from those requiring a knowledge of type and various fonts to work with logos or client-specific art such as the drawing of Colonel Sanders for Kentucky Fried Chicken. Sometimes there is a crossover so that a single frame graphic, type, for example, appears to move on screen. That brings graphics into the area of animation. There will be more about animation later in this chapter. For now, we'll address the basic use of graphics in commercials at both the low and top end of the production scheme.

Let's consider the history of graphics as they are used in television. Apart from offering a sense of the development of the use of graphics in television, it may suggest solutions to modern problems by adopting techniques that were current 35 or 40 years ago.

The first graphics were "show cards," used to open and close programs and to identify the participants. The early studio had two cameras.

- Camera 1 had an art card on an easel. Type on a designed background spelled out the name of the show.
- Camera 2 had an art card on an easel. It, too, was on a designed background but spelled out the name of one of the hosts.

The director started on Camera 1 and then dissolved or cut to Camera 2.

- While Camera 2 was on the air, a stagehand removed the top card from the easel holding Camera 1's card to reveal the second card in the stack—the other host's name.
- When that card was ready to go on the air, the director put that camera on the air and released the second camera to the hosts to start the show.
- Somewhere in the program, a lower-third super with the talent or the guest's name was needed. The director released a camera from the set and sent it over to an easel. Then a black card with white type on the lower part of the card would be dissolved on over the host or guest revealing their name.

The cards were black cardboard, usually 11×14 with white press-on letters. The graphics to be supered were contained in an 8×10 area of the card. This allowed for a "shoot-off" area. It also allowed the material to be placed within the "safe area" portion of the screen. Television screens are mounted in frames that are not uniform in the percentage of area they cut off from the total transmitted picture. Some sets cut off more than others, so a generally accepted area, measured from the center of the screen out, has been adopted as "action safe," and a somewhat smaller area, again going from the center of the screen, has been adopted as a "graphic safe" area. The expectation is that *all* sets will be able to see the material in the "safe" area.

Black art card and press-on letters are still available in many art stores and may still be useful. Press-on type and various other graphic products designed to be transferred came in many sizes and styles and were pressed onto the card letter by letter—a time-consuming task. It was also fraught with terror for the graphic artist, who had to work very carefully to place each letter on a straight line, with appropriate spacing between each letter. A black Pentel to cover mistakes was a handy tool.

Major advances in television consisted of:

- A switcher that could not only "super" but could also "key." One of the first improvements over the simple dissolve was the key. That's almost always the way a person's name is handled when it appears in white letters in the lower third of the picture. Originally, a name was supered, and you could see the person's clothing through the white of the super. With a key, the letters seem to be placed on top of the person's clothing. As the switchers became more sophisticated, the white letters could be colorized with any number of colors.
- A third camera for the director.
- The transfer of the material to slides, which afforded better access to the graphics and didn't require that cameras be taken away from the live action to go to art cards.

- Assorted machines to produce formatted type. The type could be stripped onto a card or a roll of paper. Devices with variable speed controls existed to "roll" or "crawl" hot-pressed white copy on those long specially prepared rolls. Stations used the same technology for programs so that end tags could be set at variable speeds, which usually translated into fast, medium, or slow settings to control the timing for live shows. For those on the lower end of the commercial production scale, graphics still consisted of white letters rubbed onto a black card. When post-production became a reality for commercials, the artwork would be placed under a "graphics camera." Usually the graphics camera was a less expensive or old camera mounted on a converted still camera enlarger base. The camera could be lowered or raised, later zoomed in or out, and the type could be angled on the base board.

- The first really significant change in the handling of simple graphics both for commercials and for general television use was the advent of the computer-generated graphic. While early and limited systems of character generation date back to 1964, the leading company to manufacture and install a significant number of character generators was the Chyron company, which claims to have introduced its first character generator in 1970. The original Chyron system allowed a facility to quickly access a wide variety of fonts and some simple graphics such as an arrow, a circle, and a square. The system integrated directly with the switcher and was soon "the way to go." Chyron made it easy and fast to include the legal requirements on a spot. It was also easier to make spots that included copy such as "Sale Ends Midnight" and to add and delete store names. It also came with special fonts that could be used with buzz phrases like "You'll love it!" "Refreshing!" and "New!" Soon after its introduction, various fixes, upgraded programs, and even new switchers came on the market that allowed the type and material shot from a "graphics camera" to be manipulated. The graphics could zoom in or out; be angled on an x, y, or z axis; and finally could crawl or roll.

Practically speaking, setting up the specific programs for commercials took a lot of time. The producer was charged on a half-hourly or quarter-hourly basis for the use of the graphics camera. The same was true for the use of the Chyron and the Chyron operator. As competition for the market increased, other graphics program were developed. All of the programs became easier to use and cheaper to buy.

Today an extraordinary number of tools are available to the client, agency, and producer who need to include graphics in their commercials. While the new tools enable access to a wide variety of easy-to-get-at graphics, time is still required to set up even the most simple graphic.

At all levels of commercial production, no matter how simple or complicated, the graphic artist will have to:

1. Input the material to be used: type, logo, drawing, or picture.
2. Size and position the type, logo, drawing, or picture.
3. Perhaps redraw, recolor, or distort material in some way.
4. Get approval or corrections.
5. Make the revisions.
6. Get final approval.
7. Assist in the integration of the approved graphics into the commercial, sometimes frame by frame at 30 frames per second of airtime.

At the very simplest level, existing camera-ready material or computer-generated appropriate material will need to be input, sized, positioned, and integrated into the commercial.

At the least expensive end of commercial production, the editor uses the graphics programs inherent in the editing program they are using to create and include graphics in the commercial. Adobe, Apple, and Pinnacle have graphic tools that are adequate for a surprisingly large number of tasks. Further up on the ladder, there are specific tools for graphics. This includes Adobe's After Effects and Photoshop, Apple's Shake, and Discreet's Combustion, which offers the graphic artist a wider range of tools to manipulate type and still images.

At the top of the graphic ladder are programs and tools that offer a great deal of control, in many layers and in close to real time. These are programs such as Flint, Flame, and Inferno, as well as updated, but not as popular, programs from companies such as Quantel. Many versions of older programs are still in use. These are programs such as Harry, which handles single layers, and Henry, which handles multiple layers. Quantel's Paintbox is still being used at numerous sites and, as is the case with many of the older programs, still turns out significant work.

Along the way to creating effective graphics, the client, the agency, and the production company will play a significant role.

The Client: The agency and the producer want the client to get the facts early enough that there is sufficient lead time to complete the project. That means getting the actual copy or logo as it is to appear on the air. If special artwork is needed for the commercials, and the artwork is housed with the client, the client needs to get it to the agency or to the producer, who can work with it early enough to discover if any accommodations need to be made. Is it a giant piece; perhaps a logo that hangs in corporate headquarters? Is it color correct? Does it have to do anything special like stay underwater, for example? The producer and graphic artist will also need to be prepared if any changes need to be made. They may need to track down the crucial information and then get approvals for all the information and the actual artwork.

Bottom Line: Get it together!

Horror Story 3743

We're in the edit suite . . . a Smoke suite, and it's costing $600 an hour. An address is needed for a tag. The address is in Florida. The client is asked: "Do you spell the name of that town: "Ft. Myers" or "Ft. Meyers"?

"I'm not sure. I'll call the store."

As it happened, the sales associate on the floor isn't sure either nor is the assistant manager, and the manager is out, and yes, that is the city in which they live; nevertheless, they are not sure about how to spell it. Only the client knew that that address was to be used.

Time is passing at $10 a minute.

We call Information for the city and casually ask how Information spells the city's name.

We do the same thing with FedEx.

Now at least there is consensus.

The Agency: Help the client. Suggest a realistic time line for having all graphic materials in hand. Make sure the client is aware of what's needed and, at the very least, explain, if necessary, the consequences, both financial and artistic, of not working with sufficient lead time. This may help the client gather what is needed expeditiously. Make sure that the approvals are in hand early enough that the creative and production arms of the team can take care of any problems. Make sure there is some one person who is in charge.

Bottom Line: Make sure that what's supposed to be together is, in fact, together.

Horror Story 3744

We're in the edit suite . . . working on the graphics.

The graphic artist is told by the art director: "Make the background blue."

"No," the copy editor/creative director says. "Make it red."

They're both running the show and sharing the responsibility.

The client isn't there and really shouldn't be put in the position of having to make that creative decision. Shouldn't this have been decided prior to entering the graphic artist's suite?

What should the graphic artist do?

What he did do was turn around, ask them to make a decision, and then waited.

The Producer: Sometimes being away from the heart of the matter can lead to creative solutions. Be sure as the commercial producer/director that you are aware of what graphics are needed and their due dates and that the agency is aware of those needs. Encourage face-to-face meetings because graphics are very specific, and very much a part of the details that can be sloughed off. Direct communication can catch problems before they occur. And lastly, anticipate problems.

Bottom Line: Be creative! Cope!! Help!!! (Strictly alphabetic order. . . .)

Finally, look at the spot on a black and white monitor as the editing process is going on. Make sure the graphics and other elements of the commercial "read" in black and white as well as in color. Sometimes, color choices work well in color but are too close in hue, chroma, or intensity when viewed in black and white, and the client's message becomes obscured.

Animation

Commercials that are totally animated are out of the scope of this book. How to make animated commercials is at least a volume unto itself. Nevertheless, it would be impossible to investigate the creation of commercials without acknowledging the part of animation in the world of commercials. It is also impossible to gloss over the use of animation in even the most fundamental commercials.

There are many definitions for animation because there are so many ways in which animation is created and used. Some definitions are:

- Animation is anything that moves that isn't live action.
- Animation is anything that is shot one frame at a time.

Alternatively, it's

- The process of taking a series of individual pictures—called frames or panels and stringing them together in a timed sequence to give the appearance of continuous motion.

©GRANTASTIC DESIGNS, grantasticdesigns.com, all rights reserved

- The movement of the created image in recorded time.

Dan McLaughlin, Chair, UCLA Animation Program

If you make commercials, you will be dealing with animation. To some people animation simply means cartoons. Cartoons! Cartoons are those wonderful cel animation films from Disney, The Walter Lantz Company, Warner Brothers, and independent small studios such as Bob Kurtz and friends and the Hubleys. In fact, there are studios that do feature films and big works, and there are many studios that work in commercials and also work on smaller films. Each coast, and Chicago as well (at least partially because of the Leo Burnett Company and all the children's products they handle), has animation studios that are a part of the commercial scene. The animators gave us Mickey Mouse, Donald Duck, The Simpsons, The Roadrunner, and many characters associated with popular cereals. For a long time, cel animation ruled, but today there's a great deal more than that to animation.

Here are some of the popular animation formats.

1. *Cel character animation: Mickey Mouse* or *The Simpsons.* Artists draw on separate pieces of artwork called cels. They are usually photographed at 12 cels per second for full movement or animation, though they may be photographed at other frame rates, which may distort the sense of action happening in real time.

2. *Computer animation: Finding Nemo* or *Toy Story.* The animation can be anything from full character animation to digital effects derived from computer animation programs. It also includes flying type and logos.

3. *Stop motion:* Portions of *King Kong,* or the California Raisins commercials. Things such as miniatures, clay or other plastic substances, any physical entity rather than drawings or photographs seem to move. A doll's head is moved from left to right in 12 increments. Each increment is photographed. When the film is played back at the "normal speed" of 24 frames per second, the doll's head appears to move from left to right in a second's time.

Some common offshoots of stop motion photography are:

3a. *Clay, puppet, or sculptural animation:* Nick Park's *Wallace & Grommet* and the Chevron gas commercials. Clay, or for that matter any pliable substance, is shot, moved, and shot again at 8, 10, 12, 16, or 24 frames per second.

3b. *Miniatures:* Although work with miniatures and models is often done in real time, there are times when the material is shot one frame at a time and may then be considered to be a part of stop motion or animation.

3c. *Pixelation:* Actors or objects are shot as stills or at less than 24 frames per second. This was a popular technique used in commercials in the late 1960s and early 1970s. Charlie Chaplin films were shot at a time when 18 frames per second was the standard for shooting and projection. Later they were projected at 24 frames per second and seemed to have a jerky kind of quality, which is what we think of when we deal with pixelation.

3d. *Time-lapse photography:* This technique is commonly seen as day turning to night or clouds moving quickly across the sky. It's accomplished by shooting any natural event at a speed that is less than the normal speed of 24 frames per second. The shutter may be opened just once every 30 seconds or every minute, or in the case of building construction, perhaps once a day. It's a technique that's often used to indicate the passage of time.

4. *Rotoscoping: Cool World* or *Lord of the Rings*. In rotoscoping a drawing is made from a photograph of live action, or "motion capture." The photograph is projected on the artist's drawing board. It's traced and then shot. This was patented by Max and Dave Fleisher in 1917. It was first used in an animated film based around a character named *Koko the Kop*. Its later use in Disney's *Snow White* solidified its use in the world of animation. Today, rotoscoping usually refers to matte cutting and frame-by-frame painting in the computer using tools like Pinnacle's Commotion or Avid's Matador.

Inevitably experimental or less traditional animation forms must be mentioned. These include many of the techniques mentioned here and also involve other approaches to animation such as painting on or scoring the actual film.

Apart from those commercials that are entirely animated, some form of animation is integral to almost every commercial. When type moves onto the screen, it's animated onto the screen. The logo moves from left to right across the screen bringing a banner with the client's name. It *animates* to the screen.

At the lowest end of the commercial production scale, commercials using nothing but animated type and graphics with a voice-over are still used and still successful. The following commercial and others like it are successful and popular with clients and agencies with low budgets. This copy requires nothing but a music bed, a voice-over track, animated type, and some clip art and stock manufacturer's photos.

Audio	Video
1. From New York to Los Angeles. From the major cities in between.	1. Zooming type with city names.
2. Truckloads of _____ are coming . . . (furniture/men's clothing/brown and white goods)	2. Dissolve or wipe to photos of merchandise.
3. To store name (client's chain of stores)	3. Wipe to client's logo.
4. You'll find savings of 20%, 30%, 40%, and even 50%.	4. Dissolve to zooming numbers.
5. Save on an incredible array of (furniture/ men's clothing/brown and white goods, etc.). Save on (sofas and bedroom suites, or suits and sports jackets, or TVs and refrigerators).	5. Dissolve or wipe to photos of clothing, merchandise.
6. From manufacturers such as _____ (Insert names of manufacturers)	6. Wipe/dissolve to manufacturers' logos.
7. Yes, save 20%, 30%, 40%, and even 50%.	7. Wipe to zooming numbers.
8. And it's only at _____ (client's store name/chain of stores name).	8. Store logo and address top-half of screen.
9. But the sale ends _____ (insert date). Be there!	9. "SALE ENDS" and dates.

Clients, advertising agencies, production companies, and producers who specialize in making commercials that are totally animated are in a separate category unto themselves. Many of the concerns they have are the same as those for live action commercials. They need approvals. They need to create the audio track, which is usually done first in animation. They need to create or find a music bed and then go through test stages and final drawings or models to come up with the video that will go before the camera to become the commercial. The significant difference between full animation and real-time production is, primarily, the time line. The specific time line to any animation project is unique to that project; however, animators need approvals much earlier in the process because creating the commercial frame by frame takes more time than live action. It also costs more to redo.

Additionally, the very nature of animation requires a different thought process regarding the overall production than that which is needed for live action. Unlike live action, animation requires that editing decisions be made prior to creation. The shooting ratio in animation is 1 to 1 or very close to it. The shooting ratio in live action is much higher. In live action the take, and the specific in and out point of a particular scene, is chosen *after* the scene has been shot in a number of different "takes." With animation the decision about when to begin and end a scene takes place *before* the animation begins.

Type and graphic movements, which are a part of almost all commercials, are now handled, as are the commercials themselves, in a digital computer environment. At the low end of the scale, the most recent editing programs from Apple and Adobe have built-in programs for type and some limited animation. Moving up the scale, editors using Avid systems also have the ability to animate type and simple cels or frames.

Where major moves or graphic/animation decisions are to be made, artists using various computer-driven animation tools work with programs capable of rendering graphics consisting of multiple levels of work. The high-end tools may offer layering of two or three layers in real time. More layers can be seen once the program has rendered the material. The speed of the rendering is tied to the program, the complexity of the material to be rendered, and the hardware handling it all. The output of such high-end work will more than likely be edited using a digital program that imports graphics and animation and is then easily transferred to the commercial.

Ultimately the process in all forms is the same. Create an image, move it incrementally, shoot it again, move it again, and shoot it again. The input from the client and agency are the same throughout. The client or agency needs to establish strong communication ties with the animators and work within a clearly defined time line and strong key check-off points along the way.

Research

Creative Director 1:

You watch behind the mirror and you start to pull your hair out because you go, wait a minute, you're asking the wrong questions. And you want to jump in there and save your spot. But it's dead. It's not gonna go anywhere.

Creative Director 2:

Pure good advertising from my viewpoint is going to sell product based on what the focus group says.

Research Executive:

Well, the advertising agencies are dealing . . . with an emotional level of the consumer. When the ads are not liked, when they're disliked, they're not happy. And they often try to find something wrong with what we've done. Like we didn't get the right people in here, we didn't ask the right questions, whatever the case may be. They have to own up to the fact that the whole idea of doing this is to find out if their idea's a good idea, and if in fact three groups of people come in here and tell you it's a bad idea, you probably should listen to that.

Client:

Three words I try not to use are "always," "never," and "research."

Some people involved in the creation of commercials love testing, and some hate it and sometimes they are the very same people. Nonetheless, research and testing are parts of the process of making commercials. Sometimes the best research indicates the world is waiting for a car like the Edsel. The Edsel was introduced by the Ford Motor Company in the late

1950s after a great deal of research indicated that it was exactly what the public wanted and that it could be expected to break all sales records. It received an enormous amount of publicity and advertising and generated such a positive response from the media that it appeared on the cover of *Life* magazine. It was, nevertheless, a monumental failure. At other times research saves a product, shows a line of thought that helps create moving and powerful commercials, or stops an ineffective or detrimental commercial from airing.

Simply stated, research is a methodical attempt to get answers to questions. It is, according to *Webster's Collegiate Dictionary*, a "studious inquiry, a careful or diligent search." The data gathered in trying to answer questions for clients and their agencies affect production and may guide the following:

1. The product or service's creation
2. The marketing strategy created to deliver the product or service
3. The creative package that's used to sell the product or service
4. The commercial's effectiveness
5. The commercial's placement

Research that involves various forms of testing, such as focus groups, onsite interviews, telephone interviews, dial tests, etc., is important at a number of steps along the way to creating a commercial.

1. Research is useful to the client. Decisions are made based on research. Should we manufacture this product or that? Should we offer this service or that? Can we expand our market? Those decisions often govern what material an agency is given to create a campaign and a commercial.
2. Research is important in determining the goals of the commercial.
3. It's important to the creative group that uses the research to help create the commercial.
4. Completed spots are subjected to further research prior to being released.
5. Once the completed commercial is on the air, it is again subject to testing to determine the nature of its impact: How well it is remembered, and, ultimately, how successful it is in achieving its goals.

At the lowest end of the production scale, research and testing are often considered unessential luxuries. As soon as substantial production and air cost are involved, research and testing begin to play an important part in all the steps involved in the process.

Clients want to know the answers to a wide variety of questions such as:

- What should I manufacture?
- What products should I be selling?

- Can I add sportswear or a women's line?
- What are kids looking for in a new product?
- How big or how small should the product be?
- Is my new sandwich going to appeal?
- Is this campaign going to sell?
- Is there a new audience?
- Should we tweak it? How?

Advertising agencies use research to determine possible approaches to the commercial. Is this board or animatic going to work as a production? Once the commercial has been shot, answers are sought to questions such as: Is there a positive response to this commercial or that commercial? Should we change anything? What? Will it work in all markets? Should changes be made for different markets? What should be changed?

The testers want to be as accurate as possible no matter what the results show. How they get the answers may be controversial. They may be accused of asking the wrong questions or questioning the wrong population, but ideally, like Sgt. Friday of TV's *Dragnet* fame (circa 1967) they are "just trying to get the facts." To just get the facts, the testers may be helped by knowing what information is being sought.

> Some clients will let you know what they're getting at. What's the purpose of having these people here, and that gives you a better sense of what you're looking for than just, I need men and women twenty-five to forty-five who drink coffee. That doesn't tell me a lot. But if they're really looking for people twenty-five to forty-five who drink coffee because that's how they get up in the morning or because they can't live without it, that's a whole different thing than just, people who drink coffee. So the more information we know about a study, or the more about what they're trying to find out, usually the better we are at getting those right people into our office.
>
> Debbie Schlesinger of Schlesinger Associates

Often, the problem is that the client hasn't clearly identified what they want to know. In *A New Brand World* by Scott Bedbury with Stephen Fenichell, an incident is recounted regarding the naming of General Motors' Saturn cars. When the cars were in the development stage, a great deal of money and time were spent trying to come up with names for the new cars. After spending $150,000 on research, "Aura" and "Intrigue" were chosen as the names for the two basic Saturn cars. That sounded, according to the advertising team at Hal Riney Associates, like traditional GM sorts of names. That didn't address the revolutionary aims to which the Saturn team was committed. The Saturn team did some more work on the name and decided to use the very simple "Saturn Coupe" and "Saturn Sedan." In fact, they did research on those names too, and fortunately those names fared very well.

The question is how could the first set of research, costing $150,000, be so far off the mark? What parameters were set, or weren't set, that could lead to names like Aura and Intrigue, instead of Coupe and Sedan? Clearly asking the right questions is a major consideration. How that's done is different in every situation, but this anecdote is recounted as a cautionary tale. Objective research came up with two different answers to the same basic question—What do we name the car? The material used to get to those two different answers was surely not the same. Computer technology has lent us the term GIGO— Garbage in. Garbage out. It certainly has relevance in framing the research team's process.

Let us take a hypothetical situation in which a food chain, one known for selling hamburgers, is ready to introduce a new product because they want to increase their business. They've decided to explore selling a product outside of their perceived specialty. They decide to do some research to find out what new product their customers would like. At this point they may call in a research group to help them with the new product choice.

There are a large number of variables that can come into play when doing research, so specificity is enormously important. Is the company trying to find out if the product will sell in a limited area or across the country? Is the new product geared to a particular slice of the population, and if so, who is the target audience? As the specifics of the question are decided, "I want to sell more product" becomes "I want to sell more new product to a broad range of customers." A broad range of customers in our example means both men and women. Both men and women becomes men and women 18 to 49. Specifically: "I want to sell more of a new product to men and women, age 18 to 49, living on the East Coast or West Coast, or all over America, who will probably be buying the product between the hours of 11 AM to 1 PM Monday through Friday on workdays, who traditionally only thought of us for hamburgers, etc."

There are two major kinds of research:

1. *Qualitative analysis:* Qualitative analysis uses focus groups and other direct contacts in the research process. This kind of research strives to come up with in-depth responses. The overall sample may be limited, but the kinds of answers sought tend to go beyond the questionnaire and deliver responses that are qualitative in nature.

2. *Quantitative analysis:* Quantitative analysis implies a less in-depth study. It uses tools such as telephone or in-person interviews with questionnaires. It might also include panel studies or control test studies. This kind of analysis seeks answers based on a large quantity of respondents and responses.

Let's go back in time to the early 1990s and assume we have a hypothetical client in the fast food business, someone like McDonalds. The client has decided to explore enlarging their business by appealing to a larger fast food group and wants to investigate the creation of vegetarian sandwiches, which they hope will sell well on the West Coast. In 1990 this would probably have been seen as a poor idea. Hamburger eaters weren't seen as the kind of people who would go to a fast food restaurant for a vegetarian sandwich. But that was then.

The client is going to want to know:

1. Does their clientele want this product?
2. Will it bring in new clientele?
3. Will it turn away existing clientele?
4. Will it be profitable?

At this point a quick *quantitative* study might be in order, so two or three geographic areas might be chosen for the study. In this example let us say that three areas are chosen, and 150 phone interviews are conducted in each location. That's a total of 450 calls. If each call took just 10 minutes, including the time to enter notes, it would take 45 uninterrupted hours.

The interviewer will first screen the person being interviewed to determine eligibility for the study. For example, questions may include: Do you go to fast food restaurants? How often do you go? Three or more times a week? Once a week? Two or three times a month? If you do go to fast food restaurants, do you: a. sometimes, b. always, c. never, have a vegetarian meal? The goal is to determine whether follow-up questions regarding our vegetarian sandwich will get a meaningful response.

The results of these interviews will be used to determine the feasibility of creating and selling vegetarian sandwiches. The same methodology might be used for many other product questions. Later, the specifics of the responses here, and in the testing that continues, may inspire the creative efforts that become commercials.

Continuing with our imaginary product, we'll assume that the company decides that there *is* an interest in the sandwiches and the client wants to do a taste test. Here, a *qualitative* study is probably best. That will mean finding or creating an environment where the sandwiches can be tested. In such a case we'll assume that the research company chooses a hotel, which can provide the kitchen facilities that are needed. Three groups of 50 people will be tested. If it were required, smaller groups of people might be used. They might be invited to a testing room where videotapes of their responses might be part of the research. In fact, an important ingredient built into many of the major research facilities is the ability to record the testing.

The client wants to try out three different kinds of sandwiches to determine which has the greatest chance for success. The research company will create a questionnaire and ask which is the favorite. They might want to know what could be improved. How? After the data came back there might be a decision to make changes in the ingredients and try again to see what kind of response the new sandwich gets.

Let's say the client is now satisfied with the results. They've decided which vegetarian sandwich to try out and now want to know what kind of response the sandwich is getting in the field. A test market is chosen, and in the first week, in-store representatives from the research company attempt to solicit information from those who ordered the sandwich. They may also interview those who didn't order the sandwich.

If all goes well, the client may decide to proceed with a television campaign showcasing their new product. They then go to their account executive at the agency, share the results of their testing, and give the go-ahead for a marketing campaign for the, as yet, unnamed new product.

The advertising agency then begins to work on the new campaign. If the agency is large, it will assign a marketing group to create a strategy for the marketing of the new sandwich. The marketing group, too, will need research to determine what's the best way to get to core customers. To do this they may institute their own research efforts and will certainly want to see the results of the research that has already been done on the project. From that research, and their own, the agency team devises a few different media strategies and campaigns that they feel would be appropriate. It may include television commercials but might just suggest the use of billboards, radio and billboards, or most likely, a combination of all media.

Here's how it works from the agency perspective. Having evaluated the research, the creative group begins the serious process of creating the commercial or commercials. They will have read through, listened to, and viewed the results of its own and perhaps other agencies' panels, phone interviews, and onsite interviews. They may have their own perception of the client's product, brand identity, and position in the market, and they will want to know even more. In fact, the creative team may get involved in some of their own research by spending time at the client's outlets. They'll want to get their own perspective on the food that's served, on the clientele, and on the locations. Somewhere in the research, perhaps in the transcribed statements or in tapes of responses, there may be a kernel that sets the tone for the creative efforts.

> . . . that spot I created is now in the Smithsonian Institute because I created an ad campaign that came right out of the focus groups. And that is, I created an ad campaign that said computers are cool for girls. Where that ad line came from was right out of one of the kid's mouths, and I recognized that what they were saying was, boys are always allowed to play with computers, and then the girls are saying, wait a minute. Computers are cool for girls.
>
> Tom Sylvester, Edendale Films

This creative process is the same no matter what the level of production. Even the production process represented by a one-man team who serves as the creative-director as well as the writer/director/gaffer/grip/editor still must confront:

1. *Client background:* Who is the client? What is being sold?
2. *Target audience:* Who is the product/service for? Men/women, age range, location
3. *Competition:* Who else is trying to do the same thing? How are they doing it?

4. *Position:* What position should this client take? The cheapest? The most convenient?

5. *Tonality:* Will this be funny? Serious? Light? Hard driving? etc.

6. *Key selling points:* What is the most important part/sell of the message?

At the simplest level, the research is the writer or director's experience with similar clients and situations.

As the level of sophistication increases, greater resources are called into play. Beyond the simplest level, the creative group uses the research as an aid as it goes about the task of creating the commercial or commercials. It may mean that a few people get together and throw out ideas, or as is the case in some organizations, the process is carried out alone and then ideas are pitched to one another.

Typically, two or three ideas emerge and a mode of presenting them to the client is sought. There is no one way that that process is completed. At the lowest end of the scale, a script and perhaps a board might be presented along with a reel that showed similar commercials. At this stage no testing is involved.

In a typical scenario at higher levels of commercial production, research and testing play a part. It begins with the choice of ideas to be presented. In some agencies the ideas or storyboards might be presented to a focus group with a moderator. The aim is to determine which spots rate highest with which populations and to find out what parts of the storyboards need reworking.

The results of this research may play a part in the presentation of material to the client. In the past, boards alone might be used with a limited number of participants. The danger with this approach is that a lay audience is really not equipped to visualize the commercial based on the boards.

A more vigorous approach consists of creating animatics and seeing how they test. These are usually videotape versions of the storyboards. A track is created with the audio portion of the boards, and the panels of the board are then shot and edited to the audio track to make a kind of animated version of the commercial. The boards are then presented to a panel who is asked to comment on various aspects of the commercial as presented by the animatic version. The goals are set before the panel begins. The panel itself may or may not be videotaped. A recording and transcription of the session is likely to be a part of the testing package. The skill of the facilitator or moderator is extremely important in qualifying the commercial and in guiding the conversation to elicit responses that will be of use. Here, too, a lay audience has a difficult time imagining the commercial as a live action, rather than as an animated production.

Richard Goldman of The Men's Wearhouse tells about showing a proposed commercial in animatics form to a focus group. Someone in the focus group said: "I didn't like the guy in the green hat. I wouldn't trust someone like that." Of course, there is no "guy in a green hat." It's a drawing meant to indicate that someone would be saying those words. The animatic artist simply drew a picture with a man wearing a green hat. Others on that panel agreed with the comment, and before the moderator could get them back on track, the commercial was dismissed. An explanation would have sounded defensive, and it was too late.

Eventually, commercial boards are chosen and presented to the client. If there has been research based on the particular boards, then that research may be offered along with the rest of the presentation. However, the agency may choose not to share that research. They may want to hide any negative reactions. They might, for example, have wanted to use the research to refine the commercials and feel that now that the spots have been fixed, the research becomes irrelevant. The manner in which the results of research is handled has a lot to do with the particular client-agency relationship.

Once the commercials are made, there is often another round of tests. Focus groups are formed, and their opinions regarding the spot or spots are solicited. Reactions are sought to discover if the spots ought to run or if they need to be revised. Some spots may be appropriate for some parts of the country and not work in others. Some spots may work well only during daytime, for example. Others are suitable for prime time or late night. Different versions of the same spot may be tested to see which works best, where it works best, and with whom it works best. Finally, the research will be used to suggest further actions regarding the spots. Another way in which companies research spots is to run similar or identical spots in different markets and then see which spot yields the greatest sales.

Once the spots are put on the air, they are tracked to see what kind of impression they've made and whether they're successful in achieving the goals for which they were made. In another way, the Arbitron and Nielsen research ratings regarding homes using television, share of the market, etc., help determine the placement and cost of running the commercials.

Perhaps the most significant user of testing of spots are those commercials that demand immediate action: the spots for records, knives, slicing machines, and the like. If there's a number to call, and the switchboard is flooded. That's the final bit of research.

Jason Haikara, Senior Vice President of Marketing for Fox Broadcasting Company, said, "I can speak from experience that testing can be paralyzing. You ultimately have to go with your gut in a lot of cases. But testing is just one more piece of information to help you make a decision."

Additional material regarding testing and market research can be found at the Market Research Association web site *www.mra-net.org.*

9 Specialists

Commercial production utilizes some of the most creative minds in the world. Their task is to create little messages intended to capture the attention and then appeal to the fantasies and desires of a wide and varied audience whose program they've just interrupted. They have no time to leisurely set the stage or mood. There's no time to introduce or develop characters or plot. In spite of this, their message must instantly appeal to the viewer, remain in the viewer's mind, and impel the viewer to go out and buy or use something they weren't thinking about at the time of the interruption. It's no wonder that many different skills are called upon to create eye- and ear-catching concepts in television's very cluttered marketplace. The client's business has to stand out, be remembered, and then be acted upon—soon. No doubt, there is someone right now who is perfecting some new way to throw a pizza in the air. That specialist will surely be discovered, recognized as a standout talent, and featured in a soon-to-be-made commercial. This chapter is about some of those specialists.

Sometimes commercials are made by one person who conceives the project, sells it to the client, budgets it, shoots, edits, and finally delivers copies to the stations. That's unusual anywhere but on low-budget commercials. However, there *are* a lot of low-budget commercials, and many are made that way. Most of the time, even with a medium-budget commercial, there are a *few* contributors. With expensive productions there are usually *many* contributors and many specialists who lend their skills to the project. Most come and go. Their work is needed for some unique aspect of the production, and they leave after their work is done and go on to the next project.

Inevitably, some specialists will be left out of this chapter. Hopefully, those unlisted are so specific, and their talents so unique, that inclusion is unnecessary. For example, if you worked on one of the old Marlboro ads, you would have had to hire a horse wrangler. That kind of specialty is not covered in this book. Other personnel have been left out too, such as the third and fourth electrician, third and fourth grip, second home economist, nurse, fire safety officer, and effects foreman. For an example of how extensive that group can be, consider the list of below-the-line specialists working in IATSE positions in just one area of the country (the West Coast) as listed in Chapter 10, Useful Forms and Reference Material.

Many of the job descriptions have been discussed at some length in earlier chapters. Where that is the case, the description in this chapter will be very brief. I've organized the job descriptions by areas whenever possible so that the director, the producer, and their staff are all listed under one heading. Those significant jobs that are not a part of most productions, such as animation and greenspeople, are simply alphabetized.

Main Production Staff

Director

In most cases it is the director who is hired to make the commercial. On the low end of the scale, the director may also write, produce, edit, and, for that matter, make the dubs for the commercial. Once past that level of production, it is the director who is the main reason a production company is hired. The director is responsible for the filming or taping of the script or storyboards. It is his or her vision or method of work that affects the look of the commercial.

Producer

The most current definition of the commercial producer is probably that he or she manages the production on behalf of the director. At one time the producer ran the show and hired the director. In some cases that is probably still true, but it is rare in commercial production.

On the low-budget end of the production scale, the producer typically directs and may even edit as well. In higher end productions, there are a number of people who "produce" the commercial.

1. At the upper end of production, there may be a client producer who usually doesn't carry the title "producer." This person may be a company liaison, production supervisor, production coordinator, etc. He or she represents the client and works directly with the agency and the production company on all matters pertaining to the production of commercials.

2. The agency producer (AP) functions as the link between the client, the various departments within the agency, and the production company.

3. There are production company producers who serve as the link between the advertising agency and the production company. These producers assist the director by supervising those areas of production outside of the strictly creative function of the director. They are the contact people for contracts and are the first line to the agency producer. They arrange for the rental of gear, the hiring of crew and facilities, and the creation and maintenance of the schedule.

    During the shoot they facilitate the production and continue to be the liaison between the agency producer, the client, and the director. Along the way, they maintain or supervise those responsible for the record keeping needed for sound fiscal management of the production.

4. A third producer oversees the production in its postproduction stages at an editing facility. They are the link between the production company that shot the commercial, the agency who hired the production company to turn the footage into a final commercial, and the editing company for whom they work.

   Ordinarily this simply means creating a paper trail of facilities and personnel needed to complete the commercial. It also means arranging for the timely delivery of all the elements in a form that expedites the production. However, they also consult with the production company on how the boards will be shot. They need to understand all the elements of the job and are expected to catch and help solve potential problems. Sometimes they are called upon to help resolve specific production or even interpersonal issues. Most of the time the work calls upon their knowledge of the business: A commercial in which a character is supposed to fly warrants a discussion of how that is to be handled. Will the talent be hung by wires? If so it might be best to paint the wires bright orange so that it will be easy to digitally paint them out. What company will paint them out? With what process? On what schedule?

5. Specialty producers such as audio producers, music producers, graphic producers, etc., exist to shepherd their area of expertise through from beginning to end. They usually work in conjunction with the agency or production company.

In each case, the producers are responsible for pulling together all the pieces of the commercial. They make sure that all the material, facilities, and crew that should be available are available when needed and that the finances are tracked.

Assistant and Associate Producers

The assistant/associate producer (the title is often interchangeable) helps with the production in many ways. There is no one job description for this category. Each organization uses their assistance in a unique manner. Traditionally, they are on hand to facilitate both the personnel and hardware concerns of each area. They are often the first to initiate contact for casting sessions, booking a recording studio, arranging for special props, etc. Additionally, they are the actual record keepers. Often their notes are called upon to reconstruct discussions regarding terms of contract, amount of hours worked, personnel, etc.

Assistant Director

Assistant director is a specific job category under the Directors Guild of America contract. The assistant director works with the director on a *film* shoot and has duties that are different from those of an associate director who works with a director on a *tape* or *live* shoot.

The assistant director, working on a film shoot, is the link between the unit production manager, the director, and the various crews and talent working on the project. The assistant director makes up the call sheet for the cast and may assign dressing rooms. The assistant director anticipates issues with regard to time or materials and either attends to them on his or her own or calls on the proper parties, either the director, the producer, or the unit production manager, to resolve the problem.

Second Assistant Director

The second assistant director usually works under the assistant director. He or she often serves the same function as a stage manager in a theatrical production, making sure that talent is in place for each shot and that the set is ready for film or tape to roll. For example, you might see the second assistant director with a headset in charge of controlling the release of extras in a street scene a block away from the camera position. He or she might be posted at 81st Street, while the camera rolls with others in the cast on 80th Street.

Associate Director

The associate director works with the director on live or taped shoots. Essentially, the work on commercial shoots is very similar to that of the assistant director on a film shoot, except that the associate director is more likely to become involved in matters to do with slating and logging of material. Sometimes the associate director will serve as a stage manager.

Floor or Stage Manager

The floor manager, or stage manager, which is the term used in the Directors Guild basic agreement, is the liaison between the director, the crew, and the talent in video production. In a film production, much of this work is done by the assistant director. Stage managers assign dressing rooms; call the cast; call props, lighting, or construction to the stage; and generally assist the director. Originally, the stage manager's task was to be the representative of the director on the shooting floor while the director was in the control booth. As single camera production came to be the norm for commercials, the task of the stage manager was often filled by the associate director.

Unit Manager

Unit managers serve in much the same way as line producers do on feature or episodic television productions. Their responsibility is to track the production unit's day-to-day costs. The term "unit" came from the idea that each production was a unit unto itself. There was the morning news unit, the evening news unit, the home show unit, etc. Each of those units has an individual responsible both to the station and to the producer to assist in maintaining the budget and who sometimes serves as a source for locating either freelance or full-time personnel. Usually they deal with below-the-line personnel. Commercial production needed the same day-to-day consideration. Unit managers work with the producer and director on budgetary affairs and on hiring of the crew. They may be responsible for crew calls.

Location Scout/Location Manager

Location scouts maintain lists of locations and then serve as an agent between the production company and the space to be rented. They may act as, or be employed by, a location service company.

Location companies find locations for production companies, arrange for the use of the location, and may act as the go-between for the production company and the location. Initially they provide photographs, Polaroids, or digital pictures of the location. They may specialize in one kind of location, for example, suburban homes, or more likely will have a storehouse of many different kinds of locations from all types of sites. Some location companies are strictly local, specializing in civic buildings, such as libraries, jails, courtrooms, railroad stations, etc. Some specialize in international services with locations and managers across the globe. They may provide a location manager.

A location manager is to the location as a studio supervisor is to a particular studio. On location the location manager is invaluable. In the preproduction stages, they deal with location concerns such as permits, power, maps, parking, bathrooms, trailers, catering, and other matters that are essential to the smooth operation of the production. During the production phase, they help coordinate and assist in the location schedule and work with vendors such as location owners and caterers. They may also serve as an additional source for finding local crew members and local facilities, such as prop rental, camera rental, and gaffer equipment. Working closely with the unit's production manager, they approve invoices specific to the location.

Horror Story 39
A location scout who was new to the job rented a large cruise ship, but pleaded poverty to save money for the film company. He arranged for a very low price based on the premise that it was a student film. When the owner of the ship discovered a full-scale major Hollywood production on board, he forced the production to leave immediately. No amount of discussion or offer of more money after the fact swayed the captain, who felt, rightly, that he had been deceived.

Production Manager

Production managers are responsible for the day-to-day, minute-to-minute operation. They are often headquartered at the home base of the production company. They make sure that all manner of calls are made, that field office supplies are where they need to be, and that the comings and goings of various crew members as well as inventory such as props, lights, and dollies are handled in a timely manner. Production managers are totally involved with the production end of the work, leaving aesthetic and many interpersonal questions to the producers. They often work with a production coordinator who is at the actual shoot.

Studio Supervisor

When a production company uses a sound stage, a studio supervisor is usually included with the package. Studio supervisors function as the liaison between the production company and the rental facility. They are aware of the particular characteristics of the facility. They'll know where the power outlets are, where the bathrooms are, phone costs, etc. They're also knowledgeable about stage crews, rentals, and even, or especially, where one can send out for food.

In the major markets the production company is often required to hire at least one crew member who has worked at the facility for a while—a kind of house crew member. House crew members know the peculiarities of the facility and save the facility from unnecessary problems as each new user tries to figure out the location of fuses, wiring schematics, access buttons, levers, etc. They save the production company time and money. The cost of the studio supervisor is built into the cost of the rental. The cost of the crew members may or may not be built in, depending on the facility. In my experience the studio supervisor and studio crew person are valuable additions to the smooth operation of a production.

Script Supervisor

Script supervisors keep track of what has been shot. They need to know the location of all the material shot in a production: On which roll? At what point in the roll can it be found? What is the time code for a particular shot? How long did run? What peculiarities are there about the take? Did the talent pour the coffee before, during, or after they spoke? Was the actor on the left leaning forward in the yesterday's take? The script supervisors notes and the video tap are invaluable at the shoot and later at the edit.

Camera Personnel

The camera personnel are the director of photography, camera operator, and assistant camera operator. These jobs are described in more detail and in context in Chapter 5, Production.

Tape or Digital

On a tape or digital shoot it is usual for either the camera operator or the facility to provide the camera. Since most shoots are single-camera shoots, only one operator is necessary. If there is a camera control unit, a video shader who controls the hue, chrominance, and value of the colors may be part of the camera crew.

Film

Film offers a number of models. In the simplest form, there is just one person who serves as the director of photography (DP), camera operator, assistant, and loader and who is responsible for the camera, lenses, and filters, as well as the lights and the various logs and reports to the lab and for editing. A single DP on a job may indicate that it's a low-budget shoot, a simple shoot, or a shoot with specific one-operator requirements such as skydiving or underwater shots.

More often there are at least two and as many as four people involved. The additional tasks to be completed by someone, no matter what the size of the budget, are caring for lenses and filters, loading the camera magazines, checking for malfunctions, ensuring a clean film path so that there are no hairs in the gate, operating the zoom, pulling focus, holding slate, logging takes, and facilitating lab and editing reports, as well as delivering and picking up material from the lab.

DP

The DP is the person in charge. In very expensive productions, the DP's purpose is to design and implement the lighting, choose the lenses and filters, and order the placement or design the movement of the camera, leaving various parts of the operation to the camera operator and his or her assistants and dolly or crane crew.

Camera Operator

The second camera crew member most likely to be on the camera crew is a camera operator who actually operates the camera.

First Assistant Camera Operator

The first assistant camera operator loads the camera, deals with lenses and filters, and is responsible for actually changing them and keeping them clean. He or she holds slate; pulls focus; and after the shot is made, checks the gate, keeps the logs, and sometimes delivers the film.

Second Assistant Camera

The second assistant camera operator is the fourth person involved. He or she takes over the job of loading the camera, holding slate, checking the gate, logging takes, and delivering film to the lab. The first assistant still pulls focus and is responsible for lenses and filters.

Engineering

Commercials shot in a television studio or on location with a production company will usually have an engineer assigned to the project. The engineer is responsible for keeping everything going at peak performance. There are many problems that can occur, from something as simple as a faulty cable or poor connection to something more significant such as a software glitch in some part of the studio facility. Any problem anywhere in the system can slow down or totally stop a shoot.

Audio

There are a number of audio areas to be considered for in studio or on location, and film or tape or digital media.

The Recordist

The recordist is the person who is responsible for the sound recording. He or she listens to what is being recorded and makes sure that it is being recorded at the right level, without any interfering extraneous sounds. If it is a film shoot, he or she is also responsible for ensuring sync with the film. The title "recordist" might also be attributed to someone in charge of videotape recording, although the term "videotape operator" is more likely.

Mic Handler or Boom Operator

If sound is to be recorded, a microphone needs to be placed out of range of the camera and close enough to the speaker to get good sound. The mic handler or boom operator is responsible for the placement of the mic or mics. Occasionally, a lavalier, stand, or desk mic is used and is put in place by the mic handler. A parabolic or reflecting mic may be directed from some distance by a microphone handler. This is often used at sporting events such as at football games to listen to coaches' advice or comments from across the field.

Most often, however, the task of recording dialogue is accomplished by a microphone attached to a boom, or a fish pole, and operated by a boom operator. The fish pole is a lightweight pole with a microphone on the end. Often it is designed so that it is capable of being extended. It is usually held above the operator's head, out of range of the camera but as close as possible to the speaker to record the dialogue.

There are a number of booms other than the handheld fish pole audio boom. Both a tripod or giraffe boom and a big or perambulator boom are devices on wheels that are most suitable for work on sets rather than on location. The tripod or giraffe boom is simply a three-legged wheeled stand with a boom arm that can be extended and swung into place over actors. The perambulator boom is similar but is large enough to accommodate a platform on which an operator can stand. From this perch, the boom arm can be panned or tilted. The perambulator boom also allows the operator to point the microphone from side to side. Both units afford the operator ease of operation and precise placement of the microphone. With either of these two booms the microphone can be simply set and left in place . . . ideal for a scene at a desk, for example. One of the great advantages of this type of boom is the recordist's ability to place the microphone where it's needed and simply leave it in place out of range of the camera. If necessary, these booms can pan and truck with the same ease as a camera's crane mount. The boom's bulk, however, is more likely to be in the way. Additionally, if movement is required during a shot, two crew members are required. One operates the boom, and the other repositions it.

Audio Playback Operator

If playback is needed, an audio playback operator will be on the crew. Situations that require this might be commercials in which the cast is moving or singing to a prerecorded track. They need to hear the prerecorded voices to be able to be in sync with them. There are many other specialized cases where a playback operator is essential. Any kind of live concert, for example, requires an operator to feed the orchestra's and singers' audio to the public address system. Then, there are times when a director requires that the cast hear previously recorded material, for a dance scene, for example, or that the cast be filmed reacting to material played back for the first time.

Talent

Anyone who performs on or off camera is considered talent. Unionized *film* commercials are subject to agreements with the Screen Actors Guild (SAG), while unionized *tape and live* commercials are subject to agreements with the American Federation of Radio and Television Artists (AFTRA). Commercials that use talent covered by AFTRA or SAG are usually national or large regional spots. In such cases the terms regarding talent auditions and second auditions, working conditions, minimum fees, and payments are all defined by contract, as are the rules governing owner spokespeople and employees. Production companies with agreements with the unions are required to maintain the standards to which they have agreed.

When children are to be used, specific union rules apply to their participation, as do rules governing their use that are established by state and local governments. They may also fall under scrutiny from the Society for the Prevention of Cruelty to Children (SPCC). Animals, too, are protected by state and local governments as well as by the American Society for Prevention of Cruelty to Animals (ASPCA).

In smaller markets or major markets working with production companies that are not signatories to any agreement, the use of talent, as well as the conditions under which they will work (travel pay, hours on the set, delayed lunches, etc.), and their fees are entirely negotiable. Often suitable nonunion performers can be found, particularly where there are agencies whose roster represents only nonunion talent. Finding excellence among nonunion talent, however, is often an arduous and unrewarding task.

Agents

Talent agents represent talent. They seek employment for them and negotiate on their behalf. They are paid a portion of the artist's wages. The fee is usually 10%, but in an unregulated market the percentage may vary. There are a number of agencies that specialize in representing talent specific to commercials. The clients they represent are usually easy to typecast. Agent's tend to list their clients under specific heading such as: "Spokesman," "Spokeswoman," "Moms," "Dads," "Characters male/female," and "Children." Agents also represent musicians, variety talent, circus acts, announcers, and voice-over talent.

Casting Director

The casting director helps to cast the production. He or she works with a number of agents to help find the right performer for the commercial. A talent agent represents the talent and is paid a percentage of the talent's salary for that representation. Casting directors are paid by the production company for their assistance in locating and sometimes offering advice about the talent. Most of the time, the casting director gathers pictures and résumés prior to having a casting call. He or she schedules interviews, arranges the audition/interview sites, and then maintains pertinent records of the audition. Most of the time the casting director is responsible for making videotapes of the audition and may supply the camera and operator, tape deck, and tape, as well as someone to audition with the talent.

Animal Handlers

Even here specialization is expected. Handlers who work with dogs and cats may not be appropriate if the commercial calls for lambs and monkeys. The major production areas, New York and Los Angeles, have animal handler services that can lead you to the right animal and handler for your commercial. Other areas may require a creative approach. Local veterinarians and the zoos are places to start. Although friends and neighbors may have lovely dogs, cats, and birds who look just right for the commercial, it has been my experience that, whenever possible, it's best to work with professional animal handlers. You can expect that the handler will keep the animal comfortable and looking right for the shot. You may also discover that the animal comes with the handler, the animal's owner, and, at times, a member of the ASPCA, who is there to ensure the animal's welfare.

Professional animal handlers have a variety of techniques to achieve the effects needed for the commercial, but it's still best to communicate with an animal handler early on within the process. In a commercial I worked on, one of the actors was instructed to rub a hot dog over his palm to get Fido to lick his hand. At a different shoot, a sheep was prevented from wandering away by penning the animal with a portable fence just outside of the camera's view. Other effects, however, may require training. It's best to confer with the animal trainer early to ensure sufficient lead time to accomplish the task.

Designer/Art Director

There are a variety of specialists and designers who work on commercials in many areas.

Set Designers

Set designers are the people who create sets, usually at a studio. They confer with the director and client and draw up a set, which is then constructed at a shop, shipped, and put up at a rental facility. This is usually quite costly and is most often done only when a location cannot be rented to cover the needs of the boards. Locations services, which find working rental kitchens, bathrooms, bars, warehouses, jails, hospitals, etc., can be found in most markets. In such cases the designer or art director is hired to dress the set.

In instances where the set must be made, a scene shop will most likely bid on the construction of the set. They then build the set, perhaps ship it to a paint shop or have it painted at the construction site, and finally ship it to a rental studio, where a crew accepts the set, loads it in, and then constructs it in place. Depending on the size of the production, either the same crew or separate expert crew members do any touch-up painting that's required. The set is then lit and dressed. After its use, the set either goes into storage, is returned, or is destroyed.

Art Director

The art director often has the responsibility of creating a "look" for a project. In commercials, art directors are also more likely to oversee the dressing of the set, that is, to arrange for the acquisition or rental, and placement of all the parts of the set that are not part of the architectural elements. In a kitchen, for example, they bring in the lighting fixtures, chairs and tables, cutting boards, pots and pans, and appliances. They would also bring in the touches such as false switches for the lights, phones, a radio, old newspapers, a "greeked" calendar, which means that the large bold type is doctored so that no actual material can be read.

Art directors are aided by the prop department, which consists of "outside props," those who get the props, and "inside props," those who maintain the props. They all deal with just two kinds of props.

Set props are props that appear as part of the set. This includes the physically heavy ones such as chairs and couches, as well as lighter ones such as the books in the library, the paintings on the walls, and the electric toasters and microwave ovens in the kitchen.

Hand props are those props that are handled by talent. It includes items such as folders, food, glasses, and phones.

Prop Rental

Most art directors have a working relationship with prop rental houses as well as furniture dealers. There are some standard fee structures that pertain to the rental of items for motion picture and television shoots. A substantial fee is paid for the first day's use, and there is usually a sliding fee scale thereafter. The production company usually arranges shipping and handling to ensure a timely delivery. Insurance is essential. Often the items rented are enormously expensive, and the high cost of insuring these props is still a small fraction of the replacement cost if an item were lost or damaged.

Sometimes, however, expensive products are used without charge. This is when their appearance in the commercial will enhance the product. General Motors, makers of the Cadillac, for example, might loan a Cadillac to a company that was making commercials for the Ritz-Carlton Hotel because the placement of the Cadillac in such a setting would enhance the viewer's perception of that car.

Makeup

Almost all commercials with casts in them require a makeup artist. At the very least a makeup artist's job is to powder the talent because the lights used in production can emphasize the skin's natural sheen in an unnatural way. Under the normal circumstances involved in lighting for film, which is not a normal lighting situation, makeup is used to achieve a natural look and adds appropriate color to both men and women. Makeup is used to hide blemishes on both men and women. Should the shoot be a "glamour" shoot, the makeup artist's skills are crucial to the look of the commercial. On commercials with special effects, horror or clown makeup, for example, the production company will certainly need to have a makeup designer.

Hair Designers

Hair designers are mandatory for "glamour" shoots and are often needed for any commercial that uses people. Ordinarily we aren't as conscious of people's hair as we are in a closeup. The challenge is to keep hair looking good despite the rigors of a shoot. Making sure all strands of hair are in place without appearing to be plastered down requires that the hairstylist be close at hand as each take is about to start. Sometimes hairstylist skills are required for special projects such as period pieces or commercials using wigs.

Costumes

Costume Designer

Costume designers design costumes and arrange for them to be created, fitted, and adapted to whatever is needed for the commercial. They may be called on to create anything from a period evening gown to a walking hamburger and anything in between. Usually they work on more expensive commercials, although imaginative creations are not limited by budget. Most of the time, designers find traditional costumes, such as those for a fireman or hospital orderly, in the vaults at various costume houses or at specialty supply sources. Sometimes the designer will be the one on set who manages the costumes, functioning as the wardrobe person. However, wardrobe is really a different and specialized function.

Wardrobe

The wardrobe crew maintains the costumes. Where there is a small cast, this may be easy. Should the commercial require a shot with many soldiers or policemen, for instance, keeping track of which hat goes with which member of the cast can be daunting. Their job includes cleaning and pressing items that may become dirty or rumpled during the day. They make repairs when necessary.

Additionally, the wardrobe crew, the wardrobe stylist, and wardrobe attendant are responsible for making all adjustments necessary for the shoot. When I directed a commercial on location in Boston for a company called Gentlemen's Wearhouse, the model looked wonderful from the front. The back, however, was a totally different story. The suit that had been delivered to the set was incorrect. It was too large. The wardrobe crew then performed a miracle of fitting by using pins in the back of the suit, which brought the suit size down by two whole sizes and which was undetected by the camera. Lastly the wardrobe team arranges to return all borrowed costumes or merchandise.

Special Effects Designers

Often commercials will require special effects. The effects are limited only by what an imaginative creative director can dream up. From a house falling down on cue and then going back together again for the next take to a jumping hamburger, the people who arrange for that to happen are special effects experts. Special effects designers deal with either electric, chemical, optical, or physical effects. These effects are often referred to as "gags." Sometimes there is a standard way of achieving an illusion, and any special effects firm can handle the job. But there are instances when a creative solution is required. At such times, particular specialists are called upon. For example, there are some special effects firms that specialize in cars, customizing them to look like Batmobiles, or arranging for them to bounce on cue. Other special effect houses have the hardware necessary to manufacture large panes of breakaway glass and specialize in glass and glass-like products.

Production Crew

The stagehands (in television) or grips (in motion pictures) are responsible for:

Construction/stage crew grips/rigging crew: They construct the set, rig it, and make set adjustments as needed. They may help with placing set props such as couches and chairs. Dolly grips move camera dollys.

Electric/lighting crew: The head lighting technician in motion pictures is called the gaffer or "best boy." In television it's head electric or chief electric. Electric is responsible for all lighting and electric needs on the set; this can be as simple as supplying power for guitar amps or as complex as lighting several stories of a skyscraper with Christmas tree lights.

Paint crew: They paint the set. Sometimes they are also on the set as standby or touch-up artists.

Specialized Production Crew Members

Animation

In addition to the traditional roles in creating animated commercials, computer animation has its own set of specialists, including but not limited to (from *Animation Rules* by Dan McLaughlin):

Modeling—builds the three-dimensional model
Set-up—makes the model ready for animation, strings the movement
Lighting—designs the lighting for three-dimensional models
Background—builds and texture maps the three-dimensional background
Scanning—inputs the art into the computer
Compositing—assembles the different levels or files onto one level or file

Technical director—coordinates the computer production between the art and the technological concerns

Programmer—creates the programs

Support—maintains equipment, often daily, to keep systems functioning and running

Explosive Experts

Commercials that require weapons and/or explosions of any kind require a specialist to supervise that area. These specialists rent or purchase whatever is needed and maintain security. They rig and instruct where necessary. The devastation a blank pistol can inflict is often surprising to those who are unaware of the force and intensity of the powder wad that is shot out with the firing of each round, even in weapons that are used strictly for motion picture and television.

I worked as a child actor in a Western series, and a sound effects man introduced me to the dangers of the guns that were so much a part of our productions. He placed a plate of glass against a wall and fired a blank at the glass. The impact from the wad shattered the glass; it was a smart way to convince me to keep away from the weapons.

Generator Operator

Generators and generator trucks come in a variety of sizes and supply power to productions, usually when they are on location. The generator operator maintains them. The operator's responsibility is to keep the generator powered and to maintain a consistent supply of power.

Graphics

Commercials often use graphics such as company logos, slogans, prices, legal requirements, and deadlines. Graphic artists, using specialized programs, are brought onto projects to create or place the graphics into the commercial. Super graphics such as special signs that appear in stores or on locations are usually handled by a scene shop.

Greenspeople

Greenspeople are responsible for maintaining any greenery that is part of the set or location. On sets they assist the prop crew in dressing and maintaining live plants that are on the set. (Plastic plants are strictly props.) On location, greenspeople trim and dress the greens to suit the shots. Additionally, they may paint natural plant life to create a required look. On moving car shots, they may place leaves on the road to help enhance the picturization of movement as the car speeds by.

Home Economist

The home economist is in charge of food on the set. At some facilities the prop crew brings in food and dresses it for camera. More often, if the food is to be used in a commercial, a home economist or chef is brought in to handle the job. They usually have contacts in the various food markets and bring in "hero" products for on-camera appearances. Also, they are familiar with techniques designed to enhance the way food looks on camera.

Insurance

Production insurance and liability insurance is a major cost consideration to a production company. There is a lot of costly specialized gear used on a shoot and many potentially hazardous conditions under which work will be performed. The cables, cable runs, electric tie-ins, and instrument placements used for lighting creates inherently dangerous situations. Large companies maintain their own policies or may be self-insured. They may also purchase special insurance for particular projects. Smaller companies either take out policies for particular projects or, more often, share in a blanket policy in which a number of production companies participate. Most rental companies require proof of insurance before they'll rent gear or props.

Lab

A film laboratory processes film. Different labs have different processing techniques, and while the process procedures are the same, each lab seems to yield different negatives and prints. The variances are caused by the particular lab's approach to the process. Film may be processed using different chemicals or processed at different temperatures. Even within the same lab, material processed early on Monday morning after the chemicals have been updated a few times may look different than material processed at 7 PM on Tuesday night with fresh chemicals. The director of photography or cinematographer is the link to the lab. Presumably he or she knows the characteristics of the particular lab and can get consistent results from them.

Usually material is brought in to be processed during the evening after the shoot day is finished. A work print is struck from the selected takes. This first copy is referred to as "the dailies" and is the print used for the next day's viewing. This print is unlike the final master print because it is made with a simple single pass, whereas a final print may be processed in such a way that each scene, or shot, is individually handled for maximum effect. An alternative way of handling film material for commercials is to go directly to a digital process so that all the material that's shot is transferred to digital media and continues to be worked on in digital format.

Management Services

Management services companies handle that part of the production that pertains to the managerial aspects of the commercial. They are the location finders, paymasters, accounting services, and sometimes legal adjuncts to the production. They work for the production company, and sometimes the advertising agency.

Martial Arts

Commercials sometimes require specialists in martial arts who are proficient in staged boxing, wrestling, knife fights, swordplay, or any one of a number of different martial arts. They have a working knowledge about camera movement and placement and know how to stage a fight so that it looks real. In the productions that required staged fights, I regret only the first one I ever did. I presumed to stage a fight, based on having taken a class in the subject at school. Fortunately, no one got hurt, and it was over quickly, but it didn't look very good. I engaged fight masters to choreograph all succeeding fights.

Miniatures

While miniatures are not a major part of most commercials, they are very important when they are used. Specialists exist who can create everything from a forest to a city. Since the camera can be very unforgiving, expert work is demanded. Work with miniatures is usually time consuming and costly, although they are a cost-saving device. Their use requires skilled builders and special camera mounts and lenses.

Music and Sound Effects

Most commercials use music either in the background or as part of a jingle for the spots. Music libraries and sound effects libraries abound. There is a surprisingly wide variety of "stock music," which is original music composed, produced, and sold for broadcast and other uses through stock music houses. One usually pays a small fee for listening time, which is assisted by someone who knows the library's material. The jingles or music pieces are called music cues. Once a cue is found, it's prepared for the producer in whatever format is most convenient, $1/4$-inch, DAT, etc., and a fee is then paid for its use. The fee for clearance of the cue will be based on the markets in which the cue will be heard and covers a predetermined block of time, usually 13-week runs. The composer is then reimbursed through royalties paid to the music publisher by the stock house. The client, in this case the production company, will regularly be billed for additional uses.

Sometimes a piece of music is specifically written for a spot. The composer and production process can vary from a friend with a guitar or synthesizer to a full-blown production done by a "jingle house." When a new jingle is required, a number of cues will be proposed. One is chosen and then produced. The production is handled with the same care as would go into the production of a major CD. Talent is auditioned, unless a known voice or set of voices are to be used, and a recording session is booked. The agency producer, the production producer, and a music producer are usually in attendance as is the client or its representative. A number of takes are made of the jingle, and often the jingle will be produced in a number of different styles and lengths to support radio as well as the television versions. The recordings of the instruments and the voices are then handled at a later session in an audio mix, which is discussed in Chapter 7, Post-Plus.

Sound effects are handled in much the same way. Extensive stock libraries exist, and custom effects can be created by many of the sound effects houses.

Rental Facility

Inevitably, production companies rent a facility or some piece of gear or prop for a short term. This can be a fully equipped sound stage, or simply a camera or audio rental, gaffer or grip rental, prop rental, costume rental, or car, van, or truck rental. Whatever the case, the renter or the production company needs to be very specific about what it is . . . exactly . . . that they want, and for how long they want it. Most of the time the production or renter needs to be insured and may need to pay for a portion of the rental prior to actually using the rented material. In some cases a company may need to post a bond to guarantee payment.

Still Photographer

The still photographer takes still pictures. This may be a position that is under union jurisdiction. Since the work is associated with production stills, the photographers need to be aware of the particular requirements of the set. They need to have a silent shutter and be aware of set procedures. They have to be sensitive to the needs of the talent. They may have to work very quickly and, of course, take good pictures.

Teleprompter Operator

A teleprompter is a device that is used to allow talent to look into the lens of a camera and read copy that, to their eyes, appears to be in front of the lens. In reality the unit is mounted on a camera and uses special glass that allows the copy to appear in front of the lens while allowing the reader to be photographed. In the original version of the teleprompter, which was mechanical, the teleprompter operator used a rheostat to run the copy past the center of the lens line. Now the operation is, for the most part, done entirely with computer-generated text and controls.

Transportation

On Camera
Picture vehicles, all of which need drivers, are those vehicles that appear in the commercial: cars (of all vintages), vans, buses, motorcycles, scooters, road vehicles such as bulldozers, trucks, airplanes, helicopters, and trains. Any of the vehicles may be rigged in any way. A car, for example, can be made to appear to have sustained a crash, it can hop or roll over, or do anything that the boards call for—even taking wing and flying. Early Hertz commercials featured the slogan: "Let Hertz put you in the driver's seat." The idea was illustrated by having the driver fly into a car while the car was traveling down the road. The flying driver was matted in, but the car had been specially rigged to give it the appearance of driving without a driver.

Drivers are used in the on camera mode, most notably driving for automobile commercials. The drivers who do this are professional drivers and observe rigorous safety precautions and rehearse carefully. They are usually in contact with one another at all times to be able to communicate any variances and to count off the execution of a particular movement. Often they are under the supervision of a lead driver.

Off Camera
Drivers are used in the off camera mode to ferry people and equipment. They take cast, crew, and some equipment to and from locations. Specialty drivers may also drive large-scale camera rigs. They have to know the operation of the camera vehicle they are driving and be masters in the vehicle's use. Large crane trucks, for example, need to carry the camera and crew gently and smoothly. These drivers also are knowledgeable with regard to the various mounts that are available for their vehicle and how to operate the vehicle with a wide variety of configurations.

Apart from moving stock, location shoots require a number of other vehicles and personnel to maintain them. Some of the vehicles and drivers are:

Camera and sound: To house the necessary gear for camera and sound services. This may be as small as a panel van or as large as a 10-ton truck with air compressors and a built-in darkroom.

Gas and oil: To refuel vehicles if spots are to be shot at a distant location. Car commercials shot at desert locations, for example, may find it cheaper to have refueling facilities handy rather than to have to tool down to the nearest gas station.

Generator: To supply major amounts of power for lights and electronic gear.

Grip/electric: To house the necessary lighting gear and sometimes light generators for lights and electricity on remotes.

Honey-wagons: To house dressing rooms and bathrooms on location. These facilities are housed in vehicles called "honey-wagons," which can be a bus, a van, or a trailer. As the size of the production increases, the number of vehicles required as honey-wagons goes up. Where "star" talent is involved, the honey wagon can become quite elaborate.

Props/makeup/costumes: To drive members of the props, makeup, and costume departments, and their equipment. These areas may be served by one vehicle and driver or may each have its own vehicle and driver, depending on the complexity of the production.

Water: To sprinkle water on streets and roads. This changes the color of the street or road from gray or tan to black, and changes the f stops at which the camera shoots. The cost of the truck and driver is offset by the gain in grip equipment that's not needed and the look of the shot.

Security

Almost all sets and locations require security to prevent pilferage, to secure the site from unwanted visitors, and to keep a record of the comings and goings of staff, clients, cast, and crew. In larger cities police notification is mandatory, and a police officer or a contingent of officers are assigned to the production. The production company pays for this service. It is unwise to try to avoid this since productions without the proper permits and security are simply shut down.

Where fire or the potential for fire is a part of the commercial, a fire warden, usually a fireman, is required for the production. In some cities a first-aid or medical standby person is required.

Stunt Work

A stunt coordinator or stunt person is needed when any major stunt is required, such as a car chase, work with fire, or leaps from building. Prudence and insurance concerns mandate the use of stunt performers for stunts as seemingly simple as a scene in which an actor or actress falls off a ladder while hanging curtains in a living room. Sometimes a specific known performer is hired for a particular stunt. Otherwise a stunt coordinator may be engaged to review the boards and makes recommendations for effecting the stunt. The stunt coordinator is knowledgeable about cameras and angles and will make recommendations regarding the shooting. Stunt coordinators either perform a stunt themselves or make recommendations for a particular stunt person to perform the actual stunt. Usually stunt performers are paid at the same rate as an actor, but with an added fee based on the difficulty and danger of the stunt and the number of times they must repeat it.

Teachers

In New York and Los Angeles, productions that use children must adhere to very strict rules regarding the use of children in film and television. The number of hours that children may be made available for shooting is strictly enforced with a sliding scale for younger children. A teacher is required on the set and the level of certification of the teachers is governed by a strict set of rules. In New York permits are required from the Society of Prevention of Cruelty to Children (SPCC) and the Mayor's office. In Los Angeles the California State Department of Industrial Relations division of Labor Enforcement has jurisdiction over child labor.

10 Useful Forms and Reference Material

This chapter is essentially composed of lists of people, organizations, Internet sites, and other information relevant to making commercials. Browse the headings and see if it has the list, site, or direction for which you were looking, or that arouses your interest.

You might also explore the notion of exploring the material available on the Internet. Go to Google, or a similar search engine. Type in the word "Advertising" and get sent to a list of more than 60 million sites. Those appearing first are enormously useful. *AdAge* will probably be one of the first. It's the advertising world's most widely read trade paper. If you want to know what's happening now and what the dreams of those in the industry really are, this is the site and magazine to read.

The site for the American Association of Advertising Agencies is *www.aaaa.org*. This organization is, as its name implies, the major association for advertising agencies. 4A agencies are major advertising agencies, so while you won't find most small agencies or many middle-sized agencies, there's a wealth of material both on the site and on the numerous links. Pick a city that interests you, look up the 4A agencies listed in that city, and link to an Internet site for one of them. You're likely to get a glimpse of their reel, a feel for the kind of image the agency wants to project, and a brief description of how they work. Many of these useful sites change names or addresses frequently; therefore, this list is subject to change.

Guilds, Unions, Associations, and Internet Sites

AAAA—American Association of Advertising Agencies—*www.aaaa.org*

AAF—American Advertising Federation—*www.aaf.org*

AdAge—A trade magazine—*www.adage.com*

ADG—Art Directors Guild—*www.artdirectors.org*

Adweek—A trade magazine—*www.adweek.com*

Advertiser and Agency Redbooks Online—*www.redbooks.com*

AFM—American Federation of Musicians—*www.afm.org*

AICE—Association of Creative Editors—*www.aice.org*

AICP—Association of Commercial Producers—*www.aicp.com*

AFTRA—The American Federation of Television & Radio Artists—*www.aftra.org*

AMPAS—The Academy of Motion Picture Arts & Sciences—*www.oscar.org*

AMPTP—The Alliance of Motion Picture and Television Producers—*www.amptp.org*

ANA—Association of National Advertisers—*www.ana.net*

ARF—American Research Foundation—*www.arfsite.org*

ATAS—The Academy of Television Arts & Sciences—*www.emmys.org*

ACVL—Association of Cinema and Video Labs—*www.acvl.org*

CAB—Cable Television Advertising Bureau—*www.onetvworld.org*

Clio Awards—*www.clioawards.com*

DGA—Directors Guild of America—*www.dga.org*

FCC—Federal Communications Commission—*www.fcc.gov/cgb*

IAA—International Advertising Association—*www.iaaglobal.org*

IATAS—International Television Academy of Arts & Sciences—*www.iemmys.tv*

MRA—Market Research Association—*www.mra-net.org*

MVPA—Music Video Production Association—*www.mvpa.com*

NATAS—National Academy of Television Arts & Sciences—*www.emmyonline.org*

NATPE—National Association of Television Program Executives—*www.natpe.org*

NCTA—National Cable Television Association—*www.ncta.com*

Nielsen Media Research—*www.nielsenmedia.com*

PERA—Production Equipment Rental Association—*www.pera.ws/index.lasso*

PGA—Producers Guild of America—*www.producersguild.org*

SAG—Screen Actors Guild—*www.sag.org*

SMPTE—Society of Motion Picture & Television Engineers—*www.smpte.org*

TVB—TV Bureau of Advertising—*www.tvb.org*

The American Association of Advertising Agencies (*www.aaaa.org*) site lists many of these and additional sites of interest.

Entertainet Cyberspace Directory (*www.entertainet.com*) located in Dallas, Texas, is another site that lists a number of entertainment sites of local and national interest. The following address at their site lists entertainment-related organizations: *http://www.entertainet.com/orgs_uns/dfwactor/unions.htm*

For a perspective on the history of advertising in America from 1850 to 1920, visit Duke University's Hartman Center site: *http://scriptorium.lib.duke.edu/eaa*

For a similar perspective on editing, visit: *www.sssm.com/editing/museum*

A broadcast history timeline can be found at: *www.tvhandbook.com/History/History_timeline.htm*

The Canadian Broadcasting Company's (CBC) archive of editing formats is both relevant and concise and can be found at: *http://archives.cbc.ca/info/281g_en41.shtml*

The advertising department at The University of Texas at Austin has a wonderful site, including an area with quotes from numerous sources regarding various areas of advertising and commercials. The quotes can be found at: *http://advertising.utexas.edu/research/quotes*

Two good sites for reviewing current commercial work and for critical reviews are:
adcritic.com
boardsmag.com

Below the Line

The following list includes the majority of positions filled by The International Alliance of Theatrical Stage Employees (IATSE) union crew members in the film and commercial film industry on the West Coast. It does not include jobs covered by the National Association of Broadcast Employees & Technicians (NABET) or the International Brotherhood of Electrical Workers (IBEW) or guilds such as the Directors Guild of America (DGA) or any of the talent unions. Although the following is a very extensive list, similar local unions representing some portion of below-the-line crew members may be found nationwide. Some crew positions are covered by two or three unions. For example, in both Los Angeles and New York, tape and live video camera operators may be working under either a NABET or an IBEW contract, depending on which union has jurisdiction at a particular facility. Most of the very busy freelance camera operators belong to both unions. I include the list here to give the reader an indication of the diversity of positions involved in the making of any film project. Clearly, not every commercial has someone from every category working on the project; however, there *are* a great number of specialists involved in the making of a commercial.

IATSE Local #33 Theatrical and TV Stage Employees

1. Master property persons
2. Property persons
3. Lamp operators
4. Front light operator
5. Dimmer board operator
6. Bridgelight operator
7. Master carpenter
8. Grips
9. Forklift operators
10. Flyman
11. Crane operators

12. Master sound persons
13. Sound console operators
14. Floor sound (wireless)
15. Tape deck operator
16. Chemical effects operators
17. Pyrotechnics
18. Stage managers
19. Visual console
20. Performance operating crew
21. Turntable and winch operators
22. Truck loaders or unloaders

Basic Craft #40 International Brotherhood of Electrical Workers

23. Electrical foreman
24. Air conditioning foreman
25. Sound installation foreman
26. Electrical gang boss
27. Air conditioning gang boss
28. Cable splicer
29. Electronic technician
30. Journeyman wireman
31. Air conditioning engineer
32. Production van driver/operator
33. Apprentice wireman
34. Sound installation/maintenance
35. Sound gang boss
36. Construction gang boss

IATSE Local #44 Affiliated Property Crafts Persons

37. Prop maker foreman
38. Prop maker gang boss
39. Prop maker journeyman
40. Special effects foreman
41. Special effects gang boss
42. Special effects journeyman

43. Licensed powder man
44. Assistant licensed powder man
45. Foreperson-greensman, draper, property
46. Property sewing, upholsterer
47. Draper foreman
48. Upholsterer gang boss
49. 3rd prop
50. Upholsterer
51. Draper
52. Property sewer foreperson
53. Property swing person
54. Property foreperson
55. Property master
56. Asst. property master—daily
57. Property gang boss/leadman-greensman
58. Draper upholsterer gang boos
59. Property person-property swing person
60. Draper, upholsterer, greensperson, prop
61. Sew, set construction
62. Construction coordinator

Basic Craft #78 Plumbers & Pipefitters

63. Plumber foreman
64. Assistant foreman
65. Journeyman plumber
66. Hyphenate driver/craftsperson

IATSE Local #80 Motion Picture Studio Grips

67. Key grip
68. Grip foreman—daily
69. Grip foreman
70. Grip sub foreman
71. Head camera crane operator
72. Camera crane electric control operator
73. Dolly grip (crab dolly operator)

74. Blue goose operator
75. Grip gang boss
76. Grip
77. Key grip
78. Best boy grip (2nd company grip)
79. Grip trainee (canvas room grip)
80. Crafts service foreperson
81. Crafts service gang boss
82. Crafts service person
83. Sand blaster
84. Roofer
85. Tar pot person
86. Pneumatic tool operator
87. Tool room keeper

Basic Crafts #399 Teamsters Transportation Drivers

88. Transportation coordinators
89. 1st on production driver gang boss
90. All other gang bosses (except 3551 & 3581)
91. Drivers: auto (station wagon, minivan, motorcycle)
92. Drivers: class c (pick-up, 5 ton, lot tractor)
93. Drivers: class a (trailers 600 lb., cranes, bulldozer)
94. Camera car driver
95. Production van driver-operator
96. Chapman crane operator
97. Auto service person
98. Auto service person—thru 1991 agreement
99. Dispatcher
100. Ramrod
101. Wrangler gang boss
102. Driver/wrangler
103. Wrangler (pick-up)
104. Trainer (domestic animals)
105. Trainer (stable)
106. Wild animal trainers
107. Wild animal handlers

108. Auto gang boss
109. Auto mechanic
110. Dog trainer
111. Dog handler
112. Location managers
113. Director of photography
114. Camera operator
115. Portrait photographer
116. Still photographer
117. 1st assistant photographer
118. 2nd assistant photographer
119. Videotape operator
120. Film loader
121. Kodak Panavision prev. Sys oper
122. Publicist

IATSE Local # 683 Film Technicians of Motion Picture Industry

123. Laboratory contact—lab employee
124. Negative timer & developer or machine foreman
125. Hazeltine timer
126. Neg cutting foreman—lab employee
127. Sensitometry
128. Chemical foreman
129. Positive developer or machine foreman
130. Printer foreman
131. Positive daily assembly foreman
132. Release assembly foreman
133. Vault foreman
134. Stripping foreman
135. Film shipping foreman
136. Customer service employee
137. Analytical chemist
138. Scanner operator
139. Shift boss negative developer or machine operator
140. Shift boss sensitometry
141. Shift boss chemical

142. Shift boss positive developer or machine operator
143. Shift boss printer
144. Shift boss negative assembly
145. Shift boss positive daily assembly
146. Shift boss release assembly
147. Shift boss film shipping
148. Shift boss vault
149. Shift boss color control
150. Operator negative developing machine
151. Special effects printer
152. Operator pre-develop negative breakdown
153. Hazel and/or timer trainee (90 days)
154. Operator new generation printer
155. Fade maker
156. Densitometrist
157. Shop expediter
158. Operator cinext tester
159. Color conformer
160. Daily, release and/or dupe printer
161. Magnetic sound striper
162. Operator magnetic sound striper
163. Matte cutter
164. Operator negative assembly
165. Operator process, negative polisher & cleaner
166. Operator color control
167. Negative process machine (hardening & coating)
168. Vault clerk
169. Operator C positive develop machine
170. Operator C positive assembler and/or slitter
171. Operator C tape puncher
172. Operator C release inspector
173. Operator C reprint and/or replacement clerk
174. Operator D positive developing machine
175. Operator D positive waxer
176. Operator E positive make-up for developing machine
177. Operator E positive release splicer

178. Operator E rewinder
179. Operator E assistant film shipping clerk
180. Operator E film machine clean-up
181. Negative cutter
182. Operator E negative rewinder
183. Still department foreman
184. Still department shift boss
185. Special effects assembly/splicing
186. Still department projection & contact point
187. Still department developer
188. Still department chemical mixer
189. Still department retoucher
190. Still department photostat
191. Still department copy
192. Still department other technicians
193. Still department helper
194. Special effects learner

IATSE Local #595 International Sound/Cine-Technicians

195. Production mixer—1 daily (mixer production journeyman)
196. Engineer (supervising engineer journeyman)
197. Operative supervisor/engineer (journeyman)
198. Maintenance technician (technician test engineer journeyman)
199. Gang boss (journeyman)
200. Service recorder (service recorder tv engineer journeyman)
201. Null (location engineer journeyman)
202. Sound technician (utility sound technician journeyman)
203. Microphone boom operator (journeyman)
204. Recording machine operator (journeyman)
205. Production mixer Y-1 (mixer production entry)
206. Supervising engineer (4113) (supervising engineer entry)
207. Operative supervisor/engineer (operator supervising and/or engineer entry)
208. Boom operator (entry)
209. Dubbing machine operator (entry)
210. Sound service person I
211. Sound service person II

212. Dubbing machine operator (journeyman)
213. Audio assistant (sound department trainee)
214. Sound service person II

IATSE Local #700 Motion Picture Editors

215. Music mixer
216. Supervising engineer
217. Sound engineer
218. Service recorder
219. Utility sound technician
220. Microphone boom operator
221. Recording machine operator
222. Sound service person
223. Re-recording mixer
224. Supervising re-recording mixer
225. Supervising engineer
226. Sound engineer
227. Service recorder
228. Utility sound technician
229. Recording machine operator
230. Sound department trainee
231. Editor
232. Serial editor
233. Montage editor
234. Sports editor
235. Trailer editor
236. Engineer
237. Supervising sound editor
238. Head music film editor Z-4a
239. Record machine operator
240. Sound effects editor 1st 6 mos.
241. Sound effects editor 2nd 6 mos.
242. Sound effects editor—thereafter
243. Music film editor 1st 6 mos.
244. Music film editor 2nd 6 mos.
245. Music film editor—thereafter (Z-9)

246. Music editor (Z-3)
247. Assistant editor 1st 6 mos.
248. Assistant editor 2nd 6 mos.
249. Assistant editor
250. Chief projectionist (supervising)
251. Projectionist gang boss (working)
252. Projectionist gang boss (supervising/working)
253. 3rd editor
254. First engineer
255. First process projectionist
256. Scoring projectionist
257. Projectionist
258. Process projectionist
259. Projection engineer
260. Trainee projectionist
261. Process librarian daily
262. Head librarian Z-6
263. Supervising librarian
264. Librarian 1st 6 mos.
265. Librarian 2nd 6 mos.
266. Librarian thereafter

IATSE Local #700 Motion Picture Editors Guild

267. Trailer supervisor 1st 12 mos.
268. Trailer supervisor 13 to 24 mos.
269. Trailer supervisor 25 to 36 mos.
270. Trailer supervisor 48 mos.
271. Jr. trailer supervisor 1st 6 mos.
272. Jr. trailer supervisor 7 to 12 mos.
273. Jr. trailer supervisor 13 to 18 mos.
274. Jr. trailer supervisor 19 to 24 mos.
275. Jr. trailer supervisor 25 to 30 mos.
276. Story analyst first 6 mos.
277. Story analyst 7 to 18 mos.
278. Story analyst 19 to 24 mos.
279. Story analyst 25 to 42 mos.

280. Story analyst 43 to 54 mos.

281. Story analyst over 55 mos.

IATSE Local #705 Motion Picture Costumers

282. Costume supervisor

283. Key costumer

284. Costume supervisor

285. Costumer

286. Wardrobe assistant

287. Checkers

288. Manufacturing foreperson

289. Pattern maker & fitter

290. Head beader

291. Women's garment tailor

292. Milliner

293. Table person

294. Figure maker

295. Head dyer

296. Alteration fitter

297. Draper

298. Shirtmaker

299. Dyer

300. Beader

301. Special operator

302. Millinery maker

303. Stock clerk

304. Cleaner

305. Finisher

306. Workroom apprentice

307. Men's tailor cutter

308. Men's supervising tailor

309. Special costume keyperson

310. Tailor fitter

311. Coat, vest & pant maker

312. Alteration tailor

313. Special costume manufacturer

314. Tailor's helper
315. Wardrobe specialty manufacturer

IATSE Local #706 Make-Up Artists & Hair Stylists

316. Make-up/hair dept. head
317. Make-up/hair assistant dept. head
318. Foreman
319. Make-up artist/technician
320. Make-up artist
321. Make-up artist trainee
322. Head body make-up person
323. 2nd make-up
324. Key hair stylist
325. Assistant hair stylist
326. Hair stylist
327. Hair stylist trainee
328. Wigmaker class II
329. Wigmaker class I

Basic Crafts Local #724 Studio Utility Employees

330. Laborer foreman—daily
331. Laborer gang boss
332. Gardner gang boss
333. Laborer
334. Entry level employee
335. Pot washer (paint)
336. Concrete tender
337. Plaster tender (hod carrier)
338. Sand blaster
339. Roofer
340. Tar pot man
341. Pneumatic tool operator
342. Horticulturist
343. Gardener

344. Toolroom keeper
345. Nulhyphenate driver/laborer

IATSE Local #728 Studio Electric Lighting Techs.

346. Lamp operator
347. General foreman
348. Chief lighting technician
349. Best boy electric
350. Sub foreman
351. Chief rigging electrical
352. Running repair technician
353. Special operator
354. Gang boss
355. Electric lighting technician
356. Rigger gaffer
357. Entry level electrical (technician)

IATSE Local #729 Motion Picture Set Painters

358. Head paint foreman
359. Production paint foreman
360. Decorator gang boss & decorators
361. Color mixer
362. Paperhanger gang boss & paperhangers
363. Maintenance painter gang boss
364. Painter
365. Paint shop helper & entry level painter & apprentice painter
366. Apprentice sign writer 1 to 6 mos.
367. Supervising sign writer
368. Journeyman sign writer & sign writer (entry)
369. 3rd painter/production painter

Basic Crafts Local #755 Sculpturers and Plasterers

370. Plasterer foreman
371. Modeler gang boss
372. Artist

373. Sculptor
374. Modeler
375. Plasterer gang boss
376. Model maker gang boss & model makers
377. Plasterer
378. Caster
379. Mouldmaker
380. Cement finisher
381. Improver
382. Helper & apprentice
383. Standby or keyman: hyphenate driver/plasterer

IATSE Local #767 Motion Picture Studio First Aid

384. First air/medic
385. Registered nurses
386. Nurses/first aid

IATSE Local #790 Illustrators & Matte Artists

387. Matte artist
388. 1st & 2nd assistant matte artist
389. Apprentice matte artist
390. Production illustrator
391. Senior illustrator
392. Junior illustrator
393. Apprentice illustrator

IATSE Local #816 Scenic, Title & Graphic Artists

394. Head scenic artist
395. Lead scenic artist
396. Scenic artist
397. Scenic artist assistant
398. Student scenic artist
399. Title artist—daily
400. Lead title artist
401. Title artist technician

402. Title artist trainee
403. Student artist trainee
404. Scenic artist shop person

IATSE Local #839 Motion Picture Screen Cartoonists

405. Animator-journeyman
406. Layout-journeyman & apprentice layout
407. Assistant animator
408. Color modelist—journeyman (21-5000)
409. Technical director 1st 6 mos.
410. Technical director

IATSE Local #847 Set Designers & Model Makers

411. Senior set designer—daily
412. Senior set designer—weekly
413. Junior set designer 'A'—daily
414. Apprentice set designer
415. Senior set model builder
416. Leadman set model builder
417. Assistant set model builder
418. Apprentice set model builder—daily

IATSE Local #871 Script Supervisors (Art Department Co-ord. & Accounting)

419. MOW teleprompter operator
420. Production accountant
421. Assistant production office coordinator
422. Production accountant
423. Assistant production accountant
424. Production office coordinator
425. Assistant production office coordinator
426. Art department coordinator
427. Script supervisor—1st year daily & 2nd year
428. Script supervisor
429. Teleprompter

IASTE Local #876 Art Directors Guild

430. Art director
431. Art director 2nd 6 mos. (on call)
432. Key art director
433. Assistant art director
434. Visual consultant
435. Art director-in-charge of draft room

IATSE Local #892 Costume Designers Guild

436. Costume designer
437. Assistant costume designer
438. Senior costume sketch artist

IATSE Local #884 Teachers

439. Teacher/welfare worker

Sources

These are yearly directories that update film commissions; studios and stages; and equipment, prop, lighting, and costume sources as well as listings of personnel for most production jobs. They also list associations, guilds, and unions and serve as a "Yellow Pages" for the motion picture, television, and commercial production industry.

- *Creative Industry Handbook—www.creativehandbook.com*
- *Debbies Book—www.debbiesbook.com*
- *Hollywood 911—www.hollywood-911.com*
- *Hollywood Creative Directory—www.hcdonline.com*
  Includes: *Hollywood Creative Directory, Representation Directory, Distributors Directory, Music Directory,* and the *Blu-Book Production Directory*
- *Motion Picture TV and Theatre Directory—www.mpe.net*
- *Producers Masterguide—www.producers.masterguide.com*

Most state film commissions publish listings that are helpful for location shooting. They can usually be found online or by calling the particular State Film Commission. They are also listed in the *Producers Masterguide.*

Sample Bid Documents

Figure 10.1 shows a bid form that is based on the standard form used by the Association of Independent Commercial Producers (AICP). This one was used by The Film Syndicate, in Los Angeles.

Currently the AICP demands that the Addendum A to the Standard Commercial Production Agreement (Figure 10.2) be attached.

The AICP also offers the Location Permit Checklist (Figure 10.3), which can be found online at their site, *www.aicp.com*.

Figure 10.4 shows the standard bid forms from the Association of Independent Creative Editors (AICE). The form indicates that it's from the Association of Independent Commercial Editors, which was its original name. (©2003 Association of Independent Creative Editors, Inc.)

Sample Research Questions

Figure 10.5 shows a partial set of answers to research questions posed by The Men's Wearhouse regarding its advertising campaigns.

Job Hunting

Students and recent graduates have a different task when it comes to job hunting than those who have been in, or are still in, "the business." Networking is the best way to get a job or switch jobs. However, networking usually means that you've been around long enough to have someone with whom to network. Other than that, letter writing, employment agencies, the Internet, and the newspaper are probably the best, if not the only, way to look. This book does not presume to offer advice to the people who have already entered the industry and who have personal contacts. This advice is designed for those just getting started.

There's a quote that is attributed to Eric Von Stroheim: "The most important part of directing is having a job." The same is true for television commercials. Getting the job is the most important part of working on commercials. Being in a position to keep the job, or if you choose, to leave it, is second most important.

The best advice I ever heard on the subject came from a young director of the Channel 5 Evening News in Los Angeles. She was asked about how she got her job. She said she started as an intern and then said, "Be better than average. Come early. Leave late." One had to notice that she was also creative, intelligent, sensitive, and obviously persistent; she later mentioned that good time management skills were important.

For students the most advantageous way to get a foot in the door at an agency or at a company that produces commercials is to get an internship. The agency or production company gets a college student to work at no cost. The student may prove to be valuable, and in any event can be let go easily if he or she is counterproductive. Liability risks for the agency or production company are lessened, or nonexistent. The student gets college credit and a great deal of knowledge of how that organization works. At the very least, professional networking opportunities abound. Along the way the student gets to know where the organization's copier is, where Joe the producer hides out, where Joan the writer hangs out, who all the people at the agency are, and a great deal about how the agency works. When someone needs to be hired, the intern may be a comfortable choice because he or she is a known quantity and has had the good fortune to have been at the right place at the right time.

To look for an internship, make a list of agencies in your area. You might start with the AAAA—American Association of Advertising Agencies, *www.aaaa.org*, or contact your local advertising club or find advertising agencies in the Yellow Pages. Call and explain that you want to intern at their company. Find out to whom you should apply. Write a concise cover letter and enclose a résumé, including work experience of any type. No one expects a college student to have an extensive, high-profile job history.

For help with résumé writing, go to Google on the Internet and type in the word "resume." You will find 20 million sites that deal with résumés. The top few offer free templates. You also might want to read *What Color Is Your Parachute* (by Dick Bolles, published by Ten Speed Press), which is all about job hunting. Proofread and spell check everything. Most faculty members will be pleased to review your résumé and cover letter.

Following is one suggested letter, which should have your name, address, and phone number on it.

Dear _____:
I am a student at _____ and wish to get an internship at (___ Agency). I am particularly interested in working in television production and have been taking as many classes as I can in related areas. I'd be glad to work in any area of your organization, as I recognize how important it would be for me to have a complete understanding of the advertising business.

I have enclosed a résumé and will call you in the next few days. I hope I can meet with you and discuss working at your agency or that you would take the time to offer some suggestions that might help me find a position as an intern at an advertising agency or commercial production company.

Sincerely yours,
Your Name

Finding a job is often a numbers game. The more contacts you make, the better your chances for success. Send out five letters a day and keep track of the letters you've sent out. Five days after you've sent a letter, call. Arrange an interview if possible. Expect rejections, and simply move on to the next name on the list. If after a month of this, which is 80 letters later, you haven't landed a job, start all over again, explaining that you've contacted a number of people and are still interested in a position. With hopes that the situation may have changed at the agency, you are again enquiring about working as an intern. Once you get an interview, try to find out about the agency's or production company's work. It's wise to be able to refer to what they're doing. At the very least you will be someone who has taken the time to do some research and who has some knowledge in the field.

There are no guarantees that this will work, though it has for a number of students of mine. If you're ready to get a job and *haven't interned*, you need to create a résumé and you can use a somewhat similar letter. If possible, include a statement that distinguishes some work you have done.

Dear _____:
I recently graduated from _____ and would like to work at (___ Agency, Production Company). I am particularly interested in working in television production and (majored in advertising) (took a number of classes in television production, and advertising) (took as many classes as I could in related areas). I'd be glad to work in any area of your organization, as I recognize how important it would be for me to have a complete understanding of the advertising business.

I have enclosed a résumé and will call you in the next few days. I hope I can meet with you and discuss working at your agency or that you would take the time to offer some suggestions that might help me find a position in advertising, or with a commercial television production company.

Sincerely yours,
Your Name

ASSOCIATION OF INDEPENDENT COMMERCIAL PRODUCERS
FILM PRODUCTION COST SUMMARY

Bid Date:

Production Co.:		Agency:
Address:		
		Client:
Telephone:		Product:
Fax:		Producer:
Job #:		Telephone:
Contact:		FAX:
Director:		
Producer:		
DP:		
Production Designer:		
Editor:		
Pre-Production Days: 9		Bid Name:
Build & Strike Days: 3	Hours: 10	Commercial Title	Code	Length
Pre-light Days: 2	Hours: 10			
Studio Shoot Days: 2	Hours: 13		5	:15
Location Days: 1	Hours:			
Location(s):				

SUMMARY OF ESTIMATED PRODUCTION COSTS		ESTIMATED	ACTUAL	VARIANCE
1 Pre-production & Wrap Costs	Totals A & C	58,867	91,317.90	32,450.00
2 Shooting Labor	Total B	81,183	96,267.68	15,084.68
3 Location & Travel Expenses	Total D	10,580	18,562.97	7,982.97
4 Props, Wardrobe & Animals	Total E	16,350	20,567.38	4,217.38
5 Studio & Set Construction Costs	Totals F, G, & H	173,639	227,812.83	54,173.83
6 Equipment Costs	Total I	46,050	51,524.38	5,474.38
7 Filmstock, Process & Print	Total J	26,880	17,225.88	(9,654.12)
8 Miscellaneous	Total K	700	1,815.07	1,115.07
9 Sub-total	A to K	414,249	525,094.09	110,845.09
10 Director / Creative Fees (not included in Direct Costs)	Total L	33,900		(33,900.00)
11 Insurance		8,285		(8,285.00)
12 Sub-total Direct Costs		422,534	525,094.09	102,560.09
13 Production Fee		103,560	103,560.00	
14 Talent Labor & Expenses	Totals M & N			
15 Editorial & Finishing	Totals O & P			
16 Editorial Fee				
17 Other				
18 Other				
19 Additional Billings	Overages	218,251		(218,251.00)

Contracted Total [ ]

Contingency Day [ ]

GRAND TOTAL	**$778,245**	**$628,654.09**	(149,590.91)

COMMENTS
This budget does include casting and wardrobe but no talent costs or related expenses. This budget is based upon to date information. Any changes in the project or schedule could alter the estimate.

Figure 10.1 Bid form based on the standard form used by the Association of Independent Commercial Producers (AICP). This one was used by The Film Syndicate, in Los Angeles.

A	PRE-PRO & WRAP CREW	Days	Rate	OT Hours 1.5	2.0	ESTIMATED	% PT/P&W	OT Based	ACTUAL
1	Producer	13	900			11,700	22.0	12	16,050.00
2	Assistant Director	2	800			1,600	22.0	12	1,700.00
3	Director of Photography	2	1500			3,000	22.0	12	7,500.00
4	Camera Operator						22.0	12	
5	Assistant Camera	1	500			500	22.0	12	500.00
6	Loader						22.0	12	
7	Art Director						22.0	12	
8	Prop Master	3	550			1,650	22.0	10	550.00
9	Prop Assistant	1	450			450	22.0	10	
10	Executive Producer						22.0	12	6,500.00
11	Gaffer	2	550			1,100	22.0	12	500.00
12	Best Boy Electrician	2	500			1,000	22.0	12	475.00
13	Electrian	2	475			950	22.0	12	900.00
14	Electrian						22.0	12	925.00
15	Electrian						22.0	12	1,350.00
16	Key Grip	2	550			1,100	22.0	12	1,000.00
17	Best Boy Grip	2	500			1,000	22.0	12	950.00
18	Dolly Grip	2	475			950	22.0	12	950.00
19	4th Grip	2	425			850	22.0	12	2,250.00
20	Mixer						22.0	12	
21	Boom						22.0	12	
22	Recordist						22.0	12	
23	Playback						22.0	12	
24	Makeup Artist						22.0	12	
25	Hair Stylist						22.0	12	
26	Costume Design	5	650			3,250	22.0	12	3,250.00
27	Wardobe Attendant	3	350			1,050	22.0	12	1,400.00
28	Script Supervisor						22.0	12	
29	Home Economist						22.0	12	
30	Asst. Home Economist						22.0	12	
31	VTR Operator						22.0	12	
32	Wrap Personel						22.0	12	1,015.00
33	Storyboard Artist	1	1000			1,000	22.0	12	2,826.06
34	Teleprompter Operator						22.0	12	
35	Generator Operator						22.0	12	
36	Still Photographer						22.0	12	
37	Location Scout						22.0	12	
38	Production Assistants	12	175			2,100	22.0	12	2,350.00
39	2nd AD						22.0	12	
40	Location Coordinator						22.0	12	
41	Crafts Service	1	200			200	22.0	12	225.00
42	Fireman						22.0	12	
43	Police						22.0	12	
44	Welfare Worker						22.0	12	
45	Teamster						22.0	12	
46	Production Manager	12	500			6,000	22.0	12	8,000.00
47	Production Coordinator	10	300			3,000	22.0	12	3,900.00
48	Utility PA	2	175			350	22.0	12	525.00
49								12	
50							22.0	12	
	Sub-total A					42,800			65,591.06
	PT/P&W					9,417			15,386.40
	TOTAL A					**52,217**			**80,977.46**

Figure 10.1 *Continued*

B	SHOOTING CREW	Days	Rate	OT Hours 1.5	2.0	ESTIMATED	% PT/P&W	OT Based	ACTUAL
51	Producer	3	900			2,700	23.0	12	2,700.00
52	Assistant Director	3	900	6		3,510	23.0	12	2,700.00
53	Director of Photography	3	2000	6		7,800	23.0	12	7,500.00
54	Camera Operator	3	900	9		3,915	23.0	12	2,103.57
55	Assistant Camera	3	550	9		2,393	23.0	12	1,642.86
56	Loader	3	400	9		1,740	23.0	12	1,314.29
57	Art Director						23.0	12	
58	Prop Master	3	550	9		2,393	23.0	10	2,018.18
59	Prop Assistant	3	450	9		1,958	23.0	10	
60	Steadicam Operator						23.0	12	1,850.00
61	Gaffer	3	550	9		2,393	23.0	12	1,642.86
62	Best Boy Electrician	3	500	9		2,175	23.0	12	1,560.71
63	Electrician	3	475	9		2,066	23.0	12	1,478.57
64	Electrician	3	450	9		1,958	23.0	12	1,478.57
65	Electrician						23.0	12	1,478.57
66	Key Grip	3	550	9		2,393	23.0	12	1,607.14
67	Best Boy Grip	3	500	9		2,175	23.0	12	1,560.71
68	Dolly Grip	3	450	9		1,958	23.0	12	1,526.79
69	Company Grips	3	425	9		1,849	23.0	12	2,796.43
70	Mixer	3	550	3		1,898	23.0	12	1,500.00
71	Boom	3	425	3		1,466	23.0	12	1,459.61
72	Recordist						23.0	12	
73	Playback						23.0	12	
74	Makeup Artist/Hair	3	650	3		2,243	23.0	12	6,553.58
75	Make up Assistant	3	450			1,350	23.0	12	800.00
76	Costume Design	3	650	3		2,243	23.0	12	2,659.09
77	Wardobe Attendant	6	350			2,100	23.0	12	2,270.00
78	Script Supervisor	3	500	3		1,725	23.0	12	1,571.43
79	Home Economist						23.0	12	
80	Asst. Home Economist						23.0	12	
81	VTR Operator	3	500	3		1,725	23.0	12	1,642.86
82	Meal Penalties						23.0	12	1,479.53
83	Storyboard Artist						23.0	12	
84	Teleprompter Operator						23.0	12	
85	Generator Operator						23.0	12	
86	Still Photographer						23.0	12	500.00
87	Location Scout						23.0	12	
88	Production Assistants	9	175			1,575	23.0	12	1,750.00
89	2nd AD	3	450	3		1,553	23.0	12	1,800.00
90	Location Coordinator						23.0	12	
91	Crafts Service	3	225	3		776	23.0	12	867.86
92	Fireman						23.0	12	
93	Catering Labor						23.0	12	1,706.56
94	Production Associates						23.0	12	6,750.00
95	Teamster						23.0	12	1,380.76
96	Production Manager	3	500			1,500	23.0	12	1,500.00
97	Production Coordinator	3	300			900	23.0	12	900.00
98	Utility PA	3	175			525	23.0	12	1,050.00
99	Runners	6	175			1,050	23.0	12	875.00
100	Barber for						23.0	12	1,950.00
		105		Sub-total B		66,005			77,925.53
				PT/P&W		15,178			18,342.15
				TOTAL B		81,183			96,267.68

Figure 10.1 *Continued*

C	PRE-PRODUCTION & WRAP EXPENSES	Amount	Rate	x	ESTIMATED	ACTUAL
101	Auto Rentals					
102	Air Fares					
103	Per Diems					
104	Still Camera Rental & Film					261.27
105	Messengers	1	150		150	436.56
106	Trucking					
107	Deliveries and Taxis					140.80
108	Home Economist Supplies					
109	Telephone and Cable	1	150		150	
110	Casting Director Call/Prep 1, Casting 2, Callbacks 1	1	2400		2,400	4,500.00
111	Casting Facilities	1	1650		1,650	1,650.00
112	Working Meals	1	1400		1,400	1,764.80
113	Casting Tape & Polaroid	1	900		900	1,587.01
			TOTAL C		6,650	10,340.44

D	LOCATION & TRAVEL EXPENSES	Amount	Rate	x	ESTIMATED	ACTUAL
114	Location Fees					
115	Permits					
116	Car Rentals					
117	Bus Rentals					75.80
118	Dressing Room Vehicles	1	2250		2,250	1,455.00
119	Parking, Tolls, and Gas Mileage	1	800		800	504.72
120	Trucking Production Truck	1	350		350	498.88
121	Other Vehicles Camera Truck	1	350		350	566.00
122	Makeup Trailer					350.00
123	3 Banger					400.00
124	Production Trailer					335.00
125	WB Catering Labor					1,106.50
126						
127	Gifts					481.85
128	Second Meal					372.10
129	Breakfast	120	9		1,080	
130	Lunch	175	18		3,150	3,833.14
131	Dinner					1,807.05
132	Set Security					208.00
133	Limousines	1	1000		1,000	1,494.00
134	Other Transportation					
135	Kit Rentals	1	400		400	3,410.00
136	WB Tables & Chairs					
137	Ice for Catering					
138	Craft Services	3	400		1,200	1,664.93
139	Propane for Catering					
			TOTAL D		10,580	18,562.97

E	PROPS, WARDROBE & ANIMALS	Amount	Rate	x	ESTIMATED	ACTUAL
140	Prop Rentals	1	1500		1,500	1,790.74
141	Prop Purchases	1	1250		1,250	1,986.78
142	Wardrobe Rentals					1,663.48
143	Wardrobe Purchases	1	13000		13,000	11,726.93
144	Picture Vehicles					1,948.00
145	Animals and Handlers					
146	Makeup EFX, Wigs Etc.					109.44
147	Product Color Correction					648.00
148	Kits/Misc	1	600		600	
149	Art Dept - Fuel & Park					380.47
150	Art Dept Still Film & Process					313.54
			TOTAL E		16,350	20,567.38

Figure 10.1 *Continued*

F	STUDIO RENTAL & EXPENSES		Amount	Rate	x	ESTIMATED	ACTUAL
151	Rental For Build Days	Stage 2 & 5	2	1800		3,600	13,000.00
152	Build OT Hours						
153	Rental for Pre-Lite Days	Stage 2&5	2	2000		4,000	3,600.00
154	Pre-Lite OT Hours	Stage Manager					
155	Rental for Shoot Days	Stage 2&5	3	2500		7,500	4,200.00
156	Shoot OT Hours	Stage 2&5	6	250		1,500	
157	WB Security						
158	Strike OT Hours	Stage 2&5	1	1800		1,800	2,600.00
159	Stage Phones						
160	Studio Security		7	200		1,400	525.00
161	Power Charges and Bulbs		60	75		4,500	2,775.00
162	Studio Related		7	175		1,225	1,018.80
163	Editing/Prd Off/Hair/MU/Ward						470.00
164	Hopper at WB						470.00
165	Warner Brothers/ Shoot						6,000.00
166	Power/ Warner Brothers						
167	Power Drop/ BB Elec	$27.46 x 17 phrs + $200 for dr					884.56
					TOTAL F	25,525	35,543.36

G	SET CONSTRUCTION CREW	Days	Rate	OT Hours 1.5	2.0	ESTIMATED	% PT/P&W	OT Based	ACTUAL
168	Production Designer	11	1000			11,000	24.0	10	13,000.00
169	Art Director	15	450	9		7,358	24.0	10	11,485.01
170	Decorator	10	550	9		6,243	24.0	10	6,600.00
171	Asst. Dec/Shoppper	4	350	9		1,873	24.0	10	
172	Leadman	7	450	9		3,758	24.0	10	4,832.95
173	Set Dresser	7	350	9		2,923	24.0	10	
174	Asst. Dressers	21	275	12		6,270	24.0	10	
175	Teamsters/Drivers	4	250			1,000	24.0	10	
176	Strike Labor						24.0	10	
177	PA's	8	175			1,400	24.0	10	2,100.00
178							24.0	10	
179							24.0	10	
180							24.0	10	
		87		Sub-total G		41,825			38,017.96
				PT/P&W		10,039			9,124.30
				TOTAL G		51,864			47,142.26

H	SET CONSTRUCTION MATERIALS		Amount	Rate	x	ESTIMATED	ACTUAL
181	Set Dressing Purchases		1	5200		5,200	1,180.54
182	Set Dressing Rentals		1	12500		12,500	11,705.26
183	Greens		1	1800		1,800	312.72
184	Windows/Floors		1	2000		2,000	
185	Appliances		1	800		800	
186	Backings		1	1900		1,900	
187	Outside Construction		1	66000		66,000	130,000.00
188	Trucking		1	1500		1,500	1,160.00
189	Renderings		1	4000		4,000	
190	Kit Rentals & Copies		1	550		550	304.66
191	Meals						464.03
192	Trash Bin	Trash Bins $45 /d x 7 days = $315/ Raliegh					
					TOTAL H	96,250	145,127.21

Figure 10.1 *Continued*

I	EQUIPMENT COSTS	Amount	Rate	x	ESTIMATED	ACTUAL
193	Camera Rental	1	13500		13,500	8,246.25
194	Sound Rental	1	1500		1,500	1,650.00
195	Lighting Rental	1	18000		18,000	18,703.75
196	Grip Rental	1	4500		4,500	6,298.30
197	Generator Rental					
198	Crane Rental					
199	VTR Rental	1	1750		1,750	1,500.00
200	Walkie Talkie Rental	1	600		600	500.00
201	Dolly Rental	1	900		900	578.06
202	Scissor Lift @ Raliegh $135/day					275.00
203	Camera Expendables					15.13
204	Production Supplies	1	2000		2,000	2,526.96
205	Teleprompter	1	1800		1,800	
206	Lighting & Grip Expendables	1	1500		1,500	2,070.93
207	Steadicam Sled					1,300.00
208	Warner Brothers Grip Truck					3,075.00
209	Warner Brothers Electric Pkg					4,785.00
210	Warner Brothers/ 80ft Condor					
			TOTAL I		46,050	51,524.38

J	FILMSTOCK, PROCESS & PRINT	Amount	Rate	x	ESTIMATED	ACTUAL
211	Purchase Filmstock	24000	0.6		14,400	8,877.84
212	Process Filmstock	24000	0.22		5,280	1,526.87
213	Vid Dailies/Transfer	24000	0.3		7,200	6,821.17
214	Add'l Vid Dailies /Transfer	Green Room Rush				
215	Process Filmstock	Green Room Rush				
216	Post Messenger p/u @ D/O @					
			TOTAL J		26,880	17,225.88

K	MISCELLANEOUS EXPENSES	Amount	Rate	x	ESTIMATED	ACTUAL
217	Petty Cash	1	250		250	
218	Air Shipping and Carriers	1	200		200	600.00
219	Phones and Cables					
220	Consultation					595.00
221	External Billing Costs					
222	Special Insurance					
223	Cell Phones	1	250		250	363.09
224	Florist Flowers for Talent & Client					256.98
225						
226						
			TOTAL K		700	1,815.07

L	DIRECTOR/CREATIVE FEES	Amount	Rate	x	ESTIMATED	ACTUAL
227	Director Prep	1	7500		7,500	
228	Director Travel					
229	Director Shoot	1	24000		24,000	
230	Director Post					
231						
232						
233						
			Sub-total L		31,500	
			PT/P&W		2,400	
			TOTAL L		33,900	

Figure 10.1 *Continued*

M	TALENT LABOR	No.	Travel Days	Shoot Days	Rate	OT Hours 1.5	OT Hours 2.0	ESTIMATED	% PT/P&W	OT Based	ACTUAL
234	O/C Principals									8	
235	O/C Principals									8	
236	O/C Principals									8	
237	O/C Principals									8	
238	O/C Principals									8	
239	O/C Principals									8	
240	O/C Principals									8	
241	O/C Principals									8	
242	O/C Principals									8	
243	O/C Principals									8	
244										8	
245										8	
246										8	
247	General Extras									8	
248	General Extras									8	
249	General Extras									8	
250	General Extras									8	
251	General Extras									8	
252	General Extras									8	
253										8	
254										8	
255										8	
256	Hand Models									8	
257										8	
258										8	
259	Voice Over									8	
260	Fitting Fees									8	
261	Fitting Fees									8	
262										8	
263	Audition Fees									8	
264	Audition Fees									8	
265										8	
							Sub-total M				
							PT/P&W				
266	Talent Agency Fees				20%						
267	Talent Payroll Service										
268	Talent Wardrobe Allowance										
269	Other										
270	Talent Labor Mark-up										
							TOTAL M				

N	TALENT EXPENSES	Amount	Rate	x	ESTIMATED		ACTUAL
271	Talent Air Fares						
272	Talent Hotels						
273	Talent Ground Transportation						
274	Other						
275	Other						
276	Talent Exp Mark-up						
				TOTAL N			

Figure 10.1 *Continued*

O	POST PRODUCTION LABOR	Amount	Rate	x	ESTIMATED	ACTUAL
277	Post Supervisor					
278	Off-line Editor					
279	Assistant Editor					
280						
281						
				Sub-total O		
			PT/P&W			
			TOTAL O			

P	POST PRODUCTION EXPENSES	Amount	Rate	x	ESTIMATED	ACTUAL
282	Film To Tape					
283	Tape To Tape					
284	Film Gate					
285	Neg Cleaning					
286	Telecine Other					
287						
288	Offline Edit					
289	Offline Storage					
290	Offline Other					
291						
292	Digital 2D/Paint					
293	Digital 3D/Modeling					
294	Digital Rotoscoping					
295	Digital Compositing					
296	Digital Effects					
297	Digital Other					
298						
299	Online Conform					
300	Title Camera					
301	Chyron					
302	Edited Master					
303	Sub-masters					
304						
305	Music					
306	VO/ADR					
307	Sound Design					
308	Foley Studio					
309	Audio Mix					
310	Audio Transfers					
311						
312	Tape Stock					
313	Dubs					
314	Standards Conversion					
315	Satellite Transmission					
316	Internet Transmission					
317						
318	Stock Footage					
319	Animation					
320	Film Editing					
321	Opticals					
322	Negative Cutting					
323	Add'l Lab Work					
324	Tape to Film					
325	Closed Captions					
326						
327						
328						
329						
			TOTAL P			

Figure 10.1 *Continued*

JOB REPORT

ACTUAL DATE
2/6/02

RECONCILIATION	
Difference between Logs and Actual Budget	0.00

MARKUP AND INSURANCE

		103,560.00	Total Markup
	Markup	**Insurance**	(149,590.91) Over / (Under)
Production (A to K)	0.0 %	0.0 %	13.31 % Est Margin
Director/Creative Fees (L)	0.0 %	0.0 %	32.53 % Act Margin
Talent Labor (M)	0.0 %	0.0 %	X Show this markup on line 270
Talent Expenses (N)	0.0 %	0.0 %	X Show this markup on line 276
Editorial & Finishing (O and P)	0.0 %	0.0 %	X Show this markup on Top Sheet line 16

All markup is shown on Top Sheet line 13 as the Production Fee unless otherwise noted above.

DETAIL OF ADDITIONAL BILLINGS

No.	Description	Markup	TOTAL BILLED
	1st Overage		36,050.00
	2nd Overage		182,201.00
	TOTALS	0.00	218,251.00

COMPANY NOTES

CURRENCY EXCHANGE RATE	
Exchange Rate	1.6500
Currency Reference	British Pounds £

All rates in the estimated budget will be multiplied by the exchange rate when the Update Rates button is pressed.

Figure 10.1 *Continued*

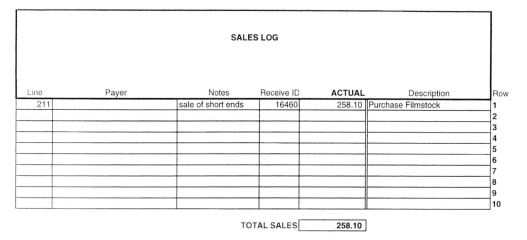

Line	Payer	Notes	Receive ID	ACTUAL	Description	Row
211		sale of short ends	16460	258.10	Purchase Filmstock	1
						2
						3
						4
						5
						6
						7
						8
						9
						10

TOTAL SALES   258.10

Figure 10.1   *Continued*

PURCHASE ORDER LOG

Line	Payee	PO	Date	Pay ID	ACTUAL	Description	Row
187		1000	12/15/00	11119	35,000.00	Outside Construction	1
187		1000	12/20/00	11116	30,000.00	Outside Construction	2
187		1000	01/02/01		65,000.00	Outside Construction	3
188		1001	01/02/01		1,160.00	Trucking	4
182		1002	12/21/00		663.03	Set Dressing Rentals	5
	DEPOSIT	1002	12/21/00	RET11115	0.00		6
182		1003	12/21/00		250.00	Set Dressing Rentals	7
	DEP	1003	12/21/00	RET11114	0.00		8
182		1004	12/28/00	2754	600.00	Set Dressing Rentals	9
144		1005	12/28/00	2753	724.00	Picture Vehicles	10
182		1006	01/02/01		4,854.44	Set Dressing Rentals	11
182		1007	12/22/00	2739	1,898.71	Set Dressing Rentals	12
182	DEPOSIT	1007	12/22/01		(1,548.71)	Set Dressing Rentals	13
182		1008	12/26/01		536.74	Set Dressing Rentals	14
182		1009	12/21/00	2736	454.65	Set Dressing Rentals	15
	DEPOSIT	1009	12/21/00	11112	0.00		16
182	Void	1010	12/25/00		0.00		17
182		1011	12/21/00	2737	550.99	Set Dressing Rentals	18
	DEPOSIT	1011	12/21/00	RET11113	0.00		19
182		1012	12/21/00	2735	1,984.00	Set Dressing Rentals	20
	DEP	1012	12/21/00	11111	0.00		21
217	Petty Cash	1013	12/13/00			Petty Cash	22
217	Petty Cash	1013	12/15/00	11118		Petty Cash	23
217	Petty Cash	1013	12/28/01	2755		Petty Cash	24
217	Petty Cash	1013	01/03/01			Petty Cash	25
161	misc	1014	12/15/00		357.50	Power Charges and Bulbs	26
151	Stage 2	1014	12/15/00		5,000.00	Rental For Build Days	27
153	Stage 2	1014	12/15/00		1,300.00	Rental for Pre-Lite Days	28
155	Stage 2	1014	12/15/00		1,600.00	Rental for Shoot Days	29
158	Stage 2	1014	12/15/00		1,000.00	Strike OT Hours	30
160	Stage 2	1014	12/15/00		0.00	Studio Security	31
161	Stage 2	1014	12/15/00		1,250.00	Power Charges and Bulbs	32
162	Stage 2	1014	12/15/00		10.50	Studio Related	33
163	Stage 2	1014	12/15/00		180.00	Editing/Prd Off/Hair/MU/Ward	34
164	Stage 2	1014	12/15/00		135.00	Hopper	35
195	Stage 2	1014	12/15/00		7,497.75	Lighting Rental	36
196	Stage 2	1014	12/15/00		2,277.00	Grip Rental	37
202	Stage 2	1014	12/15/00		135.00	Scissor Lift	38
151	Stage 5	1014	12/15/00		8,000.00	Rental For Build Days	39
153	Stage 5	1014	12/15/00		2,300.00	Rental for Pre-Lite Days	40
155	Stage 5	1014	12/15/00		2,600.00	Rental for Shoot Days	41
158	Stage 5	1014	12/15/00		1,600.00	Strike OT Hours	42
160	Stage 5	1014	12/15/00		525.00	Studio Security	43
161	Stage 5	1014	12/15/00		1,167.50	Power Charges and Bulbs	44
162	Stage 5	1014	12/15/00		1,008.30	Studio Related	45
163	Stage 5	1014	12/15/00		290.00	Editing/Prd Off/Hair/MU/Ward	46
164	Stage 5	1014	12/15/00		270.00	Hopper	47
195	Stage 5	1014	12/15/00		11,206.00	Lighting Rental	48
196	Stage 5	1014	12/15/00		4,021.30	Grip Rental	49
202	Stage 5	1014	12/15/00		140.00	Scissor Lift	50
200		1015	12/26/00		500.00	Walkie Talkie Rental	51

Figure 10.1 *Continued*

204		1016	12/19/00	PD	238.15	Production Supplies	52
	DEPOSIT	1016	12/19/00	11135RET			53
105		1017	12/20/00	est	300.00	Messengers	54
120		1018	12/21/00		498.88	Trucking	55
121		1018	12/21/00		566.00	Other Vehicles	56
107		1019	12/22/00		140.80	Deliveries and Taxis	57
143		1019	12/22/00		2,094.64	Wardrobe Purchases	58
143		1019	12/22/00		2,514.24	Wardrobe Purchases	59
224		1019	12/22/00		197.02	Florist	60
218		1020	12/13/00	est	300.00	Air Shipping and Carriers	61
218		1021	12/24/00	est	300.00	Air Shipping and Carriers	62
193		1022	12/25/00		8,246.25	Camera Rental	63
201		1023	12/26/00		578.06	Dolly Rental	64
204		1024	12/22/00		56.25	Production Supplies	65
118		1025	12/26/00		1,455.00	Dressing Room Vehicles	66
33		1026	12/27/00		1,326.06	Storyboard Artist	67
211		1027	12/22/00		13,173.49	Purchase Filmstock	68
204		1028	12/23/00		45.00	Production Supplies	69
132	Studio Facilities	1029	12/26/00		208.00	Set Security	70
164	Studio Facilities	1029	12/26/00		65.00	Hopper	71
165	Studio Facilities	1029	12/26/00		6,000.00	Shoot	72
167	Studio Facilities	1029	12/26/00		884.56	LINE NUMBER?	73
181	Studio Facilities	1029	12/26/00		400.00	Set Dressing Purchases	74
208	Studio Facilities	1029	12/26/00		3,075.00	Grip Truck	75
209	Studio Facilities	1029	12/26/00		4,785.00	Electric Pkg	76
130		1030	12/28/00	2757	3,833.14	Lunch	77
213		1031	12/22/00		6,821.17	Vid Dailies/Transfer	78
204		1032	12/26/00		1,342.13	Production Supplies	79
105		1033	12/26/00	est	20.00	Messengers	80
147		1034	12/26/00		648.00	Product Color Correction	81
	Void	1035					82
133		1036	12/28/00		1,494.00	Limousines	83
182		1037	12/27/00		133.20	Set Dressing Rentals	84
141		1038	12/28/00		649.50	Prop Purchases	85
183		1039	12/28/00		312.72	Greens	86
212		1040	12/27/00		352.09	Process Filmstock	87
212		1041	12/28/00		256.88	Process Filmstock	88
	Void	1042					89
143		1043	12/29/00		451.00	Wardrobe Purchases	90
		1044	12/21/00	RET 2738	0.00		91
140		1045	12/22/00		1,123.10	Prop Rentals	92
140		1046	12/22/00		750.00	Prop Rentals	93
140		1046	12/22/00		(550.00)	Prop Rentals	94
		1047	12/21/01	RET11108			95
140		1048	12/28/00		467.64	Prop Rentals	96
142		1049	12/28/00		313.00	Wardrobe Rentals	97
142		1049	12/26/01	RET 2744		Wardrobe Rentals	98
125		1050	12/27/00	2746	1,106.50	Catering Labor	99
131		1050	12/27/00	2746	1,807.05	Dinner	100
122		1051	12/29/00		350.00	Makeup Trailer	101
123		1051	12/29/00		400.00	3 Banger	102
124		1051	12/29/00		335.00	Production Trailer	103
70		1052	12/29/00	2758	1,500.00	Mixer	104
194		1052	12/29/00	2758	1,650.00	Sound Rental	105
212		1053	12/29/00		678.15	Process Filmstock	106
199		1054	12/28/01		1,500.00	VTR Rental	107
223		1055	12/29/00		363.09	Cell Phones	108
206		1056	12/28/00	11144	1,025.00	Lighting & Grip Expendables	109
212		1057	12/29/00		239.75	Process Filmstock	110

Figure 10.1 *Continued*

32		1058	12/27/00	2756	155.00	Wrap Personel	111
111		1059	12/23/00		1,650.00	Casting Facilities	112
113		1059	12/23/00		1,455.00	Casting Tape & Polaroid	113
143		1060	12/30/00		660.32	Wardrobe Purchases	114
143		1061	12/29/00		4,372.22	Wardrobe Purchases	115
143		1062	12/30/00		1,130.13	Wardrobe Purchases	116
143		1063	12/29/00		254.38	Wardrobe Purchases	117
135		1064	12/29/00		200.00	Kit Rentals	118
206		1064	12/29/00		600.00	Lighting & Grip Expendables	119
211		1065	01/02/00		(4,037.55)	Purchase Filmstock	120
141		1066	01/02/01		950.00	Prop Purchases	121
182		1067	12/29/00		496.83	Set Dressing Rentals	122
		1067	12/29/00	RET11110			123
220		1068	01/03/01		595.00	Consultation	124
207		1069	12/29/00		1,300.00	Steadicam Sled	125
110		1070	01/03/01		4,500.00	Casting Director	126
206		1071	12/28/01		445.93	Lighting & Grip Expendables	127
105		1072	01/04/01	2760	116.56	Messengers	128
204		25234	12/28/00		184.03	Production Supplies	129
							130
							131
							132
							133
							134
							135
							136
							137
							138

TOTAL PURCHASE ORDERS 288,346.06

Figure 10.1 *Continued*

PAYROLL LOG

Line	Payee	PO	% PT&W	OT Based	Days	Rate	1.5	2.0	2.5	3.0	Misc Taxable	Misc Non-taxable	Total ST	Total OT	ACTUAL	Description	PT/P&W	Row
1			24.0	14	6	875.00							5,250.00	0.00	5,250.00	Producer	1,260.00	1
1			24.0	14	5	900.00							4,500.00	0.00	4,500.00	Producer	1,080.00	2
1			24.0	14	2	900.00							1,800.00	0.00	1,800.00	Producer	432.00	3
2			24.0	14	5	900.00							4,500.00	0.00	4,500.00	Producer	1,080.00	4
2			24.0	14	1	800.00							800.00	0.00	800.00	Assistant Director	192.00	5
2			24.0	14	1	900.00							900.00	0.00	900.00	Assistant Director	216.00	6
3			24.0	14	2	2,500.00							5,000.00	0.00	5,000.00	Director of Photography	1,200.00	7
5			24.0	14	1	2,500.00							2,500.00	0.00	2,500.00	Director of Photography	600.00	8
8			24.0	14	1	500.00							500.00	0.00	500.00	Assistant Camera	120.00	9
10			24.0	11	1	550.00							550.00	0.00	550.00	Prop Master	132.00	10
10			24.0	14	6	500.00							3,000.00	0.00	3,000.00	Executive Producer	720.00	11
11			24.0	14	5	700.00							3,500.00	0.00	3,500.00	Executive Producer	840.00	12
12			24.0	14	1	500.00							500.00	0.00	500.00	Gaffer	120.00	13
13			24.0	14	1	475.00							475.00	0.00	475.00	Best Boy Electrician	114.00	14
14			24.0	14	1	450.00							450.00	0.00	450.00	Electrian	108.00	15
14			24.0	14	1	450.00							450.00	0.00	450.00	Electrian	108.00	16
15			24.0	14	1	450.00							450.00	0.00	450.00	Electrian	108.00	17
15			24.0	14	1	475.00							475.00	0.00	475.00	Electrian	114.00	18
16			24.0	14	1	450.00							450.00	0.00	450.00	Electrian	108.00	19
16			24.0	14	1	450.00							450.00	0.00	450.00	Electrian	108.00	20
17			24.0	14	1	450.00							450.00	0.00	450.00	Key Grip	108.00	21
18			24.0	14	1	500.00							500.00	0.00	500.00	Key Grip	120.00	22
19			24.0	14	1	500.00							500.00	0.00	500.00	Best Boy Grip	120.00	23
19			24.0	14	1	475.00							475.00	0.00	475.00	Best Boy Grip	114.00	24
19			24.0	14	1	475.00							475.00	0.00	475.00	Dolly Grip	114.00	25
26			24.0	14	1	475.00							475.00	0.00	475.00	Dolly Grip	114.00	26
26			24.0	14	2	450.00							900.00	0.00	900.00	4th Grip	216.00	27
26			24.0	14	1	450.00							450.00	0.00	450.00	4th Grip	108.00	28
27			24.0	14	1	450.00							450.00	0.00	450.00	4th Grip	108.00	29
27			24.0	14	1	450.00							450.00	0.00	450.00	4th Grip	108.00	30
32			24.0	11	1	650.00							650.00	0.00	650.00	Costume Design	156.00	31
32			24.0	11	1	650.00							650.00	0.00	650.00	Costume Design	156.00	32
32			24.0	11	3	650.00							1,950.00	0.00	1,950.00	Costume Design	468.00	33
32			24.0	14	1	350.00							350.00	0.00	350.00	Wardrobe Attendant	84.00	34
32			24.0	14	2	350.00							700.00	0.00	700.00	Wardrobe Attendant	168.00	35
33			24.0	14	1	350.00							350.00	0.00	350.00	Wardrobe Attendant	84.00	36
38			24.0	14	1	100.00							100.00	0.00	100.00	Wrap Personnel	24.00	37
38			24.0	14	1	100.00							100.00	0.00	100.00	Wrap Personnel	24.00	38
38			24.0	14	1	100.00							100.00	0.00	100.00	Wrap Personnel	24.00	39
38			24.0	14	1	100.00							100.00	0.00	100.00	Wrap Personnel	24.00	40
38			24.0	14	1	100.00							100.00	0.00	100.00	Wrap Personnel	24.00	41
41			24.0	14	1	130.00							130.00	0.00	130.00	Wrap Personnel	31.20	42
46			24.0	14	3	500.00							1,500.00	0.00	1,500.00	Storyboard Artist	360.00	43
46			24.0	14	2	150.00							300.00	0.00	300.00	Production Assistants	72.00	44
46			24.0	14	2	175.00							350.00	0.00	350.00	Production Assistants	84.00	45
46			24.0	14	2	175.00							350.00	0.00	350.00	Production Assistants	84.00	46
47			24.0	14	1	175.00							175.00	0.00	175.00	Production Assistants	42.00	47
47			24.0	14	1	175.00							175.00	0.00	175.00	Production Assistants	42.00	48
47			24.0	14	5	100.00							500.00	0.00	500.00	Production Assistants	120.00	49
			24.0	14	5	100.00							500.00	0.00	500.00	Production Assistants	120.00	50
			24.0	14	1	225.00							225.00	0.00	225.00	Crafts Service	54.00	51
			24.0	14	4	500.00							2,000.00	0.00	2,000.00	Production Manager	480.00	52
			24.0	14	2	500.00							1,000.00	0.00	1,000.00	Production Manager	240.00	53
			24.0	14	5	500.00							2,500.00	0.00	2,500.00	Production Manager	600.00	54
			24.0	14	5	500.00							2,500.00	0.00	2,500.00	Production Manager	600.00	55
			24.0	14	1	300.00							300.00	0.00	300.00	Production Coordinator	72.00	56
			24.0	14	5	300.00							1,500.00	0.00	1,500.00	Production Coordinator	360.00	57
			24.0	14	5	300.00							1,500.00	0.00	1,500.00	Production Coordinator	360.00	58
			24.0	14	2	300.00							600.00	0.00	600.00	Production Coordinator	144.00	59

Figure 10.1 *Continued*

48			24.0	12	1	150.00							150.00	0.00	150.00	Utility PA	36.00	63
48			24.0	14	2	100.00							200.00	0.00	200.00	Utility PA	48.00	64
48			24.0	14	1	175.00							175.00	0.00	175.00	Utility PA	42.00	65
51			24.0	14	3	900.00							2,700.00	0.00	2,700.00	Producer	648.00	66
52			24.0	14	3	900.00							2,700.00	0.00	2,700.00	Assistant Director	648.00	67
53			24.0	14	3	2,500.00							7,500.00	0.00	7,500.00	Director of Photography	1,800.00	68
54			24.0	14	2	350.00		1.5					1,900.00	203.57	2,103.57	Camera Operator	504.86	69
55			24.0	14	3	500.00		2					1,500.00	142.86	1,642.86	Assistant Camera	394.29	70
56			24.0	14	3	400.00		2					1,200.00	114.29	1,314.29	Loader	315.43	71
58			24.0	11	3	600.00		2					1,800.00	218.18	2,018.18	Prop Master	484.36	72
60			24.0	14	2	925.00							1,850.00	0.00	1,850.00	Steadicam Operator	444.00	73
61			24.0	14	3	500.00		2					1,500.00	142.86	1,642.86	Gaffer	394.29	74
62			24.0	14	3	475.00		2					1,425.00	135.71	1,560.71	Best Boy Electrician	374.57	75
63			24.0	14	3	450.00		2					1,350.00	128.57	1,478.57	Electrician	354.86	76
64			24.0	14	3	450.00		2					1,350.00	128.57	1,478.57	Electrician	354.86	77
65			24.0	14	3	450.00		2					1,350.00	128.57	1,478.57	Electrician	354.86	78
66			24.0	14	3	500.00		1.5					1,500.00	107.14	1,607.14	Key Grip	385.71	79
67			24.0	14	3	475.00		2					1,425.00	135.71	1,560.71	Best Boy Grip	374.57	80
68			24.0	14	3	475.00		1.5					1,425.00	101.79	1,526.79	Dolly Grip	366.43	81
69			24.0	14	3	450.00							1,350.00	0.00	1,350.00	Company Grips	324.00	82
69			24.0	14	3	450.00		1.5					1,350.00	96.43	1,446.43	Company Grips	347.14	83
71			24.0	14	3	450.10		1.7					1,350.30	109.31	1,459.61	Boom	350.31	84
74			24.0	14	2	500.00		1.25					1,000.00	89.29	1,089.29	Makeup Artist/Hair	261.43	85
74			24.0	14	3	850.00							2,550.00	0.00	2,550.00	Makeup Artist/Hair	612.00	86
74			24.0	14	3	850.00		3					2,550.00	364.29	2,914.29	Makeup Artist/Hair	699.43	87
75			24.0	14	2	350.00		2					700.00	100.00	800.00	Make up Assistant	192.00	88
76			24.0	11	3	650.00		6					1,950.00	709.09	2,659.09	Costume Design	638.18	89
77			24.0	14	3	350.00		4					1,050.00	200.00	1,250.00	Wardobe Attendant	300.00	90
77			24.0	14	3	300.00		2.8					900.00	120.00	1,020.00	Wardobe Attendant	244.80	91
78			24.0	14	3	500.00		1					1,500.00	71.43	1,571.43	Script Supervisor	377.14	92
81			24.0	14	3	500.00		2					1,500.00	142.86	1,642.86	VTR Operator	394.29	93
82			24.0	14							32.00		0.00	0.00	32.00	Meal Penalties	7.68	94
82			24.0	14							8.00		0.00	0.00	8.00	Meal Penalties	1.92	95
82			24.0	14							28.00		0.00	0.00	28.00	Meal Penalties	6.72	96
82			24.0	14							28.00		0.00	0.00	28.00	Meal Penalties	6.72	97
82			24.0	14							28.00		0.00	0.00	28.00	Meal Penalties	6.72	98
82			24.0	14							40.00		0.00	0.00	40.00	Meal Penalties	9.60	99
82			24.0	11							40.00		0.00	0.00	40.00	Meal Penalties	9.60	100
82			24.0	14							32.00		0.00	0.00	32.00	Meal Penalties	7.68	101
82			24.0	14							40.00		0.00	0.00	40.00	Meal Penalties	9.60	102
82			24.0	14							32.00		0.00	0.00	32.00	Meal Penalties	7.68	103
82			24.0	14							32.00		0.00	0.00	32.00	Meal Penalties	7.68	104
82			24.0	14							32.00		0.00	0.00	32.00	Meal Penalties	7.68	105
82			24.0	14							28.00		0.00	0.00	28.00	Meal Penalties	6.72	106
82			24.0	14							40.00		0.00	0.00	40.00	Meal Penalties	9.60	107
82			24.0	14	1	803.53							803.53	0.00	803.53	Meal Penalties	192.85	108
82			24.0	14							40.00		0.00	0.00	40.00	Meal Penalties	9.60	109
82			24.0	14							20.00		0.00	0.00	20.00	Meal Penalties	4.80	110
82			24.0	14							40.00		0.00	0.00	40.00	Meal Penalties	9.60	111
82			24.0	14							40.00		0.00	0.00	40.00	Meal Penalties	9.60	112
82			24.0	14							28.00		0.00	0.00	28.00	Meal Penalties	6.72	113
82			24.0	14							40.00		0.00	0.00	40.00	Meal Penalties	9.60	114
82			24.0	14							28.00		0.00	0.00	28.00	Meal Penalties	6.72	115
86			24.0	14	1	500.00							500.00	0.00	500.00	Still Photographer	120.00	116
88			24.0	14	3	175.00							525.00	0.00	525.00	Production Assistants	126.00	117
88			24.0	14	1	175.00							175.00	0.00	175.00	Production Assistants	42.00	118
88			24.0	14	3	175.00							525.00	0.00	525.00	Production Assistants	126.00	119
88			24.0	14	3	175.00							525.00	0.00	525.00	Production Assistants	126.00	120
89			24.0	14	4	450.00							1,800.00	0.00	1,800.00	2nd AD	432.00	121
91			24.0	14	3	225.00		6					675.00	192.86	867.86	Crafts Service	208.29	122
93			24.0	14	2	200.00							400.00	0.00	400.00	Catering Labor	96.00	123
93			24.0	14	2	210.10							420.20	0.00	420.20	Catering Labor	100.85	124
93			24.0	11	2	325.00		4					650.00	236.36	886.36	Catering Labor	212.73	125
94			24.0	14	3	450.00							1,350.00	0.00	1,350.00	Production Associates	324.00	126
94			24.0	14	6	120.00							720.00	0.00	720.00	Production Associates	172.80	127
94			24.0	14	4	120.00							480.00	0.00	480.00	Production Associates	115.20	128
94			24.0	14	5	120.00							600.00	0.00	600.00	Production Associates	144.00	129
94			24.0	14	4	900.00							3,600.00	0.00	3,600.00	Production Associates	864.00	130
95			24.0	12	1	446.58							446.58	0.00	446.58	Teamster	107.18	131
95			24.0	14	1	500.00							500.00	0.00	500.00	Teamster	120.00	132

Figure 10.1 *Continued*

PO code	Rate	Days	Qty	Hrs 1	Hrs 2	Total for PO	Description	Payroll 1	Payroll 2	Payroll 3	Total Payroll	PT/P&W	Line
95	24.0	12	1			434.18	Teamster		434.18	0.00	434.18	104.20	133
96	24.0	14	3			500.00	Production Manager		1,500.00	0.00	1,500.00	360.00	134
97	24.0	14	3			300.00	Production Coordinator		900.00	0.00	900.00	216.00	135
98	24.0	14	3			175.00	Utility PA		525.00	0.00	525.00	126.00	136
98	24.0	14	3			175.00	Utility PA		525.00	0.00	525.00	126.00	137
99	24.0	14	2			175.00	Runners		350.00	0.00	350.00	84.00	138
99	24.0	14	1			175.00	Runners		175.00	0.00	175.00	42.00	139
99	24.0	14	2			175.00	Runners		350.00	0.00	350.00	84.00	140
100	24.0	14	3			650.00	Barber for Jamie Foxx		1,950.00	0.00	1,950.00	468.00	141
119	24.0	14					Parking, Tolls, and Gas	44.52			44.52	0.00	142
119	24.0	14					Parking, Tolls, and Gas	128.05			128.05	0.00	143
119	24.0						Parking, Tolls, and Gas	20.80			20.80	0.00	144
119	24.0						Parking, Tolls, and Gas	49.40			49.40	0.00	145
119	24.0						Parking, Tolls, and Gas	80.27			80.27	0.00	146
135	24.0	14					Kit Rentals	50.00			50.00	0.00	147
135	24.0	14					Kit Rentals	250.00			250.00	0.00	148
135	24.0	14					Kit Rentals	250.00			250.00	0.00	149
135	24.0	14					Kit Rentals	90.00			90.00	0.00	150
135	24.0	14					Kit Rentals	150.00			150.00	0.00	151
135	24.0	14					Kit Rentals	350.00			350.00	0.00	152
135	24.0	14					Kit Rentals	225.00			225.00	0.00	153
135	24.0	14					Kit Rentals	150.00			150.00	0.00	154
135	24.0	14					Kit Rentals	150.00			150.00	0.00	155
135	24.0	14					Kit Rentals	45.00			45.00	0.00	156
135	24.0	14					Kit Rentals	300.00			300.00	0.00	157
135	24.0	14					Kit Rentals	400.00			400.00	0.00	158
135	24.0	14					Kit Rentals	150.00			150.00	0.00	159
135	24.0	14					Kit Rentals	50.00			50.00	0.00	160
135	24.0	14					Kit Rentals	150.00			150.00	0.00	161
135	24.0	14					Kit Rentals	350.00			350.00	0.00	162
168	24.0	11	3			1,000.00	Production Designer		3,000.00	0.00	3,000.00	720.00	163
168	24.0	11	5			1,000.00	Production Designer		5,000.00	0.00	5,000.00	1,200.00	164
168	24.0	11	5			1,000.00	Production Designer		5,000.00	0.00	5,000.00	1,200.00	165
169	24.0	11	1	1		650.00	Art Director		650.00	88.64	738.64	177.27	166
169	24.0	11	3	2		650.00	Art Director		1,950.00	177.27	2,127.27	510.54	167
169	24.0	11	5	16	7	670.00	Art Director		3,350.00	2,314.55	5,664.55	1,359.49	168
169	24.0	11	4	4		650.00	Art Director		2,600.00	354.55	2,954.55	709.09	169
170	24.0	11	12			550.00	Decorator		6,600.00	0.00	6,600.00	1,584.00	170
172	24.0	11	1			550.00	Leadman		550.00	0.00	550.00	132.00	172
172	24.0	11	1			275.00	Leadman		275.00	0.00	275.00	66.00	173
172	24.0	11	4	9		275.00	Leadman		1,100.00	337.50	1,437.50	345.00	174
172	24.0	11	7	6.5	3.75	300.00	Leadman		2,100.00	470.45	2,570.45	616.91	175
177	24.0	14	3			175.00	PAs		525.00	0.00	525.00	126.00	176
177	24.0	11	4			175.00	PAs		700.00	0.00	700.00	168.00	177
177	24.0	11	5			175.00	PAs		875.00	0.00	875.00	210.00	178
									0.00	0.00	0.00	0.00	179

Total for PO 224,839.38

TOTAL PAYROLL 3,433.04 | 170,014.79 | 7,862.70 | 181,986.53

TOTAL PT/P&W 42,852.85

PO

Total Payroll	224,839.38
Total Payroll from POs	0.00
Payroll not Reconciled	224,839.38

Figure 10.1 *Continued*

PETTY CASH LOG

Line	| PO Envelopes → 1	2	3	4	5	6	7	8	9	10	11	12	13	14	15	16	17	ACTUAL	Description	Row
104	46.66	99.61	0115.00															261.27	Still Camera Rental & Film	1
112	167.66	583.01	367.05	9.00		58.49						136.13		101.08	213.12	129.26		1,764.80	Working Meals	2
113				5.36								126.65						132.01	Casting Tape & Polaroid	3
117			75.80															75.80	Bus Rentals	4
119	12.50	109.48												37.50	22.20			181.68	Parking, Tolls, and Gas	5
127		412.84											69.01					481.85	Gifts	6
128		372.10																372.10	Second Meal	7
135			100.00															100.00	Kit Rentals	8
138					1,664.93													1,664.93	Craft Services	9
141									72.98		54.50		259.80					387.28	Prop Purchases	10
142																	1,350.48	1,350.48	Wardrobe Rentals	11
143		250.00																250.00	Wardrobe Purchases	12
144		1,224.00																1,224.00	Picture Vehicles	13
146		109.44																109.44	Makeup EFX, Wigs Etc.	14
149							96.22	45.00	74.75	38.00	126.50							380.47	Kits/Misc	15
150							276.92		29.23	7.39								313.54	Art Dept Still Film & Process	16
181		198.27					61.58	166.83	85.73	150.92	32.48		73.03	11.53				780.54	Set Dressing Purchases	17
182			620.00				162.38	49.00										831.38	Set Dressing Rentals	18
188																		0.00	Trucking	19
190				42.60						91.75		82.51				87.82		304.66	Kit Rentals & Copies	20
191							27.67	4.75	160.45	143.00	33.51		94.65					464.03	Meals	21
203				15.13														15.13	Camera Expendables	22
204	18.20	38.00	42.69				378.45				6.43				177.78			661.40	Production Supplies	23
224		31.81	28.15															59.96	Florist	24
TOTAL PC RECEIPTS	245.02	3,428.56	1,348.69	72.09	1,664.93	58.49	1,003.22	265.58	423.14	431.06	253.42	345.29	496.49	150.11	413.10	217.08	1,350.48	12,166.75		
	245.02	3,428.56	1,348.69	72.09	1,664.93	58.49	1,003.22	265.58	423.14	431.06	253.42	345.29	496.49	150.11	413.10	217.08	1,350.48	12,166.75		

0.00	Cash Received
12,166.75	Due Personnel / (Due Co)

0.00	Total PC from POs
0.00	PC Reconciled

Figure 10.1 *Continued*

Addendum A to the Standard Commercial Production Agreement

PRODUCTION SPECIFICATIONS AND ESTIMATE FORM

DATE:		**Estimated Grand Total:**	

BID VERSION:

CLIENT/PRODUCT:
AGENCY:
DIRECTOR:
LOCATIONS:

#	Hrs	Prep	#	Hrs	Shoot
		Prep/Wrap			Stage Shoot
		Build/Strike			In Zone Location Shoot
		Pre-light			Out of Zone Shoot
		Tech Scout			Distant Location Shoot
		Travel			2nd Unit
		Rehearsal			Weather Covers

	TITLE	No.		TITLE	No.
1			5		
2			6		
3			7		
4			8		

SUPPLIED BY: **A** = AGENCY/CLIENT   **P** = PRODUCER   **Blank** = NOT APPLICABLE   **X** = BID SPECS

BID STATUS	PICTURE	SOUND	LOCATION	OTHER
Firm Bid	35mm	MOS	Studio Zone	EPP Policy
Cost Plus/Fixed Fee	16mm	Sync	Outside zone	Errors & Omissions
Draft	8mm	Music Playback	Distant Location	Special Insurance
Ballpark	Analog Video	Stock Music	Stage	Gap Ins Cov
Start-Up Estimate	Digital Video	Original Music	Weekend Shoot	Wrap-Up Ins
	Print/Other	DAT	Night Shoot	Weather Insurance

AGENCY/CLIENT	FOOD PRODUCT	EDITORIAL	ART DEPT	PRODUCTION
PRODUCT	Ingredient Purchase	Contracted	Picture Aircraft	Union Crew
Purchase	Food Prep	Sub-contracted	Picture Cars	Art Director
Preparation	Kitchen	**Through:**	Props	Dailies Equip
Labels	Props	Full Completion	Props-Custom	Double Dailies
Color Correction	Shipping	Picture Finish	Puppets	Fire & Equip
Transport		Vis/Digit Effx	Set Construction	Home Ec
Shipping		**EDIT INCLUDES**	Set Design	Home Ec Asst
Delivery		Animation/CGI	Set Designer	Loc Fees/Permits
Miscellaneous		CGI	Set Sketches	Location Search
	HERO CARS	Editor	Signage	Meals -Bk/Lunch
	Prep/Exps	Editorial Super	Special Effx	Meals-2nd
EXPENSES	Transport/Exps	2D Graphics	Storyboards	Motorhome
Return Shipping	Rigging Labor	3D Graphics		Police
Props	Rigging Exps	Music - Original	**CAM SUPPORT**	Production Stills
Wardrobe	Vehicle Ins	Music-Stock	Aerial Mount	Special Security
Product	Customs	Paintbox	Aircraft	
Signage/Art	Spec Handling	Screening	Camera Car	
Weather Contingency		Sound Design	Crane	
Weather Gear		Sound Effects	Gyro/Wescam	
	CREW TRAVEL	Stock Footage	Helicopter	
TRAVEL	Airfares	Stock Photographer	Hot Head	
Hotel/Airfares	Ground Travel	Stock Stills	Louma	
Per Diems	Hotel & Per Diem	Sync Dailies	Match VTR	
Cell Phones	Parking	Titles/Artwork	Video Dailies	
Cabs/Taxis/Transport	Cabs/Taxis/Transport	Tracks/Voice Over	VTR Assist	

Payment Schedule

	%	Upon signing of this agreement
	%	Upon approval of photography
	%	Upon completion and delivery of all elements and materials supplied by the production company

This estimate is based upon the following schedule:
☐ ATTACHED PRODUCTION SCHEDULE:
☐ DATES OF: _____ Through _____

Payments are due and payable as per the schedule. A late payment penalty may be assessed for payments not received within 15 days of due dates.

Terms and conditions are subject to: ☐ The AICP Guidelines   ☐ The Standard Commercial Production Agreement

Figure 10.2 Currently the AICP demands that the Addendum A to the Standard Commercial Production Agreement be attached.

TALENT SPECIFICATIONS
WHATEVER FILMS, Inc.

SUPPLIED BY: AGENCY/CLIENT = A   PRODUCER = P   NOT APPLICABLE = BLANK

☐ CASTING	☐ ANNOUNCER	☐ HAND MODELS	☐ PUPPETEERS	☐ STUNT DOUBLES
☐ PRINCIPAL PAYMENTS	☐ DANCERS	☐ MUSICIANS	☐ SPECIAL CONTRACT	☐ VOICE OVER
☐ EXTRAS PAYMENTS	☐ DOUBLES	☐ PILOTS	☐ STAND-IN	☐
☐ International BUYOUT	☐ GROUP PLAYER	☐ PRECISION	☐ STUNT COORD	☐

CAST BREAKDOWN - No. of Cast Members Per Spot

Commercial #	1	2	3	4	5	6	7	8	TOTAL
A PRINCIPAL									
B EXTRAS									
C ANNOUNCER									
D DANCERS									
E DOUBLES									
F GROUP PLAYER									
G HAND MODELS									
H MUSICIANS									
I PILOTS									
J PRECISION									
K PUPPETEERS									
L S. CONTRACT									
M STAND-IN									
N STUNT COORD									
O STUNT DBLES									
P VOICE OVER									

Commercial to Air:

Cable	National
Cinema	Other
Test	Regional
International	Spot
Digitial	

Talent Payment Notes:

CASTING
CASTING DIR
FACILITY
PREP
CAST
CALLBACK
3RD CB
Polaroids
Laser Prints
Dubs
Editing
Sets tapes
Messengers/Ship
Meals

CAST PAYMENTS	
SAG	
Non-Union	
Principal Payment	
Extra Payment	
To Include:	
3rd Callback	
Agent Fees	
Fittings	
Meal Penalty	
Night Premium	
Rehearsal Fees	
Smoke Payment	
Talent Mileage	
Wardrobe Allowance	
Weekend Premium	

CAST SUPPORT
Makeup Stylist
Overscale Makeup
Special Makeup
Makeup rooms
Hairstylist
Overscale Hair
Honeywagon
Motorhomes
Prosthetics
Rehearsal Hall
Celebrity Expenses
Celebrity Limo
Celebrity Motorhome
Choreographer
Special Security

CAST SUPPORT
Costume Designer
Wardrobe Stylist
Wardrobe Attendent
Welfare/Teacher
Xtras Holding Area
Xtras Wranglers
Xtras Meals & Craft Service
CAST TRAVEL
Hotel & PD
Meals
Transport/Miles
Air Travel

THIS BID PACKAGE INCLUDES THE FOLLOWING DOCUMENTS OR MATERIALS:

NOTES/COMMENTS:

Agency/Client Signature	*DATE*	*Production Company Signature:*	*DATE*

Figure 10.2 *Continued*

ABOUT AICP
NEWS & VIEWS
AICP SHOW
AICP COMPANIES
DOING BUSINESS
MEMBER PERKS
INDUSTRY LINKS
IMPORTANT DATES
CLASSIFIEDS
HOME
SEARCH

DOING BUSINESS

AICP LOCATION PERMIT
CHECKLIST FOR PRODUCTION COMPANY INTERNAL USE ONLY

Before you make that call to the permitting authorities, have this checklist handy as a reference when providing information to the permitting authority. Please Note: This checklist is a reference guide only, so be sure to include any other items or activities that should be disclosed to the permitting authorities. In providing this checklist, AICP does not take any responsibility for the outcome of a permit application; nor does it take responsibility for any information that a production company may, or may not, have provided in the permit application process.

THE BASICS

☐ Production Title
☐ Production Co.
☐ Producer's Name, Phone & Cell #/ Pager #
☐ Director
☐ Locations/Permitting Service Rep/Agent's

☐ Type of Film:
☐ Address: City/State/Zip /Phone:
☐ Location Manager's Name, Phone & Cell #/Pager #
☐ Assistant Director
☐ Name & Phone #

LOCATION INFORMATION

☐ Location Address
☐ Description of Location
☐ Open to Public
☐ Closed to Public

☐ Filming Dates & Hours
☐ Posting Requirements
☐ List all meter #'s to be reserved:

VEHICLE BREAKDOWN - HOW MANY?

☐ Large Trucks
☐ Vans
☐ Generators
☐ Pix Vehicles

☐ Other Trucks
☐ Mtr Homes/Dr Rms
☐ Camera Cars
☐ Cast/Crew Cars

PERSONNEL - HOW MANY?

☐ Crew
☐ Extras

☐ Cast

ACTIVITIES - BE PREPARED TO DESCRIBE SHOTS

☐ Aquatics
☐ Heli as cam ship
☐ Ship to Ship
☐ Drive-up & away

☐ Aerial Work
☐ Heli as picture ship
☐ Describe aerial work
☐ Drive-by's

Figure 10.3 The AICP also offers the Location Permit Checklist, which can be found online at their site— *www.aicp.com.*

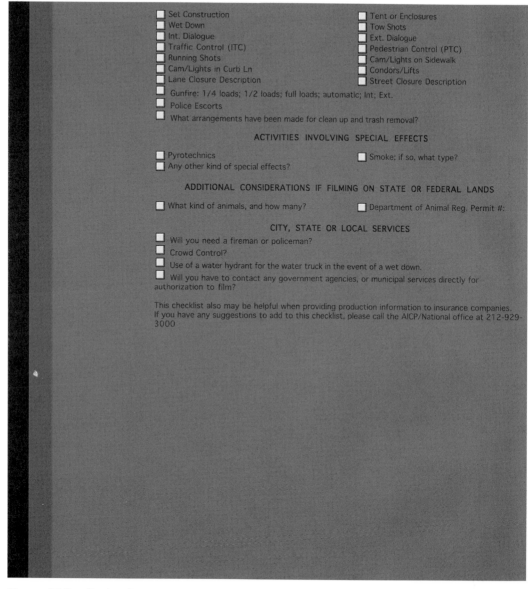

☐ Set Construction
☐ Wet Down
☐ Int. Dialogue
☐ Traffic Control (ITC)
☐ Running Shots
☐ Cam/Lights in Curb Ln
☐ Lane Closure Description
☐ Gunfire: 1/4 loads; 1/2 loads; full loads; automatic; Int; Ext.
☐ Police Escorts
☐ What arrangements have been made for clean up and trash removal?

☐ Tent or Enclosures
☐ Tow Shots
☐ Ext. Dialogue
☐ Pedestrian Control (PTC)
☐ Cam/Lights on Sidewalk
☐ Condors/Lifts
☐ Street Closure Description

ACTIVITIES INVOLVING SPECIAL EFFECTS

☐ Pyrotechnics
☐ Any other kind of special effects?

☐ Smoke; if so, what type?

ADDITIONAL CONSIDERATIONS IF FILMING ON STATE OR FEDERAL LANDS

☐ What kind of animals, and how many?

☐ Department of Animal Reg. Permit #:

CITY, STATE OR LOCAL SERVICES

☐ Will you need a fireman or policeman?
☐ Crowd Control?
☐ Use of a water hydrant for the water truck in the event of a wet down.
☐ Will you have to contact any government agencies, or municipal services directly for authorization to film?

This checklist also may be helpful when providing production information to insurance companies. If you have any suggestions to add to this checklist, please call the AICP/National office at 212-929-3000

Figure 10.3 *Continued*

Association of Independent Commercial Editors
Post Production Cost Summary

Bid Date: _____   Actuals Date: _____

Post Production Co.:	Agency:
Address:	Address:
Telephone:	Telephone:
Contact:	Client:
Editor:	Product:
Job#:	Agency Job#:
Production Co.:	Agency Prod.:
Address:	Agency Bus. Mgr.:
Telephone:	Agency Cr. Dir.:
Contact:	Agency Writer:
Director:	Agency Art. Dir.

COMMERCIAL IDENTIFICATION   **SCHEDULE**

Title	Length	Code#	
			Shoot Date:
			Dailies:
			Edit Date:
			Due Date
			Material Required:

SUMMARY OF ESTIMATED POST PRODUCTION COSTS:

			ESTIMATE	ACTUAL
1000 Prep	Total A		0	0
2000 Off Line	Total B		0	0
3000 Graphics/Video Effects	Total C		0	0
4000 Audio	Total D		0	0
5000 Finishing	Total E		0	0
6000 Miscellaneous	Total F		0	0
7000 SUB-TOTAL: DIRECT COSTS			0	0
7100 Mark-up	35% of	0	0 0	0
8000 Labor	Total G		0	0
8100 Creative Fee				
9000 TOTAL			0	0
9100 Neg. Insurance	.5% of	0	0	0
9200 Sales Tax	8.25% of	0		0
10000 GRAND TOTAL			0	0

Comments:

This bid is offered pursuant to AICE standard procedures and cancellation policies.

Figure 10.4 Standard bid forms from the Association of Independent Creative Editors (AICE). The form indicates that it's from the Association of Independent Commercial Editors, which was its original name. ©2003 Association of Independent Creative Editors, Inc.

Association of Independent Commercial Editors
Post Production Cost Breakdown

1000 PREP			ESTIMATE	MU	ACTUAL	Tx
1010 Dailies Logging	(	Hrs @	)	0		
1020 Dailies Digitizing	(	Hrs @	)	0		
1030 Negative Prep	(	Hrs @	)	0		
1040 Negative Cutting	(	Hrs @	)	0		
1050 EDL Prep	(	# @	)	0		
1060 Graphics Design Prep	(	Hrs @	)	0		
1070 Mix/Sound Design Prep	(	Hrs @	)	0		
1080						
		TOTAL A		0		0

2000 OFF LINE			ESTIMATE		ACTUAL	
2010 Off-Line Edit	(	Hrs @	)	0		
2020 Off-Line Graphics	(	Hrs @	)	0		
2030 High Res Reconforming	(	Hrs @	)	0		
2040 Rough Cut Cassettes	(	# @	)	0		
2050 Hard Drive Rental	(	Wks @	)	0		
2060 Backup/Restore	(	Hrs @	)	0		
2070 Off-Line Work Material	(	# @	)	0		
2080						
		TOTAL B		0		0

3000 GRAPHICS/VIDEO EFFECTS			ESTIMATE		ACTUAL	
3010 Graphics Designer Fee	(	Hrs @	)	0		
3020 Producer's Fee				0		
3030 Storyboards	(	Days@	)	0		
3040 Mac Graphics	(	Hrs @	)	0		
3050 Digital Load/Prep	(	Hrs @	)	0		
3060 Graphics Artist	(	Hrs @	)	0		
3070 Rendering	(	Hrs @	)	0		
3080 Digital Graphics/2D	(	Hrs @	)	0		
3090 Digital Graphics/3D	(	Hrs @	)	0		
3100 Digital Graphics/Compositing	(	Hrs @	)	0		
3110 Digital Graphics/Type Design	(	Days@	)	0		
3120 Tape Stock	(	# @	)	0		
3130 Archiving	(	Hrs @	)	0		
3140 Facility Overtime	(	Hrs @	)	0		
3150 Off-Line Graphics	(	Hrs @	)	0		
3160						
		TOTAL C		0		0

4000 AUDIO			ESTIMATE		ACTUAL	
4010 Narration Record	(	Hrs @	)	0		
4020 Dialog Replacement	(	Hrs @	)	0		
4030 Music						
4040 Sound Effects	(	# @	)	0		
4050 Digital Editing	(	Hrs @	)	0		
4060 Sound Design	(	Hrs @	)	0		
4070 Transfers & Stock	(	# @	)	0		
4080 Vis. Coded Cassettes	(	# @	)	0		
4090 Prelay/Archiving	(	Hrs @	)	0		
4100 Scratch Record/Mix	(	Hrs @	)	0		
4110 Final Mix	(	Hrs @	)	0		
4120 Audio Relay	(	# @	)	0		
4130 Satellite/Digital Transmission	(	Hrs @	)	0		
4140 Facility Overtime	(	Hrs @	)	0		
4150 Stock: DAT(s), 8mm Back-up						
4160						
		TOTAL D		0		0

Figure 10.4 *Continued*

Association of Independent Commercial Editors
Post Production Cost Breakdown

5000 FINISHING		ESTIMATE	MU	ACTUAL	Tx
5010 Film to Tape w/ Color Correction	(Hrs @)	0			
5020 Additional Machines	(Hrs @)	0			
5030 Still Store	(Hrs @)	0			
5040 Steady Gate/EPR/RTS	(Hrs @)	0			
5050 Film Cleaning	(# @)	0			
5060 Stock for Film to Tape					
5070 Tape to Tape Color Correction	(Hrs @)	0			
5080 On-Line Edit	(Hrs @)	0			
5090 Additional Machines	(Hrs @)	0			
5100 Digital Effects Equipment	(Hrs @)	0			
5110 Character Generator	(Hrs @)	0			
5120 Color Camera/Animation Stand	(Hrs @)	0			
5130 Lexicon	(Hrs @)	0			
5140 Tape Stock & Reels	(# @)	0			
5150 Generic Master	(# @)	0			
5160 Edited Master	(# @)	0			
5170 Prot. Master/Printing Dupe	(# @)	0			
5180 Finished Cassettes	(# @)	0			
5190					
TOTAL E		0		0	

6000 MISCELLANEOUS		ESTIMATE		ACTUAL	
6010 Tape to Film Transfer	(Hrs @)	0			
6020 Standards Conversion	(# @)	0			
6030 Stock Footage Search					
6040 Satellite/Digital Transmission	(Hrs @)	0			
6050 Data Transmission Charge					
6060 Delivery & Messengers	(# @)	0			
6070 Shipping					
6080 Packing/Inventory	(Hrs @)	0			
6090 Shipping to Storage					
6100 Travel					
6110 Hotel/Per Diem	(Days@)	0			
6120 Editorial Supplies					
6130 Equipment Rental					
6140 Working Meals					
6150					
TOTAL F		0		0	

8000 LABOR		ESTIMATE		ACTUAL	
8010 Pre-Production	(Hrs @)	0			
8020 Editor Labor					
8030 Editor O.T./Weekend	(Hrs @)	0			
8040 Assistant Labor					
8050 Assistant O.T./Weekend	(Hrs @)	0			
8060 Session Supervisory Fee	(Hrs @)	0			
8070					
TOTAL G		0		0	

Figure 10.4   *Continued*

Cancellation and Postponement

If Editorial Company blocks out a specific period of time with the agreement that it represents a firm commitment from the agency and/or client, then Editorial Company makes no further attempts to sell that time. If within the framework of the Guideline times specified below, I.e. less than five days, more than five days, etc., a job is cancelled or postponed, then it is highly unlikely that the time can be resold.

Editorial Company acknowledges, however, its obligation and desire to make all reasonable efforts to sell the cancelled or postponed time to another client. If the time is resold, then there is an obvious area for discussion regarding the extent of cancellation/postponment charges to be assessed, based on the relative dollars involved in the cancelled/postponed job and the job replacing it.

1. If notice of cancellation/postponment is given within <u>one to five business days</u> prior to scheduled starting date, the agency/client will be liable to Editorial Company for:

    a. All out-of-pocket costs
    b. Editorial Labor/creative fee as bid.
    c. Full (100%) mark-up as bid.
    d. Full (100%) estimated Avid time

2. If notice of cancellation/postponment is given within <u>six to ten business days</u> prior to scheduled starting date, the agency/client will be liable to Editorial Company for:

    a. All out-of-pocket costs
    b. Editorial Labor/creative fee as bid.
    c. Half (50%) mark-up as bid.
    d. Half (50%) estimated Avid time

3. If notice of cancellation/postponment is given <u>more than ten business days</u> prior to scheduled starting date, the agency/client will be liable to Editorial Company for:

    a. All out-of-pocket costs
    b. Editorial Labor/creative subject to negotiation
    c. A service charge of not less than 15% of the total bid price

rev 11/1/98

Figure 10.4 *Continued*

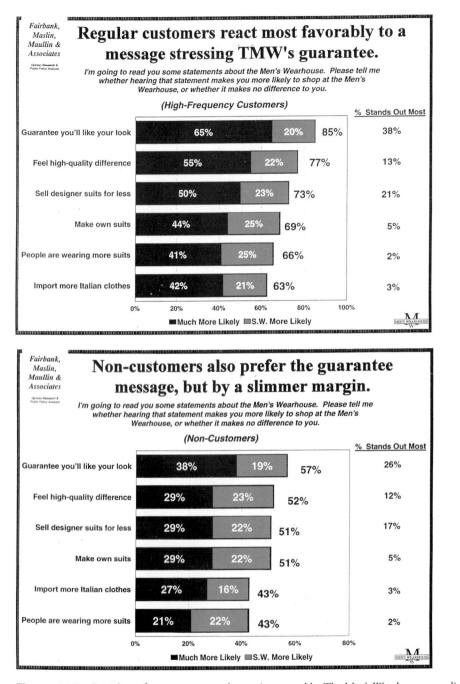

Figure 10.5 Partial set of answers to research questions posed by The Men's Wearhouse regarding its advertising campaigns.

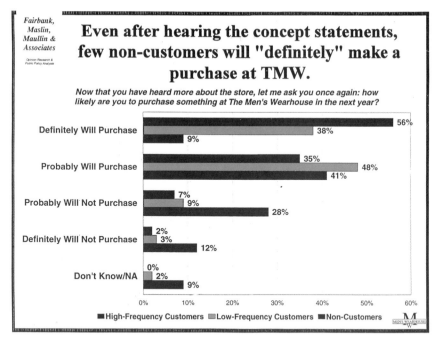

Figure 10.5 *Continued*

End Piece

I found the following while working on some forgotten project from the distant past. Nothing seems to have changed:

A Producer's Alphabetic Guide to 50 Commonly Used Advertising Agency Phrases

1. Are we going to see that cross on the film?
2. But it tested so well.
3. Can she hold it closer to her face?
4. Can they make her look more French?
5. Can we have wine with lunch?
6. Can we make the product look larger?
7. Can we pause on the bite?
8. Can we shoot it both ways?
9. Do we really have to come at 7 AM tomorrow?
10. Do you need us anymore?

11. Don't they have chairs for us?
12. He doesn't care what it costs; he's not going to pay for it.
13. How do they expect us to get to the location?
14. How do we get to the hotel?
15. I don't like what she's wearing.
16. I don't think the camera is level.
17. I don't think we should bring it up.
18. I have to have coffee . . . Now!
19. I hope we're not having Italian. We had Italian yesterday.
20. I liked it better in the animatic.
21. I'm not talking to that asshole anymore.
22. Is the video guy asleep?
23. Is this the same guy we cast?
24. It smells like something's on fire.
25. It worked fine in the kitchen test.
26. It's not in the board.
27. Nobody told me.
28. She did it in casting.
29. That's all they do is drive trucks?
30. That's not what we discussed in the prepro.
31. That's not what we wanted.
32. That's not the copy.
33. The client is very sensitive about that.
34. The drinks are great, but tomorrow can you serve the client's product instead?
35. The map is wrong!
36. This is not the original concept.
37. What about the alternative?
38. What am I looking at?
39. What happened to frame 3?
40. What happens if it rains?
41. What's the best restaurant?
42. We're not supposed to park there.
43. When is lunch?
44. Where's my Evian?
45. When you're lit, the client would like to look through the lens.
46. Which line is TV safety?

47. Which one is the eyepiece?
48. Who has the final copy?
49. Why isn't he eating it?
50. Why isn't she smiling?

Please contact me at Focal Press with some of your own gems.
Ivan Cury
Focal Press
Elsevier
30 Corporate Drive
Burlington, MA 01803
www.elsevier.com

Bibliography

Bedbury, Scott (with Stephen Fenichell). *A New Brand World.* Penguin Books, 2002.

Brown, Blain. *Cinematography: Theory and Practice.* Focal Press, 2002.

Carter, Paul. *Backstage Handbook.* Broadway Press, 1994.

Cury, Ivan. *Directing and Producing for Television: A Format Approach.* Focal Press, 2nd Ed., 2002.

Della Femina, Jerry (edited by Charles Sopkin). *From Those Wonderful Folks Who Gave You Pearl Harbor.* Simon & Schuster, 1970.

Directors Guild of America and The Association of Independent Commercial Producers National Commercial Agreement, 2001.

Donald, Ralph and Spann, Thomas. *Television Production.* Iowa State University Press, 2000.

Elin, Larry and Lapides, Alan. *Designing and Producing the Television Commercial.* Pearson, 2004.

Fauer, Jon. *DVCAM.* Focal Press, 2001.

GMM. *Creative Industry Handbook.* Author

Hampe, Barry. *Making Videos for Money.* Henry Holt and Company, LLC, Owl Books, 1998.

Hemela, Deborah Ann. *Debbies Book 18th Edition July 2003–2004: The Source Book for Entertainment Pros.* 2003.

Hornung, Clarence P. *Handbook of Early Advertising Art.* Dover Publications, Inc., 3rd Ed., 1956.

Levenson, Bob. *Bill Bernbach's Book.* Villard Books, 1987.

Lone Eagle Publishing Company. *Hollywood Creative Directory.*

Lone Eagle Publishing Company. *Representation Directory.*

Lone Eagle Publishing Company. *Distributors Directory.*

Lone Eagle Publishing Company. *Music Directory.*

Lone Eagle Publishing Company. *Blu-Book Production Directory.*

Motion Picture Enterprises, Inc. *Motion Picture TV and Theatre Directory.*

New York Production Corp. *Producers Masterguide.*

Ogilvy, David. *Confession of An Advertising Man.* Dell Publishing Co Inc., 1963.

Ogilvy, David. *Ogilvy On Advertising.* Vintage Press, 1985.

Roberts, Jerry. "Joe Pytka King of the (Commercial) World!" *DGA Magazine,* Fall 2002.

Roman, Kenneth and Jane Maas. *The New How To Advertise.* St. Martin's Press, 1992.

Sacharow, Stanley. *Symbols of Trade.* Art Direction Book Co., 1982.

Schreibman, Myrl. *The Indie Producer's Handbook: Creative Producing from A to Z.* Lone Eagle Publishing, LLC, 2001.

Schihl, Robert J. *Television Commercial Processes and Procedures.* Focal Press, 1991.

Singleton, Ralph S. *Film Budgeting.* Lone Eagle Publishing Co., 1996.

Singleton, Ralph S. *Film Scheduling or How Long Will It Take To Shoot Your Movie.* Lone Eagle Publishing Co., 2nd Ed., 1992.

Surf Producers LLC, Hollywood-911 *Hollywood 911.*

Whittaker, Ron. *Television Production.* Mayfield Publishing Co., 1992.

Zettl, Herbert. *Television Production Handbook.* Wadsworth Publishing Co. Inc., 5th Ed., 1992.

Zettl, Herbert. *Video Basics 4.* Wadsworth, 2004.

Index